THUNDER AT HAMPTON ROADS

THUNDER AT HAMPTON ROADS

BY A. A. HOEHLING

DA CAPO PRESS • NEW YORK

Library of Congress Cataloging in Publication Data

Hoehling, A. A. (Adolph A.)
    Thunder at Hampton Roads / by A. A. Hoehling. — 1st Da Capo Press ed.
        p.   cm.
    ISBN 0-306-80523-5
    1. Hampton Roads (Va.), Battle of, 1862. 2. Monitor (Ironclad) 3. Ship-
wrecks—North Carolina—Hatteras, Cape. 4. Hatteras, Cape (N.C.)—History.
5. Underwater archaeology—North Carolina—Hatteras, Cape. I. Title.
E473.2.H57 1993   92-45615
910′.9163′48—dc20   CIP

First Da Capo Press edition 1993

This Da Capo Press paperback edition of *Thunder at Hampton Roads*
is an unabridged republication of the book published in
Englewood Cliffs, New Jersey in 1976. It is reprinted by
arrangement with the author.

Published by Da Capo Press, Inc.
A Subsidiary of Plenum Publishing Corporation
233 Spring Street, New York, N.Y. 10013

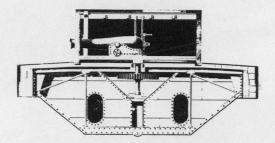

Dedicated to the sixteen officers and men of the Union navy who share a common grave with their ship the U.S.S. *Monitor*, somewhere off Hatteras.

BY THE SAME AUTHOR

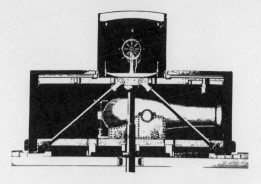

CONTENTS

FOREWORD

This is the story of a lost ship that was found after more than a century.

The U.S.S. *Monitor* revolutionized war at sea, adding "turret," "armor," and quite a bit more to the international naval lexicon. As the world's first all-iron fighting ship, she demolished forever the "wooden walls" of the fleets of oak and billowing canvas.

More than that, her history is especially unique for its inherent drama. If circumstances had deliberately contrived to produce a dramatic situation, they couldn't have done better than in the case of the *Monitor*—her conception and construction and her crucial confrontation with the Confederate ironclad *Merrimack*.

In re-creating this tale I have relied first and foremost on the words of those who actually lived through and contributed to the experience.

Finally, this is the first account in book form of how the *Monitor* was located and photographed—discovered where she had sunk 111 years ago on a stormy wintry night somewhere off Cape Hatteras.

DRAMATIS PERSONAE

Commander James Alden, USN, designate captain of C.S.S. *Merrimack*

Lieutenant John P. Bankhead, USN, last commander of U.S.S. *Monitor*

Lieutenant John M. Brooke, CSN, Chief Engineer William P. Williamson, CSN, and Naval Constructor John L. Porter, CSN, designers of the C.S.S. *Virginia* (ex-*Merrimack*)

Senator Orville Browning, of Illinois, Lincoln confidant

Flag Officer Franklin Buchanan, CSN, commanding C.S.S. *Merrimack*

James Buchanan, fifteenth President of the United States

Paymaster McKean Buchanan, U.S.S. *Congress;* brother of Franklin

Brigadier General Ambrose E. Burnside, USA, Hatteras Expedition leader

Cornelius S. Bushnell, John F. Winslow, and John A. Griswold, partners of Ericsson

Francis B. Butts, seaman on U.S.S. *Monitor*

Captain James Byers, tug *J. B. White*

Colonel Le Grand Bouton Cannon, USA, aide-de-camp to General Wool

John Cary, Confederate soldier on Sewell's Point

Salmon P. Chase, secretary of the treasury

Lucius E. Chittenden, treasury underofficial

William Cline, crewman on the C.S.S. *Virginia*

Master Rolando Coffin, tug *Mystic*

Brigadier General R. E. Colston, CSA, brigade commander of Confederate troops on James River

Frederick Curtis, seaman aboard U.S.S. *Congress*

Captain John A. Dahlgren, USN, ordnance expert and adviser to Lincoln

Commander Charles H. Davis, USN, member of navy ironclad board

Jefferson Davis, President of the Confederacy

Cornelius H. Delameter, owner of ironworks that built engines of U.S.S. *Monitor*

William F. Drake, artilleryman on C.S.S. *Merrimack*

Captain Percival Drayton, USN, commanding U.S.S. *Passaic*

Colonel Charles Ellet, Jr., USA, engineer and promoter of naval rams

John Ericsson, inventor of U.S.S. *Monitor*

Flag Officer David Glasgow Farragut, USN, New Orleans Expedition leader along with Major General Benjamin F. Butler

Flag Officer French Forrest, CSN, commanding Gosport Navy Yard

Captain Gustavus V. Fox, USN, assistant secretary of the navy

Lieutenant Samuel R. Franklin, USN, executive officer, U.S.S. *Dacotah*

Captain Ange Simon Gautier, French sloop of war *Gassendi*

Erasmus Gilbreath, soldier, 20th Indiana Regiment, at Camp Butler

Flag Officer Louis M. Goldsborough, USN, Blockading Squadron commander

Lieutenant Samuel Dana Greene, USN, executive officer, U.S.S. *Monitor*

Major General Benjamin Huger, CSA, commanding Department of Norfolk

Engineer in Chief Benjamin Isherwood, USN

Lieutenant Thomas Catesby ap R. Jones, CSN, executive officer, C.S.S. *Merrimack*

William Frederick Keeler, Paymaster, U.S.S. *Monitor*

General Robert E. Lee, CSA, commanding Army of Virginia

Rear Admiral Stephen P. Lee, USN, commanding North Atlantic Blockading Squadron

Joshua Lewis, soldier, 20th Indiana Regiment, at Camp Butler

Commodore Charles S. McCauley, USN, commandant Norfolk Navy Yard

Major General George B. McClellan, USA, commanding Army of the Potomac

Major General John B. Magruder, CSA, commanding Army of the Peninsula

Stephen Mallory, secretary of the Confederate Navy

Brigadier General Joseph K. Mansfield, USA, commanding Camp Butler and Newport News Point

Captain John Marston, USN, of U.S.S. *Roanoke,* senior officer present at Hampton Roads

Brigadier General Montgomery Meigs, USA, quartermaster general of the army

Lieutenant George U. Morris, USN, executive officer, U.S.S. *Cumberland*

Francis B. Ogden and Robert F. Stockton, early partners of Ericsson

Lieutenant William H. Parker, CSN, of C.S.S. *Beaufort*

Commodore Hiram Paulding, USN, member of navy ironclad board

Charles "Dick" Phelps, Confederate officer on Sewell's Point

Dr. Dinwiddie Phillips, surgeon, C.S.S. *Merrimack*

Commodore David Dixon Porter, USN

Captain H. Y. Purviance, USN, of U.S.S. *St. Lawrence*

Captain William Radford, USN, of U.S.S. *Cumberland*

Chief Engineer H. Ashton Ramsay, C.S.S. *Merrimack*

Corporal Thomas Ranson, USA, New York Mounted Rifles

Henry Reaney, acting master, tug *Zouave*

Lieutenant James H. Rochelle, CSN, on C.S.S. *Patrick Henry*

William E. Rogers, USA, 10th New York Regiment, Fort Monroe

Thomas F. Rowland, shipyard owner, Continental Iron Works where U.S.S. *Monitor* was built

General Winfield Scott, USA, general in chief of United States Army

Lieutenant Thomas O. Selfridge, USN, aboard U.S.S. *Cumberland*

William H. Seward, U.S. secretary of state

Dr. Edward Shippen, surgeon, U.S.S. *Congress*

Commodore Joseph Smith, USN, member of navy ironclad board; chief, Bureau of Yards and Docks

Lieutenant Joseph B. Smith, USN, commander, U.S.S. *Congress*

Commander William Smith, USN, former commander of U.S.S. *Congress*

Edward M. Stanton, U.S. secretary of war

Chief Engineer Alban C. Stimers, U.S.S. *Monitor*

Louis N. Stodder, acting master and navigating officer, U.S.S. *Monitor*

Flag Officer Silas H. Stringham, USN, first commander of the North Atlantic Blockading Squadron

Commodore Josiah Tattnall, CSN, second commander of C.S.S. *Merrimack*

Commander Stephen D. Trenchard, USN, commanding U.S.S. *Rhode Island*

Commander John R. Tucker, CSN, commanding C.S.S. *Patrick Henry*

Captain Gershon Van Brunt, USN, of U.S.S. *Minnesota*

John J. N. Webber, an acting master on U.S.S. *Monitor*

Gideon Welles, U.S. secretary of the navy

Lieutenant John Taylor Wood, CSA, C.S.S. *Merrimack*

Major General John E. Wool, USA, commanding Department of Virginia

Lieutenant John L. Worden, USN, first commander of U.S.S. *Monitor*

NOTES

Officers' ranks changed upward more rapidly in the Civil War than in any conflict before or since. Every effort is made to use ranks as they were at the time of the story. While Franklin Buchanan, for example, was known variously as Flag Officer, Admiral, Captain, and even Commodore, Richmond records then list him as Flag Officer. Rear Admiral replaced, during the war, the Flag Officer rank. The commanding officer of a ship was and is known as captain, even though his actual rank, as Worden's, might have been only lieutenant.

The Virginia *was the new name given by the Confederates to the captured Federal warship, the* Merrimack. *The ship was originally named after the Merrimack River in Massachusetts, and this is spelled with a "k." However, in the river area itself it is spelled both with and without a "k." This dual spelling was common in both the North and the South during the Civil War. Some southerners called the converted ship the* Virginia, *but most still knew it by its original* Merrimack. *Since it was in commission and existence less than three months, the new name barely had time to stick.*

Full Fathom Five thy father lies;
Of his bones are coral made;
Those are pearls that were his eyes:
Nothing of him that doth fade,
But doth suffer a sea-change
Into something rich and strange.

The Tempest

I
AN IRONCLAD IS BORN

Orders to Beaufort

CONFIDENTIAL

U.S. Flagship *Philadelphia*
Hampton Roads, Virginia
December 24, 1862.

TO: Stephen D. Trenchard
Commander
U.S.S. *Rhode Island*

Sir: Proceed with the *Monitor* in tow to Beaufort, North Carolina.
Avail yourself of the first favorable weather for making passage.
Return to this port.

Respectfully yours,
S. P. Lee
Acting Rear Admiral
Commanding North Atlantic
Blockading Squadron

A historic year in naval warfare was ending that late December 1862. The battle-scarred U.S.S. *Monitor* was preparing to depart Hampton Roads—where she had made naval history only in March—for uncertain, stormy waters farther down the Atlantic coast.

The ironclad, diminutive even by the measure of her contemporaries, was leaving for a new assignment, which, it was becoming known around the waterfront, had something to do with tightening the blockade at Wilmington, North Carolina. She remained at anchor, nonetheless, waiting for better weather and for the big, broad-beamed side-wheeler *Rhode Island* to send over a towline.

The captain of the *Rhode Island,* Stephen Decatur Trenchard, knew the perils of a winter gale, laced with snow and sleet, especially off that mariner's wasteland, Cape Hatteras. Trenchard, whose father served as a contemporary of Stephen Decatur, Oliver Hazard Perry, Isaac Hull, and other navy immortals, was both prudent and devout.

While rain slanted against the superstructure of the "blockader" vessel, Christmas had been solemnized with devotions. These were all too familiar rituals aboard what the crew had long since dubbed the "Gospel Gun Boat."

In port on a Sunday, the onetime ministerial student from New Jersey would seek out the handiest church. Upon returning, he would enter in his personal log some such entry as "felt greatly benefited by the discourse." The wardroom, too, as a captive audience, would be compelled to mix nourishment with whatever immediate recall Trenchard's memory permitted.

However, he was not so different in this respect as his irreverent crewmen tended to think. Many expressed the need for prayer in this Christmastime of the Civil War—also known as the War of Secession, the War Between the States, and the War for the Union.

For twenty-one months the conflict had seared a nation, leaving casualties—in killed, wounded, missing, and sick—that easily exceeded a quarter of a million. (Statistics, both from Union and Confederate medical and other sources, were and still are unreliable.) The major and wasting engagements had been on land, but the sea as well as inland waterways remained of crucial importance. Much of the logistics of the North was dependent upon transport by ship and barge. This explained the strategic significance of Hampton Roads, Virginia, where the broad Chesapeake Bay empties between Cape Charles and Cape Henry into the Atlantic Ocean. It is, as well, the confluence of many rivers; moving counterclockwise from the north, there are the Rappahannock, York, James, Nansemond, and Elizabeth (itself making Norfolk a great port).

Since the Potomac River, farther to the north, was lost in the brackish Chesapeake Bay waters, famed for oysters, crabs, and frequently jellyfish, Hampton Roads could be considered gate tender on the water route to Washington, the Capital of the Union. So was the James a Lorelei beckoning toward Richmond, the Confederate Capital for most of the war. President Lincoln demanded that the Potomac be guarded at all costs. If lost, the bay was a potential avenue of conquest.

For the first year of the war the control of Hampton Roads was divided between North and South. On the north banks of the Roads, the Federal strongholds were dominated by mighty and moated Fort—or "Fortress"—Monroe, the largest stone fort in North America. It was built on a land tip known as Old Point Comfort after the War of 1812 to prevent British or any other fleets from ever again steaming up Chesapeake Bay into the Potomac and attempting to repeat the burning of Washington.

Stone, earth, and brick combined into massive embrasured casemates which were considered impregnable. General Robert E. Lee, who as an engineer had aided in the final strengthening of the fort, was said to have advised against any attempts to take Monroe.

The war had inspired other encampments as satellites of the great, glowering fort. The largest of these was Camp Hamilton, two miles northwest of the mighty parent, and the second largest, Camp Butler on Newport News Point, standing guard at the mouth of the James River. In the rear of Fort Monroe was diminutive Camp Harrison in the village of Hampton, which, like Newport News, was the site of old plantations. Hampton, however, which had made its uneasy détente with Fort Monroe, was burned in August 1861 by a Virginia militia, the Old Dominion Dragoons, many of whom had lived there and thus put the torches to their own homes.

No more than a mile off Fort Monroe, a curious, navy-manned fortification raised its casemates and gun snouts out of the shallows: the Rip Raps, formerly Fort Calhoun, later to be known as Fort Wool, and man-made primarily of stone. The Rip Raps mounted at least one experimental rifle—a Sawyer gun—capable of throwing a shell the four miles across the Roads.

The total garrison of these five Federal fortifications remained at about twelve thousand (not counting various Union expeditions moving through the area), with Hamilton alone bivouacking about half that number.

Facing this considerable Union complex during most of 1861 and nearly half of 1862 were Confederate flags flying from Norfolk-Portsmouth and the Gosport Navy Yard just to the south. The principal Confederate batteries poked their muzzles from Sewell's Point, the closest land opposite Old Point from Craney Island at the mouth of the Elizabeth River, leading to the Gosport Navy Yard, five miles upriver from Lambert's Point (which was halfway up), and finally, at the mouth of the Nansemond four miles across from Newport News lay the batteries of curiously named Pig Point. The latter was lightly supported by the Town Point Battery farther up the Nansemond.

By December 1862, however, all shores of Hampton Roads were back under Federal control. This was also true of many of the southern ports that had been so integral with the Confederate cause: New Orleans, Pensacola, Fernandina (just north of Jacksonville), Port Royal (south of Charleston), and New Bern, North Carolina, on the Neuse River.

Yet the Confederacy still clung to important ports offering full docking and warehousing to blockade runners. These included—in addition to Jacksonville—Mobile, Savannah, Charleston, and Wilmington, North Carolina. A desire to tighten the blockade at the mouth of the Cape Fear River leading to Wilmington, ultimately to attack the forts themselves—Caswell in particular—that guarded this major port, had prompted the orders to Captain Trenchard, of the *Rhode Island.*

The orders, of course, had originated in Washington, from Secretary of the Navy Gideon Welles. A lawyer and former Hartford, Connecticut newspaper publisher, Welles had become a familiar sight in the Federal Capital with his shaggy beard and immense gray wig. Insistent reports—some from overseas consulates—that the Confederates were planning to break through the Federal blockade of the Cape Fear River leading to Wilmington were making the secretary increasingly nervous.

In fact, the existence and moderate success of the blockade runners had become an obsession with Welles. Now, against the advice of his assistant secretary and highly regarded career officer from Massachusetts, Captain Gustavus Vasa Fox, he was risking two precious monitors—the *Monitor* herself and the newer *Passaic,* one of a class of ten turreted warships, all somewhat larger than the Monitor—against the hazards of open sea.

The good subordinate Trenchard replied to Secretary Welles's orders as conveyed through Admiral Lee: "Sir, I have the honor to acknowledge the receipt of your confidential communication of the 24th instant and will proceed in conformity with your instructions as soon as the weather will be favorable for the tow."

The 236-foot, 1,517-ton *Rhode Island,* doubling as both a supply vessel and a blockader, was generally a happy, "good duty" ship—and she should have been. In comparison with the cramped, alternately hot and wet living aboard the monitors, the *Rhode Island* was a palace afloat. Built as a plush passenger steamer—the *Eagle*—for the coastal Charleston Line, but never having cast off in that service, she offered cabins of polished maple and walnut, wide bunks with actual mattresses and blankets, and dining refinements that included china, glassware, and table linens.

With her eight-inch guns, a special nine-inch pivot rifle, and speed, she had an apparent added asset: invulnerability. All in all, she provided eyebrow-raising contrast to the notoriously unseaworthy *Monitor,* which was 172 feet overall, with an extreme beam of 41½ feet, drawing a mere 10½ feet. This draft tended to put her in the ferryboat category, certainly an inland waterway vessel. While the *Montauk* (which belonged to the *Passaic* class) was twenty-eight feet longer and with almost twice the *Monitor*'s displacement, she was no more "deep water" than her little predecessor. Towing was mandatory outside of rivers and harbors.

In the convoy accompanying the U.S.S. *Monitor* would be the *Passaic,* with the consort *State of Georgia.* This broad-beamed steamer had distinguished herself in May by capturing the Confederate steamship *Nassau.*

Aboard the *Monitor,* her crew of sixty-three welcomed any change from what for most of the year had been "the same dull monotonous round day after day." This was the assessment of the *Monitor*'s paymaster, forty-one-year-old iron-foundry owner and partner from La Salle, Illinois, William Frederick Keeler, faithful letter writer to his "dear wife," Anna.

None, since the *Monitor*'s commissioning in Brooklyn the past January, had been such a faithful chronicler of the fortunes and trials of the novel ironclad. The monotony to which he bore testimony, however, was but one element of life aboard this "iron battery." According to her young executive officer, Lieutenant Samuel Dana Greene, a Marylander, "Probably no ship was ever devised which was so uncomfortable for her crew."

A newcomer from Rhode Island to a complement distinguished by its constant changes, young Francis "Frank" Butts, delivered his own amen as he pronounced it "the worst craft for a man to live aboard that ever floated upon water."

The *Monitor,* which had, as well, piped on several commanding officers, was now under a South Carolinian, Captain John Pyne Bankhead, who happened to be the same age as his paymaster, Keeler. Like so many of the opposing sides, Bankhead, a veteran of the Port Royal expedition, November 1861, could tick off relatives fighting under the Stars and Bars. The most illustrious of the latter was a cousin, Major General John Bankhead Magruder, who had commanded the Right Wing of the Army of Northern Virginia.

Known as "Prince John" for his courtly presence, the smartly moustached Magruder, an 1830 graduate of the U.S. Military Academy, had fought in the Seminole and Mexican wars, being decorated for bravery in the latter. He had a flair for dramatic tactics. Typical Magruder ruses and theatrics—marching a small body of troops and a brassy band around a hill—had measurably helped to stall General George B. McClellan's Peninsular campaign.

Another example of the war's divisiveness among families was fifty-one-year-old Admiral Samuel Phillips Lee, who this month had assumed command of the North Atlantic Blockading Squadron. The handsome naval officer, clean-shaven except for muttonchops, was a cousin of Robert E. Lee. He was well known in Washington society because of his beautiful and gifted wife, the former Elizabeth Blair, of Maryland.

This distinguished Virginian, who had commanded the *Oneida* at the Battle of New Orleans, declared, after being asked about his loyalty, "When I find the word Virginia in my commission I will join the Confederacy. . . ."

Meanwhile, a southwest storm continued to whip up the waters of Hampton Roads. Notwithstanding, preparations were made to get under way. Tied to a supply wharf at Fort Monroe, the *Monitor* was taking on coal and "several tons of shot and shell," by the count of Frank Butts. Her larder, too, was replenished following a Christmas feast which included turkey, fish, oysters, a selection of meats, apples, figs, plums, cherries, jellies, wines—much of it having been sent from the men's homes.

While many of the crew mistakenly believed that their little gunboat was heading for Charleston, South Carolina—disturbingly snug, it appeared, in rebel hands—correspondence continued between commanding officers of the four ships in the convoy, *Monitor, Rhode Island, Passaic,* and *State of Georgia,* as to their actual mission after arriving at the protected anchorage of Beaufort. On Bogue Sound, Beaufort was a southern cul-de-sac of Pamlico Sound. Navigation of the Cape Fear River and passing hostile batteries to attack Wilmington posed problems that were seemingly insuperable.

Since Admiral Lee adhered to the tactical theory that aggressiveness should be leavened with prudence, he leaned heavily on the opinion of his captains—those who, after all, would be entrusted with the execution of his orders. Two days after Christmas, from his flagship, the small "armed tender" *Philadelphia,* he wrote identical letters to Bankhead, to Captain Percival Drayton of the *Passaic* (monitor No. 2), and to Commander John L. Worden, former captain of the *Monitor,* now in a similar post on the yet newer *Montauk* (monitor No. 3). The latter, however, was not yet in port, although due hourly.

"Since you have examined the charts," Lee wrote, "I desire to have your opinion as to the practicability of entering Cape Fear River with the ironclad under your command. The design of the joint expedition, of which the ironclads form the effective part of the naval force for the inside attack, is to take the defenses of one or both of the entrances to Cape Fear River and capture Wilmington. . . ."

Drayton, a South Carolinian like Bankhead, was tall, angular, bearded, a formidable sea fighter both in appearance and in fearless determination. Commanding the U.S. steamer *Pocahontas* at Port Royal, he had faced, among other adversaries, his brother, Brigadier General Thomas F. Drayton, of the 4th Georgia Battalion.

When Drayton received Lee's message, he boarded a small boat for the nearby anchored *Monitor* to chat with his friend, John Bankhead. Time was short. They arrived at a speedy agreement, and Drayton replied the same day to Lee on his flagship, anchored not far off: "that after conversation with Commander Bankhead, who has been on the survey of the river, and examination of the chart, I am satisfied that for anything like my draft, the New Inlet entrance is out of the question. . . . I shall merely consider the southern one."

He then discussed the possibility of crossing the Western Bar at high tide, passing through the channel just two hundred yards in front of Fort Caswell and clearing out obstructions of pilings, concluding:

"I would say that although my convictions are decidedly against the probability of getting by the obstructions at Fort Caswell and, to a somewhat less degree of even crossing the bar, still I beg you to understand that should either or both be attempted nothing shall be left undone on my part to ensure their success. . . ."

The reply was less than to Lee's liking. Nonetheless, the ships had to slosh their way to Beaufort. On December 28 the admiral wrote to youthful Major General John G. Foster, a veteran of the largely successful North Carolina coastal campaigns and now commanding the Federal Department of that state, with headquarters at New Bern. Advising of bombardment and amphibious problems attendant to the capture of Wilmington, Lee promised to leave for Beaufort as soon as the big steam frigate and former flagship *Minnesota* arrived to transport him and his staff.

On Sunday evening, the waters of Hampton Roads flattened after four days of white choppiness. The seabirds once more flapped eastward. The pungent woodsmoke from the soldiers' dinner fires along the shore rose again straight upward. However, Trenchard, after consultation with a longtime harbor pilot, John H. Bean, advised against a night departure. Besides, they theorized, the gale might haul around again and be blowing in the morning.

Monday, the twenty-ninth, the fears of the two officers were allayed. Trenchard's quartermaster logged:

"Light airs from the south and west, mild and pleasant weather. The U.S. steamer *Connecticut* arrived during the evening and soon afterward the ironclad steamer *Montauk* came in and achored."

During the morning, Bankhead completed one trip over to the *Rhode Island*. The purpose was primarily to discuss towing plans, even though the general apprehension concerning the operations against Wilmington persisted. Neither Bankhead nor Drayton, of the *Passaic*, believed that their turrets could withstand sustained bombardment from shore batteries in the event the monitors ran aground or afoul of pilings half-sunk in the river. With Trenchard, there was no question of a vessel of such draft as the *Rhode Island*'s even attempting passage up the Cape Fear River.

Bankhead was followed to the side-wheeler by Acting Master's Mate Rodney Browne, who, with crewmen of both ships, began running out two twelve-inch-round hemp hawsers from the stern of the *Rhode Island* to the bow of the *Monitor*. They could be stretched for upwards of three hundred feet in length.

At 2:30 P.M. towlines tightened. The little convoy of four vessels got under way. The *Montauk,* just arrived, was not yet ready to return to sea. Captain Bankhead logged, as if in corroboration of Trenchard: "Wind light at S.W., weather clear and pleasant, and every prospect of continuation."

A fifth ship was also heading out from Hampton Roads to sea—the fifty-two-gun frigate H.M.S. *Melpomene.* In spite of Great Britain's manifest sympathies with the "Cotton Confederacy," her loading of blockade runners and building of such raiders as the *Alabama* (already running wild in the Atlantic under the dashing Captain Raphael Semmes), her Royal Navy subjects maintained friendly rapport with their Federal Navy counterparts. Her Majesty's officers attended social events in Fort Monroe and at such quarters as were rebuilt at the twice-razed Norfolk (or Gosport) Navy Yard. The enlisted men lifted their mugs of beer or rum at the saloons and brawled together.

One resort in the area was world-famous if not also notorious: the huge Hygeia Hotel, sprawling its rocking-chaired porches over Old Point Comfort, immediately in front of the gray ramparts of Fort Monroe. For more than two decades it had thrived as a crossroads for tough but well-heeled ship captains flying the flags of the world's merchant marine. It was by nature and location a favorite place of assignation, and inspirer of warm, rich memories.

Now it was largely commandeered as a Federal hospital, with a few of its ground-floor public rooms maintaining liaison with a more carefree, bawdier past.

There was always at least one warship flying the Union Jack in Hampton Roads, occasionally as many as four, and sometimes one under France's Tricolor as well. Today, with the spectacle of H.M.S. *Melpomene* astern of the monitors' convoy and the arrival of the *Connecticut* and *Montauk,* correspondents languishing in Fort Monroe, bored from lack of action, seized upon the marine activity as a news kernel meriting exaggeration. For one, the correspondent for the Philadelphia *Press* wrote:

> There have been stirring times here for some days past among the troops and war vessels . . . the fleet is now putting to sea and comprised about enough men of all arms to take and hold any point on the southern coast.
>
> The destination of their expedition is supposed to be North Carolina, but as a number of ironclads accompany it I presume it will go to some important southern port—say Charleston, Georgetown, Savannah, or Mobile. . . .

The scrubby pines of Lynnhaven Roads, on Norfolk's northeastern shores, gradually became a green-gray haze line in the late afternoon as the *Rhode Island*'s quartermaster logged, ". . . at 5:40 P.M. Cape Henry bore W. distance of 4 miles."

The convoy was proceeding at about five knots.

Admiral Lee, meanwhile, who had watched through his long glass the disappearing "fleet," decided he could safely advise Secretary Welles that the expedition was on its way. By the Signal Corps telegraph (completed only on March 9, running beneath the waters of Hampton Roads to Cape Charles and thence up the eastern shore of Virginia and Maryland to Harrington, Delaware, and Washington) Lee wrote:

"The *Montauk* arrived and the *Passaic* and *Monitor* went out today. *Connecticut* will be ready."

He timed the message 4 P.M. It was logged in at the War Department at 5:30 P.M. for transmittal to the navy. Not infrequently, Lincoln himself stood gravely behind the telegrapher in the signal room, a scant block west of the White House, as messages of a battle's progress or the sailing of a warship tapped in.

David Homer Bates, young manager of this office and cipher-operator, would recall how the President spent long hours in the cipher room, using it as a secluded spot for thought and rest.

The winter evening passed normally, with no appreciable change in the weather. The green and red running lights of the four ships were clearly visible to one another. A course was set along the Outer Banks, which formed a curious, sandy bulwark for several sounds, starting with Currituck, past the sparse fishing settlement of Nags Head, bulging out at Cape Hatteras for the largest—Pamlico

Sound—and ending with little Bogue Sound, on which was situated Beaufort, the convoy's destination. This strategic coast was securely in Union control after operations on land and sea that had consumed the better part of a year.

At 5 A.M. Tuesday, a swell rolled in from the south, with, according to Bankhead, "a slight increase of the wind from the southwest, the sea breaking over the pilot house forward and striking the base of the tower [turret], but not with sufficient force to break over it. Found that the packing of oakum under and around the base of the tower had loosened somewhat from the working of the tower as the vessel pitched and rolled. Speed at this time about 5 knots; ascertained from the engineer of the watch that the bilge pumps kept her perfectly free, occasionally sucking. Felt no apprehension at this time. . . ."

Two hours later, both the *Monitor* and the *Rhode Island* hove to as the towing hawsers were checked and tightened. Trenchard routinely took soundings and found 20 fathoms, or 120 feet of water, a typical depth in the Carolina shoals. At 7:30 the vessels were once more under way.

If Bankhead experienced no "apprehension," this did not necessarily reflect the emotions of his crew. Keeler, for one, watched the clouds thicken until "the sun was obscured by their cold gray mantle." It was somewhat less than reassuring to notice two sharks which had assumed their own patrol of the *Monitor,* swimming "quietly along by our sides observing us apparently with a curious eye as if in anticipation of a feast."

At 1 P.M. Trenchard took sights and logged, "Cape Hatteras lighthouse bearing W.S.W. 14 miles distant."

During the afternoon, however, there was difference of opinion on the severity of the weather, apparently depending on the individual and his nautical experience. Trenchard, the old sea dog, observed, "The sea continued smooth during the day and at sunset there was every indication of a favorable night."

Keeler, the admitted landlubber, was certain that the wind "blew quite heavy, the sea rolling with violence across our deck rendering it impossible to remain on it without danger of being swept off."

Butts was in agreement. Considered by both himself and the captain a "good hand" at the wheel—in the exposed eminence of the pilot house atop the turret—he stayed there most of the afternoon, observing that "the sea rolled high and pitched together in that peculiar manner only seen at Hatteras. The *Rhode Island* steamed slowly and steadily ahead. The sea rolled over us as if our vessel were a rock in the ocean only a few inches above water. . . . It seemed that for minutes we were out of sight as the heavy seas entirely submerged the vessel."

The *State of Georgia* watch also differed with Trenchard's optimistic assessment, logging: "From meridian [noon] to 4 P.M. weather stormy," adding, "the *Cahawba,* with ship conveying troops, and the *Rhode Island,* towing the *Monitor,* about 5 miles distant to the S.W. of us."

Most of the *Monitor* crew ate dinner at the customary 5 P.M., hanging onto table, plates, and eating utensils. Some, including the third assistant engineer, Samuel A. Lewis, were too sick in their cramped, stuffy bunks to move, underscoring anew the assessment of her executive officer, Lieutenant Greene, as to the *Monitor*'s absence of seaworthiness.

Three years out of Annapolis, Samuel Dana Greene, dark-haired and neatly moustached, who had been aboard ever since commissioning, would have been commanding officer except for his youth —twenty-two. (In the army, however, it was a different story, where George A. Custer was a major general at twenty-six. There were brigadier generals as well as brevetted brigadier generals in their twenties almost too numerous to count.)

Earlier in the year, Greene, a capable but introspective officer, had warned Secretary Welles in a formal report against seagoing missions for any ship of Monitor design, noting about the one on which he served: "She has not the steam power to go against a head wind or sea, and I think it very doubtful she could go from here [Hampton Roads] to Delaware Bay by herself, as she would be unable to make headway against a sea; she would not steer even in smooth water, and going slow she does not mind her helm readily. At sea she would be unable to work her guns, as we are obliged to keep the ports closed and calked, they being but 5 feet above water."

At dusk the swell decreased. The bilge pumps were still keeping up with the water that sloshed through the sight holes of the pilot house, hawse hole, and base of the turret. Then at 7:30 P.M., Bankhead noted, "the wind hauled more to the south, increasing in strength and causing the sea to rise; computed position at this time about 15 miles south of Cape Hatteras Shoals."

In addition, the *Monitor* was now towing very badly, yawing "and with the increased motion making somewhat more water around the base of the tower."

The *Monitor* was also equipped with the latest Worthington pump connected to a "bilge injection" and a centrifugal pump, which together could remove upwards of three thousand gallons a minute. Both were started pumping at full power, to augment the bilge pumps. Still, Second Assistant Engineer Joseph Watters observed to his dismay that the water in the engine room increased. He continued:

"I reported to Captain Bankhead that I would have to reduce the speed of the main engines in order to save steam for the use of the Worthington and centrifugal pumps. The ash pits at that time were more than half full of water, allowing but very little air to reach the fires; at the same time the blowers used for producing a current of air to the fires were throwing a great amount of water."

He watched the needle on the steam gauge drop, as he listened to the coal in the furnaces hiss, under the drenching of cold seawater.

Topsides, most of the officers were huddled in the scant shelter of the pilot house. Butts, still at the helm, decided that "this going to sea in an ironclad . . . would be the last I should volunteer for."

The motion of the *Monitor* became increasingly contorted, "riding one huge wave and, being heavier than a wooden ship, with no hold for the water to raise her, plunging through the next, and splashing down upon another with a shock that would sometimes take us off our feet, while the next would sweep over us and break far above the turret, and if we had not been protected by a rifle armor we would have been washed away."

Bankhead was worried not so much about discomfort as by the pounding the whole ship was taking, loosening her plates, removing the caulk from the base of the turret, allowing more and more water to cascade below. Each time the *Monitor* banged down into the trough of a wave, the noise, to Keeler, was "like thunder."

After 8 P.M. Bankhead signaled to the *Rhode Island* several times to stop. This was done, lines checked, and the halting, jerky progress again resumed. Trenchard, peering through the slanting rain, the spindrift from the foaming sea, thought the *Monitor*'s bow had been "brought . . . to the wind [and] appeared to make better weather."

The steamer's captain was unwarrantedly optimistic.

Bankhead perceived that with diminishing engine power and the increasing possibility that the powerful *Rhode Island* would pull the *Monitor* completely under water like some waterlogged hulk, he might actually lose the *Monitor*.

The captain hoisted a red lantern to the top of the pilot house—a prearranged signal of distress. It swayed like an erratic pendulum.

Trenchard stopped his engines and the two vessels heaved close together, like drunken companions swaying down a dark street. Bankhead shouted over the gale:

"The *Monitor* is sinking!"

Somewhere off Cape Hatteras that stormy night before New Year's Eve 1862, the U.S.S. *Monitor* was wallowing into history.

A "Big Frigate"

THE *STAR OF THE WEST* FIRED INTO
FROM MORRIS ISLAND AND FORT MOULTRIE

New York *Times,* January 10, 1861

This particular history does not commence off North Carolina, or Virginia, or anywhere on the sparse eastern coasts of the United States, but in the restless, creative mind of a man born far away—in a mining village of central Sweden with the improbable, virtually unpronounceable name of Långbanshyttan, in the province of Värmland.

At the age of ten, in the year 1813, John Ericsson was making excellent architectural/engineering drawings, including one of a complicated miniature sawmill and pump. A part of his imagination came from his mine-inspector father. Something of a loner from infancy and wholly uninterested in the common playthings and games of the other children, John preferred to improvise instruments: a drawing pen created from steel tweezers, borrowed from his mother's dressing case and ground to a point, or compasses made of birchwood sticks with needles stuck in the ends. He would himself recall that he learned at an early age "how to make and mix out of materials obtained at the druggist's for a few cents, the colors required for my drawings."

It wasn't, in this regard, overly surprising that Ericsson, at the age of twelve, was commissioned to produce drawings for the Gota Canal Company. At thirteen he confirmed his reputation as a prodigy by being employed in a full-time responsible capacity for the company—a "leveler," or surveyor.

First a cadet in the Mechanical Corps of the Swedish Navy, then an officer in the Army at seventeen, Ericsson further pursued his penchant for innovation along many lines—a better press for his engravings, for example. But his main obsession soon focused on propulsion: the development of what he described as a "flame" or "caloric" engine, something like the steam engine but using hot air instead. He explained it in a paper entitled, "A Description of a New Method of Employing the Combustion of Fuel as a Moving Power," and sent it to a newly organized civil engineering society in London.

It was already apparent that Sweden could not offer a broad enough horizon for the young man's talents. At the age of twenty-two he obtained military leave and went to London in an effort to present in person what his writings could do but mutely. The Ericsson who arrived at the Thames was good-looking if rather stony-faced, a bit under six feet, stocky, with blue eyes, brown curly hair, a "massive forehead," and a burgeoning self-confidence that hinted lustily of

16

immodesty. He would write, for example, "I was not only equal but superior to the English engineers in acquired skills."

His pride was quickly tumbled. The engine, designed for pine chips, was not suited to the hot, glowing coal fuel of England. The cylinders were burned out, and with them seemingly Ericsson's hopes for instant fame as an inventor—in an era when technology was stirring.

Undaunted, nonetheless, Ericsson built an air-compressor pump for removing water from mines. He also perfected refrigerators and coolers for breweries, "linked-motion" reversing machinery for steam engines, and new tubular condensers for marine boilers.

In fact, the Swedish inventor had a hand in devising a means whereby the entire engine system of Sir John Ross's Arctic exploration ship, *Victory,* could be placed below the waterline—itself an innovation.

Ericsson received scant thanks. Searching for a Northwest Passage, Ross became so dissatisfied with the machinery that he had it disconnected and dumped overboard—then blamed Ericsson for the "failure." The indignant Swede, by report, was prevented only at the last moment from dueling with the Arctic voyager to uphold his "honor."

After constructing several successful steam fire engines, Ericsson turned his restless talents to the railroad. The Liverpool and Manchester Line had been built for literal horsepower. Even so, the visionary owners offered a £500 ($2,500) award for the best steam locomotive design. Ericsson built his *Novelty,* the only competitor of consequence being George Stephenson's *Rocket.*

The year was 1829, and the Liverpool Line, while ambitious, was some four years too late to be the first such route, having been beaten out by the Stockton and Darlington Line. However, the public was still unconvinced. In fact, people remained in dread of the smoke- and flame-belching machines clanging down relatively soft and none-too-straight iron rails, threatening to burst momentarily into atoms. The Duke of Wellington himself, hero of Waterloo and other memorable engagements, had already denounced the railroad as an "experiment too risky," elaborating that speeds in excess of five miles per hour would surely endanger a human's "respiration." He was a very old man before he would ride in a steam-driven coach, and only then because Queen Victoria had commanded him to sit in attendance beside her.

The conditions of the 1829 contest: the engine must be capable of drawing a weight of twenty tons at the rate of ten miles per hour. Characteristically undismayed, Ericsson planned and actually constructed his *Novelty* in seven weeks. The race, held in October of that year, brought out thousands of cheering spectators.

The *Times* was ecstatic, writing, "The *Novelty* was the lightest and most elegant carriage on the road yesterday, and the velocity with which it moved surprised and amazed every beholder. It shot along the line at the amazing rate of thirty miles an hour. It seemed indeed to fly. . . ."

Then, thirty-five, forty, fifty—almost sixty miles an hour! It appeared to the spectators really the closest thing to the flight of man they had ever seen.

But it was much too fast. The *Novelty*'s boiler burst, and with it Ericsson's dreams of £500. Stephenson's sturdier but slower locomotive was the winner.

Four years later, in 1833, Ericsson succeeded in building a caloric heat engine that actually worked and could be considered a crude ancestor of the gasoline-fueled internal-combustion engine or Rudolf Diesel's similar and more powerful creation. It was hailed by contemporary and more senior scientists including Michael Faraday, who nonetheless salted his praise with the admission that he really couldn't understand how the contrivance "worked at all."

Ericsson interrupted his greater and lesser inventions (such as a file-cutting machine) long enough to marry Amelia Byam, a nineteen-year-old English girl. Wedding guests listened to the bridegroom's wry observation that this was the first time he had been in church in ten years and that he hoped it would be at least ten more before his next visit.

Back at his drawing boards within hours, the newlywed now turned to a principle first perceived by Archimedes two centuries before Christ: the rotary or screw propeller for marine propulsion, replacing the more familiar side, or beam, paddle wheels. He successfully patented his propeller and in the ensuing two years demonstrated them on the ships *Francis B. Ogden* and *Robert F. Stockton,* both named for Americans with whom Ericsson had entered into financial arrangements. Each ship was fitted with twin propellers.

The Lords of the Admiralty and other dignitaries were invited to a demonstration of the *Ogden* on the Thames. But not all would believe even their eyes. Sir William Symonds, surveyor of the Royal Navy, returned to his offices to scoff, "Even if the screw has the power to propel a vessel it would be found altogether useless in practice because, the power being applied at the stern, it would be absolutely impossible to make the vessel steer."

In spite of such skepticism, the tiny *Robert F. Stockton,* a mere seventy feet overall, crossed the Atlantic in 1839. Like the pioneering steamships before her such as the *Savannah* in 1819, she stretched her canvas for almost the entire passage.

Ericsson and his bride followed the *Stockton* to America within a few months, arriving in New York in late November 1839 aboard the *Great Western.* In service only a year, this side-wheeler was a ship calculated to impress its innovator-passenger. Designed by another inventive genius, Isambard Kingdom Brunel (who would soon build the giant *Great Eastern*), the *Great Western* was more than three times the length of the *Stockton,* 1,340 tons, and could work up to eight knots. Her great saloon displayed panels ranging from landscapes, the arts and sciences, to Cupid and Pysche, setting a precedent for yet more lavish North Atlantic decor to come. She appeared easily worth the first-class passage of $150 a cabin. Although the voyage consumed three full weeks, the *Great Western* proved a stable ocean ship as she butted through westerly gales.

Captain Stockton's earlier arrival aboard his namesake attracted more attention than Ericsson's, since the former was a well-known U.S. Navy officer.

The Ericssons quietly took up residence in the Astor House in New York, a favorite, salty meeting place for sailing captains. There, the famous Clipper masters of a decade hence—such as Nat Palmer, Josiah Cressy, and A. A. Low—would lay wagers, over their rum, on the duration of the upcoming voyage to California, to Australia, or China.

The Swede from Långbanshyttan had not planned more than a visit to the New World. His main purpose, at his friend Ogden's urging, was to "introduce my propeller on the canals and inland waters of the Union."

He also entertained dreams of a "big frigate" for the navy. Curiously enough, Ericsson had developed the desire to aid the armed forces of the United States, rather than his own country or even Great Britain. As a matter of fact, Ericsson had reasons to feel a chill toward the Island Kingdom: he had languished briefly in debtor's prison, Fleet Street, two years before, leaving England as a foreign bankrupt.

Determined not to repeat the incident, Ericsson lost no time in fulfilling the purpose of his journey. Within three years he had five propeller craft operating: two on the Great Lakes and three along the Delaware and Chesapeake Canal, linking Philadelphia and Baltimore. The latter three were so efficient that the competing Philadelphia, Wilmington, and Baltimore Railroad was compelled to reduce its fare one-half, then persuade the Delaware legislature to impose a prohibitory tariff on passengers traveling by the wonderful propeller boats.

During the period 1841–44, Ericsson's major achievement was the unconventional 600-ton iron frigate *Princeton,* approved by the farsighted Secretary of the Navy Abel P. Upshur, a Virginian. The hull was built at the Philadelphia Navy Yard, the engine in New York. The *Princeton* was noted for many "firsts"—the first "direct-acting" screw-driven metal-hulled steamship of war with all machinery below the waterline, furnaces designed for anthracite, forced draft by blowers, telescopic stack—and the biggest gun ever carried by a fighting vessel, of twelve-inch caliber.

Captain Stockton, still more or less a partner of Ericsson's, was so smitten with this gargantua of artillery that he arranged for one of his own to be forged, of the same caliber, but a foot more in diameter at the breech and altogether much heavier. It was believed to have been the largest mass of iron thus far brought under the forging hammer. The New Jersey naval officer loved his gun so much that he endowed it with a name—the Peacemaker.

But the Peacemaker, formidable and even frightening as it appeared, was imbued with an Achilles' heel, a pugilist's "glass jaw." Unlike Ericsson's gun, the Peacemaker was not reinforced with hooplike iron rings forged into the breech and extending for a partial length. In a word, roughly, it was weak "sidewise."

On February 28, 1844, a notable executive party headed by President John Tyler went on board the *Princeton* on the Potomac River for a cruise and demonstration of the wondrous Frankenstein of a naval rifle. It was a bright, unusually warm winter's day, a festive occasion with some four hundred political and social leaders and their ladies present. All held ears as the guns were fired time and again off Fort Washington (shamefully abandoned in the War of 1812). Finally, the guests retired below to toast many people and many things, including the Peacemaker. However, Secretary of the Navy Thomas Gilmer prevailed upon Captain Stockton for just one more blast from the weapon. A number of the party walked up on deck again to watch.

Stockton himself, with a confident sweep, applied fire to the fuse. There was a resounding shock, a flash, and the vessel staggered as it was wreathed in smoke.

The concussion subsided and the smoke cleared. There was the sound of groans. The Peacemaker had blown apart. Five persons lay dead, including Secretary of State Upshur and Secretary Gilmer. A score, seriously wounded, writhed in agony. Many more, including the President, were unhurt since they had been below.

The reverberations, stunning the Capital, quickly spread to the nation. No less affected than his readers, the reporter for the *Daily National Intelligencer* took pen to pronounce his own requiem: ". . . they passed from life to death by means not less fleet or fatal than fire from Heaven."

The repercussions cast their shadow as well, if undeservedly, over the Swedish inventor. The U.S. Government would never pay him the $13,930 still owed for his role in the *Princeton,* even though she steamed on to prove her usefulness in the Mexican War. The friendship of the two men, Stockton and Ericsson, was shattered. The former attempted to blame the disaster upon the Swedish inventor in spite of the fact that the Peacemaker was Stockton's design.

Not discouraged, Ericsson continued his dream of a "big frigate." However, bigness per se would not necessarily be its yardstick.

Nonetheless, he remained occupied with other projects. The 260-foot *Ericsson,* powered by his caloric engine, sank in a squall off New Jersey but was raised and refitted for steam. Steam machinery for various light tonnage vessels earned him as high as $84,000 in one year, but he lost money on the *Iron Witch,* a New York–Albany Hudson River steamer equipped with both a propeller and paddles. She vibrated so much that none wanted to embark on her pulsating decks.

Ericsson devoted much time to defending his patent rights to the screw or "spiral" propeller, especially with respect to those U.S. Government steamers found using them. He failed, however, to win a $15,000 claim. In spite of his rebuffs and shabby treatment with regard to funds owed him for the *Princeton,* Ericsson became a naturalized citizen in October 1848.

The 1840s passed into the 1850s as the Swede grew into middle age. He had moved from the Astor to a handsome house in the Wall Street area: 45 Franklin Street, its magnificence becoming a source of embarrassment. He wrote, in fact, to his mother, "Do not put faith in the gossip about our 'lavishing.' There are people who cannot understand that one can live in a grand house, wear fine clothes, and yet starve. As to my wife, her elegant garment is a black dress which I gave her five years ago. . . ."

Perhaps his lack of attention to his wife or her wardrobe was one reason why Amelia returned to England, to live out her natural life in even deeper loneliness. A hint as to Ericsson's attitude toward women found its way into a letter written by him on the occasion of an acquaintance's marriage: "I cannot refrain from giving you as a friend advice not to expect too much of your wife."

His living habits were much those of a bachelor whose interests were other than the opposite sex. Although not an early riser—breakfast was at 8:30—Ericsson, when not making business calls or stumping about a shipyard or iron foundry to supervise the transformation of his diagrams into actualities, was at his drawing board. On some days this could be as many as fourteen hours.

"John Ericsson," wrote William Conant Church, the inventor's friend and original biographer, "lived for his work, and he had no wish that anything beyond a record of that should survive him."

Ericsson boasted to his friends that he was in "good working condition" 365 days of the year. This in turn was attributable to an unusually rugged physique rather than any planned regimen of exercise balanced with rest.

When he again moved, several years after Amelia left him, to 36 Beach Street, near Canal Street and City Hall, his habits remained unchanged. His workroom with drawing boards stretched the full twenty-five feet of the second floor, bright with its five windows. His parlor and dining room, dominated by heavy chandeliers and mantel mirrors, exuded grandfatherly, old-fashioned dignity. The arts and the theater were distractions that did not intrude upon the single focus of Ericsson's life. At least one caller observed that the pins in the cushion on his bedroom bureau were arranged so that they should be in mathematical rows—and he assumed that he would probably find them so the next time he happened by. His letter file bore witness to his preoccupation with mechanical sketches and specifications.

His dress was as coldly meticulous as his home's furnishings, always formal. Invariably he could be seen in a black frock surtout coat, with rolling collar, velvet vest over a fresh shirt front, gold chain hung about his neck, looped at the first buttonhole and attached to a watch in the fob of the vest. His trousers were usually of light shade. When he walked out of his front door, a dressy beaver hat and kid gloves completed his day's habit.

Even as Ericsson in the lonely, austere grandeur of Beach Street bent constantly over his drawing board, the Union as conceived by the founding fathers was crumbling. The country, observed Charles P. Stone, a volunteer brigadier general, "was in a curious and alarming condition."

"States' rights" and the question of slavery in the "Cotton States" as well as congressional protection of slavery in the territories became issues in 1860 much too divisive to ignore.

It was manifestly beyond the capacities of the bachelor President from Pennsylvania, James Buchanan, who lamented his own inadequacies in a despairing "the office of President of the United States is not fit for a gentleman to hold."

If, as Buchanan implied, he was not up to the job, he was by the same token surrounded by weary men who could not parry the rising, impassioned dissent from the vigorous southern states or from men of stature who followed such champions of states' rights as former President John Tyler. (He died, however, before he could be seated in the Confederate Congress.)

Buchanan's general in chief of the Army, Winfield Scott, was a tired, arthritic, seventy-five-year-old relic of the War of 1812 and the Mexican War. He was a prime example of the dying flame of this Democratic administration, far too defeatist to counter the politicians below the Mason-Dixon Line.

The administration saw the clamor for secession in 1860 become active reality as the year moved forward. In June the Southern Democratic National Convention, meeting successively in Charleston, Richmond, and Baltimore, nominated its own candidates: John C. Breckinridge of Kentucky, President, and Joseph Lane of Oregon (strangely enough!), Vice-President. The *pièce de résistance* of the splinter party's plank was its insistence that it was the duty of the federal government to protect slavery.

The northern, or so-called loyal, Democrats nominated Stephen A. Douglas—"the little giant"—of Illinois, as their presidential choice. He would oppose a tall, gawky Republican lawyer, also from Illinois,

Abraham Lincoln, who had not proven to be the orator that Douglas was and cut an awkward, far-from-imposing figure.

However, Douglas, the skilled debater, was overwhelmed in the November 1860 elections. Lincoln won 180 electoral votes compared with 72 for Breckinridge and only 12 for Douglas.

Events moved swiftly. Howell Cobb, a Georgian, resigned as secretary of the treasury, and South Carolina adopted an ordinance of secession. A week later, on December 27, Castle Pinckney and Fort Moultrie, guarding Charleston Harbor, and dating to the Revolution, were seized by South Carolina.

Major Robert Anderson, commanding the Union forces, had moved his skeleton garrison of sixty-five men to strategic Fort Sumter on a built-up land spit in the middle of Charleston Harbor. There he dug in, adamantly refusing requests to surrender as the South Carolinians peremptorily seized an arsenal, the revenue cutter *William Aiken,* and other United States property in the city.

President Buchanan, more frustrated than ever and groping for some remedy, proclaimed January 4 a "Fast and Prayer Day." It didn't seem quite enough.

The tempo of history continued to pick up. A relief "expedition" involving about two hundred troops and supplies was packed aboard the Roberts Shipping Line side-wheeler *Star of the West* at New York and hurried off to Charleston. Shortly after dawn on January 9, 1861, as the vessel approached Sumter, Confederate batteries on Morris Island, at the southern approaches to the harbor, opened fire. She was hit only once—not seriously—after a total of seventeen shots was fired. The captain, John McGowan, of the United States Revenue Service, decided that prudence dictated that his course be reversed seaward.

The Charleston *Daily Courier* would headline the next day:

THE ARRIVAL AND DEPARTURE OF THE
STAR OF THE WEST

It commented: "None, therefore, were surprised when the deep-toned cannons of the batteries and forts occupied by the troops of the Commonwealth spoke in tones of thunder on Wednesday morning. . . ."

It was an understatement, as well as ungrammatical, even though the writer unwittingly chronicled the opening shots of the new war.

". . . no longer tenable"

Navy Department
April 12, 1861

CONFIDENTIAL:

Sir: The Department desires to have the *Merrimack* removed from the Norfolk to the Philadelphia Navy Yard with the utmost dispatch. The Engineer-in-Chief, B. F. Isherwood, has been ordered to report to you for the purpose of expediting the duty, and you will have his suggestions for that end carried promptly into effect.

I am, sir, respectfully, your obedient servant,

Gideon Welles,
Secretary of the Navy

TO: Commodore Charles S. McCauley
    Commandant, Navy Yard, Portsmouth, Va.

The New York *Times*, on January 10, in reporting the firing upon the *Star of the West,* observed "Great Fluttering Among the Secessionists."

There was, however, to be worse than that. Emboldened by South Carolina's militant rebellion, Florida, Alabama, Georgia, Louisiana, Mississippi, and Texas left the Union and seized government stores, forts, and other property. On March 11, a week after Lincoln's inauguration, the Confederacy, under Jefferson Davis, at Montgomery, Alabama, proclaimed its own constitution and settled down to the business of raising an army, "not to exceed 100,000 men, for 12 months' service." Davis, a West Pointer and onetime secretary of war, an icy, ingrown man, had characteristically underestimated the magnitude of the South's rebellious acts as well as the federal government's capacity to respond.

The fledgling Confederacy, at least, beat Lincoln's similar call by more than a month. Both calls revealed the nearly total unreadiness of North or South for organized hostilities. At the beginning of 1861 the Federal Regular Army was barely in excess of 16,000 officers and men. The South had its loosely organized state militia, volunteer outfits often no more than hometown drum-and-bugle corps which paraded their uniforms for the Fourth of July.

Leaders, both north and south of the Mason-Dixon Line, particularly President Buchanan, had never thought the situation would really deteriorate to *this*.

Unpreparedness was especially true of the navies. The South started with nothing more than a few stolen—"appropriated" or "confiscated"—revenue cutters, governmental survey steamers, tugs, and river craft that happened to be in ports seized by the seceding states. The *Star of the West* herself fell into enemy hands in April 1861 in Texas. The only marine asset enjoyed by the secessionists in the opening months was their fifty-year-old naval secretary, dynamic Stephen Mallory, of Florida, former chairman of the Senate Committee on Naval Affairs and early advocate of ironclad ships. By profession an admiralty lawyer, he was a pragmatist who believed Americans were "the most military people on earth." An old-fashioned disciplinarian as well, he fought a losing campaign to bring the cat-o'-nine-tails back to United States navy ships.

The Federal Navy of ninety ships furrowed a wake impressive only on paper seas. Forty of these were steam-propelled, none was an ironclad. Only eighteen could be termed relatively modern. Among the six large propeller-driven frigates were the *Merrimack* and *Minnesota*. The six-year-old ships, each more than three thousand tons, and mounting between forty-five and fifty guns, were rated, understandably, as "first-class." The coming of war found the *Merrimack* "dead" in the Gosport Navy Yard, having lain there a year upon the completion of her last and wearying cruise to Panama. Those of her crew of some five hundred whose enlistments hadn't expired deserted anyhow, many to beat the drums in their southern states for "secessh."

Decommissioned, she awaited the repair or replacement of her engines and possibly a new propeller shaft as well. It was a big, heavy one. She had been a hard-luck ship, what with previous mechanical breakdowns and discipline problems. Some averred that there had been more court martials aboard her than on any other in the navy.

Perhaps she brought along her own peculiar jinx. The whole Norfolk-Portsmouth-Gosport area seethed with secession. Gosport, named for an English town near Portsmouth, had been started as a British yard shortly before the Revolution. It had been home to the slowly growing United States Navy since 1794 and site of its first stone dry dock.

The navy, officers and sailors together with their families, learned to like the "southern" character of Norfolk, which, as a matter of fact, was maturing into an international crossroads. Ships arrived from Rio, London, Rotterdam, Le Havre, Marseilles, Cape Town, Calcutta, Sydney, Hong Kong, Manila, and Honolulu, bearing English cloth and wool, steelware, French wines and fine clothing, German and Swiss clocks, chinaware, wrought-iron furniture, sugar, and rum. They returned with tobacco and cotton, corn, pigs, pig iron, turpentine, butter, pine boards and other lumber, hides, skins, a vast assortment of raw materials that typified the New World's distinctive, lusty commerce.

There were large wooden hotels such as the Virginia, City, North Carolina, and Atlantic; specialty schools such as the Norfolk Female Institute (board and tuition, fifty dollars); pharmacies, such as Ewing's Drug Store at 29 Church Street ("Prescriptions compounded with the utmost care and promptness—no extra charge for getting up at night"); stores of every description, such as B. H. Owens, "Dealer

27

in First Class Staple and Fancy Dry Goods," on High Street, Portsmouth; an opera house, a great barter hub known as the Merchants and Mechanics Exchange, and a meeting center, Ashland Hall.

Advertisements in the *Southern Argus* and in the *Day Book* hawked such wares as matches, pepper, claret, flannel (which became "Confederate cotton"), "red padding," coffee, plows, leaf tobacco, "genuine English mustard," dry goods, tweeds, poplin boots, books, slaves, horses, cows, and a variety of patent-medicine "cure-alls."

It was as well a relatively young "town," along with its twin, Portsmouth, more frontierlike than its seaport counterparts in Europe, mellowed by the passage of centuries. Visitors from overseas found little to say that was complimentary about Norfolk's architecture, cleanliness, or waterfront aroma. Sobriety was undermined by the abundance of saloons and the availability, in barrel lots, of "Pure Mountain Rye Whiskey" and "Pure Corn Whiskey" along with the prewar flood of Jamaican rum.

However, the new secretary of the navy, Gideon Welles, was little concerned about the morals, the sights or smells, of Norfolk—just so it and its major navy yard remained under the Stars and Stripes. In fact, he had been in office but two weeks when he ordered the old sailing sloop of war *Cumberland*, 1,726 tons, mounting twenty-four guns, barnacled from several months' service in the Gulf of Mexico, to anchor off the Navy Yard, just to keep an eye on what was going on—also, what was *not* going on.

In addition to the *Merrimack* there were eight more or less major warships moored at the yard, plus the newly arrived *Cumberland*. These included the sloop *Germantown* and the ship of the line *Pennsylvania*, at 3,105 tons the largest sailing vessel ever built by the U.S. Navy and the only one with three gun decks. Authorized in 1816, she was not launched until 1837. A seventy-five-gun monstrosity, she was maintained as a receiving ship, mostly a barracks for sailors in transit, also a floating office for interminable if generally necessary "desk duty."

Considering the character of the yard's top command, bewhiskered old Commodore McCauley, of vintage similar to Winfield Scott's, Welles had ample reason for concern over the fate of the *Merrimack* as well as the entire nautical establishment. A naval observer, James R. Soley, had sniffed of the veteran officer, "an august personage who went to sea in a great flagship surrounded by conventional grandeur."

The navy secretary fired off his initial dispatch on April 13, only the day before Fort Sumter surrendered under bombardment and was evacuated. The garrison was packed aboard a small ineffective flotilla offshore commanded by Captain Gustavus Fox, a veteran of the Mexican War, distinguished by a high forehead and narrow-trimmed beard. The larger fighting ships that Fox needed for this "relief expedition" never arrived.

The Civil War had now begun in earnest.

Virginia deserted the Union—"against the monstrous despotism in Washington," as the Richmond *Dispatch* rationalized. But there were many second thoughts among the Old Dominion's citizens. For one, there was Elizabeth McIntosh Wallace, forty-five-year-old mother of four, including a twenty-year-old son, who lived at the handsome plantation Glencoe, near Norfolk on the Dismal Swamp Canal. She wrote on April 17, "It is supposed that Va. passed the ordinance of secession this morning. God have mercy upon us. I hope that I shall not live to regret that I have a grown son. . . ."

Her reaction was not far different from many thousands of Virginians, less rabid than South Carolinians or Georgians to secede.

"We are one of the most intensely excited communities," wrote another Norfolk resident, Jackson Ward, to his father. "We are now as it were in sight of a greate [*sic*] civil war. . . . We have two of the largest U.S. men of war of the hole [*sic*] Navy blockaded in. They are abreast of the Navy Yard and could blow the towns of Portsmouth and Norfolk into distinction [*sic*] if they were to attempt it. According to report, federal troops will arrive here and other points in Virginia in a few days. It is reported here today that several thousand troops from the South are now in Wilmington, N.C. on there [*sic*] way to Norfolk. . . . It is now 5 o'clock. The city is all excitement and full of people from the surrounding country . . . everybody is after me to join the Military—what shall I do?—I am bound to fight. There is no escape for any southern man except to prove himself a coward—that I cannot and shall never do. . . ."

With the fall of Sumter, panic seized Washington itself. There were riots in Baltimore, leaving a number killed, including Federal troops. The toll of the 6th Massachusetts Infantry was four dead, thirty-six wounded. Secretary of War Simon Cameron feared that the nation's capital would be invaded both from Virginia, on the southern shores of the Potomac River, and from Baltimore, less than forty miles to the northeast.

Within the week, however, the regiments marched in, noisily, double time, 35,000 strong, led by the proud, famed New York 7th. They were brought in by trains, crowded aboard box cars and passenger coaches hooked up as the locomotives had found them in the yards, from as far north as Maine. The majority came from New York, Massachusetts, Rhode Island, and Pennsylvania. Connecticut, New Jersey, and Delaware assembled their volunteers as fast as they could muster and uniform them. Even beleagured Norfolk and Old Point were denuded of some marines who were sent posthaste up the Potomac by steamer.

The soldiers overflowed the parks and open fields with their tents. Campfires glowed everywhere in the city at night. Some, not necessarily the more fortunate, were billeted in Federal buildings. The 6th Massachusetts, which had been bloodied at Baltimore, noisily pushed into quarters in the U.S. Senate Chamber, the 8th under the Dome of the Rotunda, the 7th New York (or most of it) on the House side, Rhode Island regiments in the handsome stone Patent Office. And so it went.

Along with his dispatch to McCauley, Welles hurried the young engineer in chief of the navy, Benjamin Isherwood, off to Norfolk. Then he snapped orders to the navy yards in Philadelphia and New York and to the receiving ship *Allegheny* in Baltimore Harbor to rush vessels and reinforcements of men to Norfolk. If Isherwood was to *somehow* get the *Merrimack* out of the commodore's clutches and across Hampton Roads to the safety of Fort Monroe, until she could steam to Philadelphia, he would need all the assistance that could be provided.

Isherwood was appalled at McCauley's doddering state. He found him "under the influence of liquor and bad men" (alluding both to his own southern officers and to the hard core of secessionists working in the yard, undermining the commodore's will)—also "stupefied and bewildered." Worse, the enfeebled commodore had been hoodwinked through various ruses—including the blowing of train whistles and prearranged shoutings of local citizens beyond the yard's gates—into believing that literally thousands of Confederate troops were waiting to storm the base.

Nothing could have been further from fact, with about eight hundred local militia, ill trained, poorly equipped, and overage, opposing a yard that, together with its ships, mounted hundreds of large-caliber cannon and could be instantly reinforced from Fort Monroe.

However, his own momentarily inadequate force, of doubtful loyalty, and his confused condition notwithstanding, McCauley professedly had good intentions. He replied to Welles: "I have the honor to inform the Department that the steam frigate *Merrimack* may now be taken and used for temporary service as soon as the necessary equipment can be put on board. All that is required to be done to the hull for temporary service will probably be completed by tomorrow evening [the seventeenth]."

Isherwood wasn't so certain. He found the engines "in a wretched state," the boilers disconnected, "the entire machinery . . . in a disabled condition." However, he assembled all the yard force of mechanics and boilermakers he could find and who could be counted on for at least marginal loyalty and set them hard at work—"steadily urged day and night"—toward completing a jury rig of machinery. He replaced the chain cables mooring the ship to the dock with ropes so that they could be severed with axes.

The Confederates, through their own people working in the Gosport yard, were aware of these frantic efforts. They sent steam tugs up and down the Elizabeth River to reconnoiter the possibility of scuttling old barges to block the channel. At the same time, earthworks were being shoveled up on the riverbank opposite the Navy Yard, as though cannon—if the secessionists could find any handy—would be mounted.

This was too much for a hot-blooded twenty-five-year-old lieutenant, Thomas O. Selfridge, Jr., aboard the mother hen *Cumberland*. Handsome Tom Selfridge, of Massachusetts, was a "charter" graduate of the swaddling Naval Academy, class of '51, whose father commanded the side-wheeler frigate *Mississippi* in the Gulf Squadron. He obtained permission of his own commanding officer, Captain John Marston, to pay a visit on McCauley with a plan of action. He proposed to the commandant of the Navy Yard to enter Norfolk under a flag of truce and bluntly warn that the *Cumberland* and other men-of-war in the yard would open fire on Norfolk if channel obstructions and earthwork operations did not at once cease.

McCauley, in desperation, told the very junior officer to go ahead. Holding aloft almost jauntily his white flag, Selfridge passed through a "large and excited crowd collected on the waterfront." He was taken to "the headquarters," in the Atlantic Hotel, of the commanding general, a state militia officer.

The latter observed, with some surprise, that it would be a "terrible thing" to fire on an "undefended" city. After further brief discussion, Selfridge returned to Gosport accompanied by a somber, moustached West Pointer, Colonel Henry C. Heth, recently gone over to the southern cause. Heth assured McCauley that work on the batteries across the river would cease.

Meanwhile, Welles, now possessed of the cold realization that the Navy Yard at Norfolk and all that lay there were probably lost, sent both "rank" and additional forces down the Potomac. They were led by Commodore Hiram Paulding, temporarily commanding U.S. Naval Forces in the waters of Virginia, plus the 3rd Massachusetts Infantry backed up by one hundred marines. Paulding, sixty-five, had served under Commodore Thomas MacDonough in Lake Champlain during the War of 1812. It happened to be particularly painful to him that a number of his closest associates had gone over to the Confederates—for one, Commander Matthew Fontaine Maury, eminent hydrographer and navigator. For another there was Commodore Josiah Tattnall. Paulding had been so friendly with the latter that he named a son, now in the army, Tattnall Paulding.

Isherwood, who well knew that the hour was one minute to midnight, had the engines of the prized *Merrimack* throbbing in about three days. A captain, Commander James Alden, waited to go aboard. But McCauley was succumbing to panic. The final blow to what remained of the old commodore's composure was the rumor that a steamer loaded with rebel soldiers had been sighted boiling down the James River from Richmond to seize the Navy Yard.

As Paulding waited at Fort Monroe with the small steamer *Pawnee* to take the *Merrimack* in tow, if that was necessary, Isherwood reported:

> . . . coal and engineer stores had been taken on board during this time, and forty-four firemen and coal heavers engaged for the trip. On Wednesday afternoon at 4 o'clock I called, in company with Chief Engineer Danby, on Commodore McCauley, reported the machinery ready for steam, informed him that forty-four firemen and coal heavers had been engaged and were ready to go on board, and asked him if I should fire up at once. He replied not that afternoon, adding that if I had steam on the next morning it would be time enough. Accordingly, a regular engine-room watch was kept during the night and the fires were started at daybreak. About 9 a.m. I called on the commodore and reported the engineer department ready for

leaving; that Chief Engineer Danby, the assistant engineers, the firemen, and the coal heavers were all on board, with steam up and the engines working at the wharf.

The only thing wanting was his order to cast loose and go.

He then, to my great surprise and dissatisfaction, informed me that he had not yet decided to send the vessel, but would let me know further in the course of a few hours. I called his attention to the fact that the instructions of the Department were peremptory to send her, and expressed the opinion she would pass any obstructions the enemy could have placed in the channel without feeling them, adding that if he delayed a few hours the vessel would have to remain another day, and that during the night the obstructions would doubtless be increased. To this he replied, as before, that he would determine in the course of the day.

On leaving him I requested Commander Alden to go on board with me; and pointing out to him the engineers, firemen, and coal heavers assembled in the engine room, steam being up and the engines working at the wharf, I told him that so far as the engineer department was concerned the vessel was ready to go, and that my part was done.

About 2 p.m. I again called on the commodore, when he informed me that he had decided to retain the vessel, and directed me to draw the fires. I once more asked his attention to the peremptory nature of the orders of the Department, and expressed my conviction that the vessel could then be taken out with perfect safety, volunteering earnestly my advice that the attempt should be immediately made and with the sloop of war *Germantown* in tow. He replied by reiterating his previous declaration that he should retain the vessel.

None seemed to understand; no other officer present felt he possessed sufficient seniority to countermand the infirm commodore. Tom Selfridge could only guess that McCauley was trying to avoid an "overt act"—such as getting one of his own vessels under way—to anger the Confederates.

The Navy Yard commander went further, on Saturday, April 20. McCauley ordered the whole installation and all the ships, including the *Merrimack,* scuttled by smashing and by the torch.

Welles would fix responsibility not only on McCauley but on Alden as well. The latter, whom he thought of as his personal emissary, was "timid but patriotic, wholly unable to act," lacking "audacity" and "moral courage," when, the secretary of the navy believed, he had every prerogative to do so. Isherwood came off blameless in Gideon Welles's own recapitulation of right and wrong, of effectiveness and bumbling ineffectuality.

Commodore Paulding hauled in too late. McCauley's little fleet, sea cocks opened, was either in the river mud and muck or slowly settling. There was nothing for the newly arrived senior officer to do except hasten the job of destruction and evacuate the yard.

Lamenting the inability and/or impossibility of removing or fully wrecking the big cannon, Paulding would report:

> One hundred men worked for an hour with sledge hammers, and such was the tenacity of the iron that they did not succeed in breaking a single trunnion. In carrying out the orders of the Department it was my intention to have placed the vessels named in the channel to protect it from further obstructions, and at my convenience take them under the guns of Fortress Monroe, or send them to sea, as might be most expedient.
>
> Greatly to my regret, however, I found that these vessels had all been scuttled about two or three hours before my arrival, and were sinking so fast that they could not be saved. In view of this condition of things there were but two alternatives presented to my mind—the first, to leave the navy yard and ships in the hands of people hostile to the Government, for it was apparent that the yard could not be held by our available means of defense; or, using the power with which I was invested, destroy the public property of every description. I was not long in adopting the latter expedient. . . .

The *Pawnee*'s quartermaster would log the dismal story:

> April 21.—Commences and till 4 a.m.; making preparations for setting fire to the ship houses, ships, and storehouses, and destroying the dry dock. Landed all the turpentine, powder, and waste received on board from the *Anacostia* on Friday last. Reembarked the marines and the Massachusetts regiment. Sent parties in charge of Captain Wilkes, Commanders Sands, Rodgers, and Alden, and Captain Wright, of U.S. Engineers, for carrying on the preparations above mentioned. At about 2 a.m. the marine barracks were set fire to. At 3:30 hauled off from the wharf and prepared to take the flagship *Cumberland* in tow. At 4:15 a.m. the *Cumberland,* having the steam tug *Yankee* alongside, succeeded in getting a hawser to this ship and slipping her cable. We got underway and commenced steaming

down to Hampton Roads. At 4:20 sent up a rocket, and the ships, buildings, etc., were fired. Sent all hands to quarters, opened the magazine and shell rooms and manned the starboard battery, the marines being all on deck under arms. Steaming slowly down, passed by the cities of Portsmouth and Norfolk unmolested, the flames of the burning buildings at the yard illuminating the vessels and the town perfectly. Steaming slowly to allow the boats to come alongside.

"The scene," according to Tom Selfridge, "was most impressive. The great conflagration made it as light as day. Norfolk was in the hands of an armed mob, which lined the shores, angry at the destruction which was taking place. . . ."

The correspondent for the Charleston *Courier* filing from Norfolk early Sunday, April 21, 1861, at 1:40 A.M., saw the spectacle:

"I have just come up from the wharf and from looking at the fire. It is a great puzzle to me. It does not spread at all—nor is the Yard ignited at other places. The fire is about the size of a burning of a large dwelling. Now and then it brightens up as if tar barrels or other combustible matter were thrown upon it."

The reporter, whose presence in the port proved at least that this was a well-covered war, journalistically, added three hours later, "I woke up to find the Navy Yard one universal sea of flames which in their wild leaping, lick the very clouds with their tongues of fire. The noise is . . . like the deep-toned roar of Niagara."

It was really worse than a Niagara—a thunderous $10 million dirge. McCauley's almost treasonable act ("treachery or imbecility!" cried *Leslie's Illustrated Weekly*) had placed in the South's hands several imperfectly scuttled warships—preeminently the *Merrimack*—some three thousand pieces of ordnance of all calibers including three hundred of the latest big eleven-inch Dahlgren cannon (named after their inventor, ordnance wizard Captain John A. Dahlgren), thousands of rounds of ammunition, powder barrels, food (including 991 barrels of pork, six tons of bread), clothing, uniforms, an intact stone dry dock and many other buildings. . . .

The list rolled depressingly on.

A dazed and uncomprehending McCauley would take pen aboard the *Cumberland,* anchored in the lee of the Rip Raps' huge guns, to inform Gideon Welles, ". . . the yard was no longer tenable."

His was one of the more profound understatements of the war.

"This warmed me up . . ."

The *Merrimac* is still in drydock, and it is expected that she will be ready for service by the first of the coming month. Some of the mechanics in Norfolk have expressed an opinion that, in consequence of the large amount of iron on her upper works, she will be so top heavy as to be unmanageable.

Philadelphia *Inquirer*, October 5, 1861

Lincoln, during the debacle at Norfolk, had ordered a blockade of all southern ports. The navy, perhaps, could carry it out. But even so, this strategic resolve could scarcely compensate for the loss of Gosport. The Union had not done an effective job even of demolition in spite of the pyrotechnics. There were indeed those who thought that some of the soldiers and sailors entrusted with the task had deliberately tamped out fuses or thrown them into the water.

One who appreciated the prize that had fallen to the Confederacy by default was Davis's Secretary of the Navy Mallory, who arrived in Norfolk by river steamer and train. In less than three weeks, on May 10, 1861, he was writing the South's congressional naval committee, which was still located in the provisional capital, Montgomery, Alabama:

> I regard the possession of an iron-armored ship as a matter of the first necessity. Such a vessel could traverse the entire coast of the United States, prevent all blockade and encounter, with a fair prospect of success their entire navy. If to cope with them upon the sea we follow their example and build wooden ships, we shall have to construct several at one time. . . .
>
> Naval engagements between wooden frigates, as they are now built and armed, will prove to be the forlorn hopes of the sea, simply contests in which the question, not of victory, but of who shall go to the bottom first, is to be solved.

Armored ships, however, were not, in concept, new. They dated much farther back than any contemporary efforts, to the sixteenth century when Admiral Yi, of Korea, created his little metal-topped "turtle ships," propelled by rowers. And as the 1850s ended, both France and Great Britain could each point to an iron-armored war vessel. H.M.S. *Warrior,* the largest, was a mammoth 9,200-ton juggernaut, 380 feet long. Similar ironclads, including the *Black Prince,* were being built or ordered. The Tricolor flew from the smaller, less impressive *Gloire.*

French Forrest, the new commandant of the Gosport Navy Yard, took it upon his own authority to order a local salvage/wrecking firm, Baker Brothers, to start sealing and pumping the *Merrimack,* since it was the newest and most likely Federal hulk left behind. The complicated, muddy operation was watched by an erstwhile resident of Buffalo, New York, Captain James Byers, of the tug *J. B. White,* who had arrived the previous autumn to assist in building the Albemarle Canal, running south to Albemarle Sound. Byers, however, busy running his tug for new employers, neglected to put in writing *how* Baker was going about its historic task.

On the west shores of Hampton Roads, Flag Officer Silas H. Stringham, first commander of the hastily organized North Atlantic Blockading Squadron, underestimated the salvage potential of at least the *Merrimack*. Such a picture of charred timbers, gnarled rigging, and enveloping mud was conveyed to the arthritic old sea dog that he pronounced the vessel "worthless" in a routine dispatch to Secretary Welles.

Either Stringham did not know about the strenuous efforts of Baker Brothers (his informants themselves did not), or else they were deliberately deceiving him. The South already had attached a premium to deception in military undertakings.

While Gosport's wonderful Federal cannons, many of them rifled, were being entrained southward to North Carolina, Tennessee, Georgia, Louisiana, and other sections of Virginia, all impatient to arm against the Union, the salvagers worked fast and efficiently. Two weeks after Mallory's pronouncement, the new commandant of the Navy Yard wrote to General Robert E. Lee, as the senior official of the Confederacy in the area, "We have the *Merrimack* up and just pulling her in the drydock."

The yard itself was being cleaned up and repaired, its environs fortified. Hospital Point, so named because of a naval hospital long on the site, Craney Island, and Sewell's Point all bristled with guns and earthworks while new batteries sprang up along the Elizabeth River to protect both Gosport-Norfolk and the men-of-war expected to be home-ported in this latest lair of the Confederacy.

It was altogether a heady, exciting spring for Norfolk, hotbed of secession second only to Charleston. Military boots thudded down the dusty streets as troops were trundled in over the Seaboard and Petersburg railways, carrying the bright, impudent flags of Virginia, North Carolina, South Carolina, and Georgia. The soldiers crowded the hotels and rendered it all but impossible for customary platoons of traveling salesmen to find rooms.

Residents wildly cheered new units, sometimes accompanied by fife-and-drum corps. The ladies of the city gave the soldiers fruit and other edibles and mended their uniforms. The newspapers were filled with notices of concerts in the Opera House, picnics, and lesser socials. At the same time, problems attendant to the swelling of a population by military presence inevitably arose—not only brawls and fights but scarcities compounded by the increasingly effective blockade. Flour, for example, soared to an unheard-of $8.50 a barrel.

Curiously, communication continued across the Roads, and not necessarily under flags of truce. Citizens traveled back and forth with surprising nonchalance, bearing newspapers of North and South and shopping in each other's stores. There was an evident thirst for gossip of what the other was doing, both militarily and in the mundane limbo of chit-chat, the "punctuations" of existence.

In spite of Stringham's estimate of the future of the *Merrimack,* Gideon Welles had collected enough tidbits through the Hampton Roads grapevine to be aware that his counterpart in Richmond was not asleep. Although he had never met John Ericsson and possessed not even a rudimentary understanding of the "foundry" concept of warships as opposed to traditional timber, he had a hunch that the day of the ironclad had arrived.

He called attention at a special session of Congress, on July 4, to the fact that England and France had accorded much study to the subject, then recommended "the appointment of a proper and competent board to inquire into and report in regard to a measure so important; and it is for Congress to decide whether on a favorable report, they will order one or more iron-clad steamers, or floating batteries, to be constructed, with a view to perfect protection from the effects of present ordnance at short range, and make an appropriation for that purpose."

Time, however, was running out. Exactly one week later, Mallory, whose Navy Department had now officially moved to Richmond, approved plans that had been drawn up for the alteration of the *Merrimack* into the ironclad *Virginia.* The three designers were Chief Engineer William P. Williamson, Lieutenant John M. Brooke, who had resigned from the U.S. Navy, and Naval Constructor John L. Porter. Mallory then wrote Commandant Forrest:

"You will proceed with all practical dispatch to make changes in the *Merrimack* and to build, equip and fit her in all respects . . . as time is of the utmost importance in this matter, you will see that the work progresses without delay to completion."

Then, as if to underscore his sense of urgency, he proposed to

President Davis "to shield her [the *Merrimack*] completely with 3-inch iron placed at such angles as to render her ball proof, to complete her at the earliest moment, to arm her with the heaviest ordnance and to send her at once against the enemy's fleet. It is believed that thus prepared she will be able to contend successfully against the heaviest of the enemy ships and to drive them from Hampton Roads and the ports of Virginia."

Estimating the cost at $172,523, the Confederate naval chief concluded that he was not waiting on approval—conversion had begun already.

It was a fateful July. On the twenty-first occurred the Union rout at Manassas Junction, Virginia, which came to be known as Bull Run. Residents of the District of Columbia, who had foolishly journeyed to watch what had been previewed as General Irvin McDowell's smashing of the rebellion, turned their horses and stampeded back toward the Capital, fearful that the Confederates would pursue them the whole distance, possibly across the Potomac to their own doorsteps.

Lee would pen, emotionally, "I almost wept for joy at the glorious victory."

It wasn't really that "glorious," or even much of a "victory."

The losses were relatively small—in the hundreds—on both sides and about equal. The battle served the constructive purpose of alerting the United States to the seriousness and long-term magnitude of the task ahead.

On August 3 the Navy Department, stunned but not wholly dismayed at the army's defeat, secured presidential approval for "one or more iron-clad steam vessels of war."

Four days later the department publicly advertised for bids for the ships, "either of iron or wood and iron combined for sea or river service to be of not less than ten nor over sixteen feet draught of water; to carry an armament of from eighty to one hundred and twenty tons weight . . . the vessel to be rigged with two masts with wire rope standing rigging, to navigate at sea."

In the *Evening Star* of Washington, the ad was tucked at the bottom of a page beneath an advertisement for women's clothing: French Sacque Coats (starting at $5.50, with matching dress), straw hats, mantillas, etc.

A senior board was appointed to consider the submissions that were confidently and speedily expected. It was composed of Commodores Joseph Smith and Hiram Paulding, together with the some-what lesser known and more junior Commander Charles H. Davis. Commodore Smith, a midshipman in 1809, and now somewhat infirm, was chief of the Bureau of Yards and Docks.

At 36 Beach Street in New York, a man nearing sixty but still vigorous opened a small box and dusted off a pasteboard model that had lain there seven years.

"I imagined," Ericsson would recall, "that I had a very valuable idea and kept it secure accordingly."

It was a curious sort of naval vessel: small, iron-plated, almost no freeboard, with just one revolving turret—virtually nothing else except for a small pilot house forward. The inventor had offered it to Emperor Napoleon III to use in the Crimean War against Russia, not so much because John Ericsson was sentimental about France but because he hated the czars, as traditional enemies of the Swedish. The Treaty of Paris, in 1856, made it unnecessary for any of the powers to continue weaponry buildup, much less explore technological innovations.

Nonetheless, a court correspondent wrote Ericsson a courteous letter of rejection, declaring, "The Emperor himself examined with the greatest care the new system of naval attack . . . he has found your ideas very ingenious." Then he explained that His Majesty was concerned about the expense as well as "the small number of guns which could be brought into use."

Ericsson labored over his old drawings for three weeks, then wrote a letter to Abraham Lincoln, dated August 29, 1861:

> The writer, having introduced the present system of naval propulsion and constructed the first screw ship of war, now offers to construct a vessel for the destruction of the rebel fleet at Norfolk and for scouring the Southern rivers and inlets of all craft protected by rebel batteries . . . please look carefully at the enclosed plans and you will see that the means I propose to employ are simple—so simple indeed that within ten weeks after commencing the structure I would engage to be ready to take up position under the rebel guns at Norfolk, and so efficient too, I trust, that within a few hours the stolen ships would be sunk and the harbor purged of traitors. Apart from the fact that the proposed vessel is very simple in construction, due weight, I respectfully submit, should be given to the circumstance that its projector possesses practical and constructive skill

shared by no engineer now living. I have planned upward of 100 marine engines and I furnish daily working-plans made with my own hands of mechanical and naval structures of various kinds, and I have done so for thirty years. Besides this, I have received a military education and feel at home in the science of artillery. You will not, sir, attribute these statements to any other cause than my anxiety to prove that you may safely entrust me with the work I propose. If you cannot do so then the country must lose the benefit of my services. . . .

I cannot conclude without respectfully calling your attention to the now well-established fact that steel-clad vessels cannot be arrested in their course by land batteries, and that hence our great city is quite at the mercy of such intruders, and may at any moment be laid in ruins, unless we possess means which, in defiance of Armstrong guns, can crush the sides of such dangerous visitors.

(Ericsson was alluding to British-made cannon, some rifled, patented by the English inventor William A. Armstrong.)

Ericsson signed it, then postscripted:

p.s. It is not for me, sir, to remind you of the immense moral effect that will result from your discomfitting the rebels at Norfolk and showing that batteries can no longer protect vessels robbed from the nation, nor need I allude to the effect in Europe if you demonstrate that you can effectively keep hostile fleets away from our shores. At the moment of putting this communication under envelope, it occurs to me finally that it is unsafe to trust the plans to the mails. I therefore respectfully suggest that you reflect on my proposition. Should you decide to put the work in hand, if my plan meets your own approbation, please telegraph and within forty-eight hours the writer will report himself at the White House.

However, Ericsson, in naïvely trusting the postal system, was competing with time. September 3 had been set as a deadline for submissions.

Moreover, there were those in Washington's bureaucracy with long memories. They still, inaccurately enough, blamed the Swedish inventor for the *Princeton* tragedy. In any event, the wartime deluge of letters, schemes, requests for favors, and similar mail inundated all governmental offices. Ericsson's was in likelihood simply sidetracked by a White House clerk.

Probably only a quirk salvaged Ericsson's proposals—which were really a *plea*—from final and eternal interment. Cornelius S. Bushnell, a thirty-one-year-old aggressive New Haven shipbuilder and formerly a successful wholesale grocer, was in Washington. He had secured in early September a contract to build the *Galena.*

This was an unimaginative ironclad, of 3,296 tons, not much different from existing steam frigates except for plating and the inward slope of the sides so that shells might ricochet off her. With only six cannon, the *Galena* was undergunned.

However, while giving Bushnell the go-ahead, some naval engineers voiced an obvious concern: was the *Galena* sufficiently big and sturdy to carry the armor stipulated? Since Bushnell was builder, not the architect, he was objective. In fact, he welcomed a suggestion, made at the Willard Hotel before he left Washington to return to New Haven, that he consult "the engineer John Ericsson" on the question. It was obvious that none in the Navy Department was aware of the letter of August 29 to President Lincoln.

Bushnell again submitted to the slow, jolting train ride. It required transfers involving four separate, single-track lines to travel between New York and the nation's Capital—also two ferries plus the unique annoyance of two special taxes levied by the states of New Jersey and Maryland. Even the track gauge varied from line to line, making it a physical impossibility for the same car to roll between the major northern East Coast cities.

One could not go by train even from one end of Baltimore to the other. Four lines arrived on the sprawling, ugly city's perimeters at four separate stations. In fact, it was the transfer of the 6th Massachusetts Infantry—by horse and afoot—from the President Street Station twenty-five blocks to the Cameron Station the past April that had incited the secessionist-minded mobs to riot.

Ericsson received Bushnell and asked him for a day to study the *Galena*'s plans. When the New Haven shipbuilder returned the next afternoon as requested, Ericsson met him with the news, "She will easily carry the load you propose and stand a six-inch shot at a respectable distance."

"At the close of the interview," Bushnell would recall, "Captain Ericsson asked me if I had time . . . to examine the plan of a floating battery, absolutely impregnable to the heaviest shot and shell. I replied that this problem had been occupying me for the last three months, and that considering the time required for construction, the *Galena* was the best result I had been able to obtain. He then produced a small, dust-covered box and placed before me the model and plan of the *Monitor,* explaining how quickly and powerfully she could be built."

Bushnell, "perfectly overjoyed," found Ericsson's enthusiasm contagious. Instead of hurrying the cardboard model to Washington, he made a northeasterly detour to Hartford, where Gideon Welles was at home, ailing. There he assured the Navy secretary that at last "the country was safe," because he had "found a battery which would make us masters of the situation so far as the ocean was concerned."

If this was an oversimplification, it at least won Welles's go-ahead. While the Connecticut publisher, eager to return to bed, had no idea whether the ship described would so much as float or not—indeed if it could support a couple of guns together with their ponderous turret—he believed Bushnell should pursue the idea in Washington.

The latter then contacted two partners, John F. Winslow and John A. Griswold, owners of foundries in Albany and Troy, who happened to know Secretary of State William H. Seward, another upstate New Yorker. Bushnell, introduced to Seward by them, thus secured "a strong letter of introduction" to Abraham Lincoln. This was something Ericsson himself had been unable to do, at least had not done. He couldn't even get so much as a letter through to the White House.

Noted for his impulsiveness, the President was impressed by the model, but asked, "Why do you bring this matter to me?" He told his young caller that he would accompany him the next morning across the street to the Navy Department to present the matter, model and all, to the Board of Ironclad Ships.

At 11 A.M. September 12, Lincoln appeared with Bushnell before Commodores Smith and Paulding and Commander Davis, plus other naval advisers of lesser rank. Bushnell found "all . . . surprised with the novelty of the plan. Some advised trying it; others ridiculed it." Finally, Lincoln, in his wry, often enigmatical humor, quipped:

"All I have to say is what the girl said when she stuck her foot into the stocking. It strikes me there's something in it!"

The next day Bushnell returned to continue pleading for the Ericsson "battery," as the navy officers preferred to label it. The air had become "thick with croakings," while some gloomily foreboded "another Ericsson failure."

The New Haven builder denied that the inventor had ever "made a failure," and he reviewed the Swede's successes. He was certain he had won over all opposition when Commander Davis, a crusty diehard for wooden ships of sail, exploded in what he intended as devastating sarcasm:

"Take the little thing home and worship it, as it would not be idolatry, because it is in the image of nothing in the heaven above or the earth beneath or in the waters under the earth."

The *Monitor* model was rejected.

Bushnell prudently did not argue. He thought that since Ericsson was himself "a full electric battery" he could in person accomplish what a third party had not been able to do. So he again entrained for New York.

There he abruptly appeared at Ericsson's house. Deliberately concealing the fact that the navy had rejected the revolving turret design, Bushnell, with a mixture of cajolery, candor, and half-truths, convinced his colleague that his own appearance at the Navy Department was imperative.

Ericsson agreed. He quickly packed—no great task since he wore the same sort of clothes every day—and took the night train (or trains) that very night, the fourteenth. He would report on his experience:

> . . . on going to Washington and entering the room occupied by the Board over which Commodore Smith presided, I was very coldly received, and learned to my surprise that said Board had actually rejected my *Monitor* plan . . . indignant, my first resolve was to withdraw, but a second thought prompted me to ask *why* the plan was rejected. Commodore Smith at once made an explanation showing that the vessel lacked stability.
>
> This warmed me up, inducing me to enter on an elaborate demonstration proving that the vessel had great stability. My blood being well up, I finished my demonstrations by thus addressing the Board:
>
> "Gentlemen, after what I have said, I deem it your duty to the country to give me an order to build the vessel before I leave the room!"

It didn't work out quite that swiftly. However, the board went into conference, asking Ericsson to return at 1 P.M. When he did so, Paulding, "in a very friendly manner," complimented him, saying,

"Sir, I have learned more about the stability of a vessel from what you have said than I ever knew before."

Ericsson would repeat what he had boasted many times—that "the sea shall ride over her and she shall live in it like a duck."

Later that same day, September 15, while shadows from a waning sun slanted over the low brick buildings and smoke pots of Washington, Ericsson was told to go ahead. The contract, for $275,000, would be drawn and forwarded to him.

He accepted the officers' word on faith and hastened back to New York, thinking only of how fast he could lay the keel—for that matter, in what yard? Nowhere in the world had such a craft "grown" on a shipyard ways.

The cautious navy watchdogs, however, were already framing a clause to the effect that if the *Monitor*'s invulnerability were not proven, all of the money advanced was to be refunded. Ericsson would declare that, had he known of this provision, "the *Monitor* would not have been built."

The "Impregnable Battery"

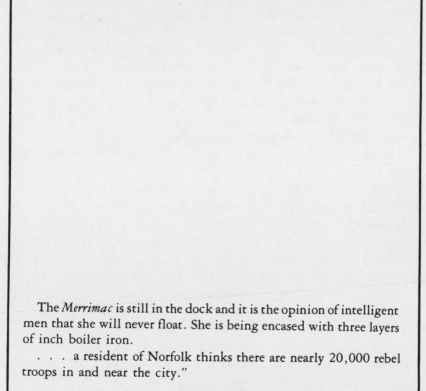

The *Merrimac* is still in the dock and it is the opinion of intelligent men that she will never float. She is being encased with three layers of inch boiler iron.

. . . a resident of Norfolk thinks there are nearly 20,000 rebel troops in and near the city."

New York *Herald,* November 17, 1861

As the crisping winds whispered of October, the navy could count, all at once, three ironclads building or in final blueprint out of some twenty proposals seriously considered.

Besides Ericsson's *Monitor* (which would not, however, even have a name until January), there was the *Galena,* taking shape in New Haven, and the *New Ironsides.* The last was a big ship, 232 feet long, 4,120 tons displacement, and mounting a main battery of sixteen powerful eleven-inch Dahlgrens plus smaller cannon. Under construction with little fanfare in Philadelphia by Merrick and Sons, she was destined to be a tough, active, and efficient man-of-war, a harbinger of true battleships to come.

And as a bonus that salved the biases of the old canvas-and-rigging brass hats, she was fitted with auxiliary masts.

After signing the navy's contract on the fourth, Ericsson spent that first October of the war planning the keel-laying. All he possessed was the dusty pasteboard model, some rough old sketches plus one trump—indomitable faith in what he now constantly referred to as "my impregnable battery." However, he could point to partners Bushnell, Griswold, and Winslow, who compensated for his own shortcomings in the day-by-day realities of engineering and construction. To this trio was added an essential fourth: a young shipbuilder, Thomas F. Rowland, who had bought out the failing Continental Iron Works in the industrial Greenpoint-Williamsburg section of Brooklyn on the East River, roughly opposite Twenty-third Street on the Manhattan side.

Bushnell, since he was in the same business, knew of Rowland. Paying him a casual visit, he broached the subject, much as one might bargain for a sack of potatoes. Would Rowland consider the construction of this "impregnable battery," plans unseen and unready, for "four or four-and-a-half cents a pound"? Tom Rowland, who, incidentally entertained the idea of creating such a ship of his own, had no pricing yardsticks at all, and the sum out of hand sounded to him ridiculously low. The two said good day and parted.

However, neither Bushnell nor Ericsson was willing to let the matter rest there. The next day Ericsson invited Rowland to a conference. At his charming best, he asked, "Tom, my boy, what are you going to charge me to build my iron ship?"

Ericsson was not too subtly putting the thought in Rowland's mind that building his ship was already a foregone conclusion. He thereby seized the initiative from the younger man, who replied, without seemingly a great deal of conviction, "nine cents a pound."

"Tut, tut, Tom!" Ericsson was quoted as responding, "it must be done for seven-and-a-half cents." And so the initial agreement was made.

Now, while Rowland prepared the ways inside his great wooden "ship house" at river's edge, Ericsson hit on a method, well ahead of the times, for hastening construction: subcontracting. Other than the hull itself, the components of his warship would be manufactured in scattered locations and then assembled at Greenpoint. Iron plates and other parts, including "stoppers" for the twin gunports, would be forged, not only at the two partners' foundries in Albany and Troy, but at North Adams, Massachusetts; Nashua, New Hampshire; and Buffalo and Baltimore.

The engines and other machinery were to be produced at the Delameter Iron Works located across Manhattan on West Street at Hudson River edge, and owned by a friend of Ericsson's, plump, extrovert Cornelius H. "Harry" Delameter. The aptly named Novelty Iron Works, in Manhattan, would build the novel turret.

By terms of the navy's contract, the complicated parts of this metallic jigsaw puzzle must be assembled, coaxed, riveted, or hammered into seagoing form within one hundred days.

With seeming but not actual deprecation, the navy, using bulk as a yardstick, had already listed this coming addition to the fleet as a "third-class screw steamer" of 776 tons. By later calculations, the tonnage would be set at 990. Other principal specifications were scribbled in Ericsson's nearly indecipherable scrawl on sheets of paper and hurried off, as they became individually ready, to Rowland and to the other contractors for decoding. It was a challenge.

The hull, unique among nineteenth-century warships, was composed wholly of hot-riveted ⅜-inch iron plates—a departure from the conventional concept of ironclad, which implied just that: iron sheathing on a wooden hull. This boxlike, flat-bottomed creation was but 124 by 34 feet.

Of more military significance was the "armored raft," or main deck, slightly better than 172 feet long, 41½ feet beam, resting atop the hull. The all-important side armor, five feet in height, and extending partly below the waterline, was composed of five layers of one-inch plates against twenty-seven inches of white oak (the principal wood used in the *Monitor,* along with some white pine). The armored deck was described as "7 inches of timber laid on wooden beams 10 inches square: the whole covered by two plates of ½-inch iron."

The relative thinness of deck armor resulted from Ericsson's reasoning that shots hitting there would be at a shallow angle and roll off, much as spent balls along a bowling lane.

The turret, with a twenty-foot inside diameter and nine-foot height, carried the corpulent thickness (and weight) of eight inches of armor, rivets only six inches apart—a formidable 120 tons. These curved plates and their many junctures especially tested the skill of the foundry, the Novelty Iron Works. There were but two somewhat oval gunports, six feet above the deck, just large enough to permit the protrusion of the muzzles of twin eleven-inch Dahlgren smoothbores. Iron "stoppers," suspended from above, closed the ports when not in use.

The guns recoiled in their carriages, which in turn moved along slides of forged iron. The big "columbiads" (which were heavy, reinforced cannon) fired an 184-pound shot, propelled by fifteen pounds of powder. This charge, set by an overly cautious Navy Department, was exactly half of the designed capacity of thirty pounds of powder.

Originally, Ericsson had specified huge fifteen-inchers, but these could not be forged in time. There had also been the question of whether the "turret gang" could withstand the concussion and recoil of two such immense naval rifles. The top of the turret was covered with railroad bars and a plate of iron with perforations to allow for air. Resting on a flat bronze ring slightly indented in the deck, the turret was connected by a central vertical shaft and gears to a twenty-five-horsepower steam engine belowdecks, controlled by one man.

If the turret was the reason for being of this strange new warship, it was also its critical point, in some respects an Achilles' heel. It was designed to mesh closely with its bronze deck ring in order to act as a seal against water, since the vessel would have only some two feet of freeboard. However, its very "snugness" meant that the turret must be "jacked up" before it could be turned, even by the "donkey" engine.

This plus the slow speed of which the little engine was capable would, critics charged, impede its flexibility in battle. Ericsson, nonetheless, continued to echo that "impregnability" was the most important quality.

Turrets were not Ericsson's discovery. Both the French and the English at the turn of the nineteenth century had committed to paper crude conceptions of what resembled castle towers placed upon barges. In 1841 one Theodore R. Timby, of New York, presented to the War Department plans for a revolving tower or turret, for use on either land or water. Ericsson's partners, learning of its existence, decided, whether it was patented or not (it was *not* until September 1862), they had better secure rights to it. This they did, for five thousand dollars.

Other than the turret, vents, a telescopic smokestack (or stacks), and a small, boxlike "pilot house" toward the bow, everything else was belowdecks—and this Ericsson considered his real innovation. Two Ericsson horizontal steam "vibrating lever engines," developing 320 horsepower and supplied by two boilers, drove, by a single shaft, a nine-foot-diameter propeller. Well back under the stern and thus shielded within a cavity, the large screw seemed out of proportion to the modest-sized vessel, being only two feet less than the *Monitor*'s total draft.

Other units of the engine department included two centrifugal blowers, driven by separate steam engines, furnishing "7,000 cubic feet of atmospheric air per minute by the process of suction through standing pipes on deck," and a supposedly more-than-adequate series of emergency pumps, including the latest high-power Worthington, a "bilge injection," and a centrifugal with the total capacity of three thousand gallons or more a minute.

Ericsson was especially proud of his protected anchor well, allowing the crew for the first time to raise or lower anchor completely protected from enemy fire. There was even a compressed-air flush toilet, ancestor of plumbing on the coming century's submarines.

In total, the inventor and his associates estimated forty separate patentable contrivances involved in the ironclad.

The forced-air ventilation was essential for a ship whose crew existed below the waterline. The complement lived in the forward part of the craft with headroom that was, at the very least, vexing to the tall.

The enlisted men's quarters, with accommodations for about forty, consisted of one large fo'c'sle. Ahead of this were eight officers' "state-rooms," about six by four feet, on each side of a central wardroom, and the captain's much larger cabin and state-room forward of these.

If the "C.O." was provided a bonus in space, he also would receive the maximum effects of the ironclad's pitching, since he dwelt so far forward.

As construction progressed, concern mounted at Fort Monroe over the presumed readying of the monster ironclad *Merrimack* under her new possessors. Major General John E. Wool, seventy-four-year-old white-haired patriarch of the War of 1812, commanding the Department of Virginia and senior Federal officer in the tidewater area, began anxiously requesting more troops.

The new commander of the blockading squadron, Flag Officer Louis M. Goldsborough, from his handsome flagship *Minnesota,* on October 17, put his own concerns on paper to Secretary Welles:

> SIR: I have received further minute reliable information with regard to the preparation of the *Merrimack* for an attack on Newport News and these roads, and I am now quite satisfied that unless her stability be compromitted by her heavy top works of wood and iron and her weight of batteries, she will, in all probability, prove to be exceedingly formidable.
>
> The supposition of the insurgents is that she will be impregnable, and a trial of her sufficiently to resist shot of the heaviest caliber, at a short range, is to take place before she is sent out to engage us.
>
> She is still in the dry dock at Norfolk, and yet needs a goodly quantity of iron to complete her casing, all of which is furnished from Richmond. She has her old engines on board, and they have been made to work tolerably well. They are not expected, however, I understand, to afford anything more than a moderate velocity.
>
> On coming out, she must, necessarily, proceed as low down as about Sewell's Point before she can shape her course to the westward for Newport News, and this will bring her within 3½ miles of us. My present purpose is to let her get well over toward the *Congress* [another sailing frigate, newly arrived] and *Cumberland,* off Newport News, and then to put at her with this ship and everything else that may be on hand at the time, with the view of bringing her between the fire of those ships and these, and cutting off all retreat on her part. It is understood that she is to be assisted by the two steamers now up the James

River, but as they can not be made very powerful I attach no very great consequences to this intention.

Nothing, I think, but very close work can possibly be of service in accomplishing the destruction of the *Merrimack,* and even of that a great deal may be necessary. From what I gather, boarding is impracticable, as she can only be assailed in that way through her ports, of which she has, in all, but fourteen.

If I could be furnished with a couple of tugs, or small steamers, to attend upon the *Congress* and *Cumberland* in season, so as to tow them promptly into position in case of necessity, they might prove of very great service. It will be, I infer, at least a fortnight before the *Merrimack* will make her attempt, but in the meantime I could employ those tugs or steamers very advantageously in the way of guard vessels at night, dispatch and tow vessels by day, etc. On the 9th instant an attempt, no doubt, was made by the insurgents to get an infernal machine among our shipping here, but it was happily foiled by the alertness of the *Lockwood,* which they tried to cut off with their two tugs engaged in the nefarious business. The night was dark and boisterous. Since then, they dispatched a tug with six armed boats in tow, toward Newport News, during the night; but, after proceeding a considerable way in that direction, concluded that it was too light for their purposes. I only mention these things to show the utility of active guard steamers.

Goldsborough, a husky, three hundred-pound Washingtonian who entered the navy as a cadet in 1812 (appointee of President Madison), distinguished himself fifteen years later when he led a boarding party onto a "piratical brig," killing or capturing most of those on board. At the time, Goldsborough was serving on the sloop *Porpoise.*

In the period 1853–57 he was superintendent of the U.S. Naval Academy. Gruff but knowledgeable, he cut an enormous and, to most subordinates, a formidable figure. He was a pioneer in introducing close-cropped hair among men, in marked departure from his immediate Revolutionary War forebears.

While Goldsborough's calculations, for the secretary of the navy, of a "fortnight" gave exaggerated credit to the speed of the Confederate naval engineers, the race between North and South for the first major, operational ironclad was fast and close. Trains chugged through the night on the Norfolk and Petersburg Railroad and even along roundabout routes as far west as Danville laden with iron plates from the Tredegar Works in Richmond. The foundry was admittedly "pressed beyond endurance" for this order. Located on the James River and the Kanawha Canal (near Belle Isle), Tredegar was the South's best and largest foundry.

Mallory thought he had ordered 1,000 tons of armor, even though Tredegar would bill the Confederacy for less—725 tons, for a tab of $123,615. In addition to the shipping problems caused by rail routes in poor repair, Tredegar also was encountering difficulty in locating sufficient sturdy flat cars to haul the unaccustomed weight.

The Confederate designers had called for two layers of 1- and 2-inch-thick rolled railroad iron, 8 inches wide, 10 feet long, to cover a 172-foot housing or "shield" (out of the vessel's approximate 262-foot overall length), 30 feet wide at the base, 7 feet high, one layer to be placed horizontally, the other vertically as a crosshatch pattern. The armor was against the frigate's 2 feet of oak-pine casemate with a thirty-five-degree slope. In addition, a 1,500-pound iron ram extended about 2½ feet beyond the prow, 2 feet underwater, a throwback to the most ancient days of sea warfare.

There wasn't much space to walk on deck or even to "con" the *Merrimack* except on her "promenade," a twenty-foot-wide iron grating atop the central armored housing.

Armament was formidable: four special Tredegar "Brooke" rifles, named after one of the vessel's three designers, Lieutenant John Brooke. Two were 7-inch (pivot guns at bow and stern) and two were 6.40-inch, plus six smoothbore 9-inch Dahlgrens "borrowed," like the *Merrimack* herself, from the Federal Navy.

With her great weight—a gross of at least 4,000 tons!—the ship's draft would be no less than twenty-two feet. Old sailors could speculate, Jeremiah-like, as to channels available for her navigation. Hampton Roads was a pilot's nightmare of shallows, especially around Newport News and Fort Monroe. The ten-mile length of the Elizabeth River to the Navy Yard, the ironclad's sole avenue of sortie, was navigable only in one narrow channel.

By the same token, how far up the James could the *Merrimack* steam to the defense of Richmond?

Already the *Merrimack,* according to Dr. Dinwiddie B. Phillips, an earnest secessionist who would be ship's surgeon, "bore some resemblance to a huge terrapin with a large round chimney about the middle of its back."

As a matter of fact, save for her bulk and magnitude, she was not altogether unique. In basic appearance and concept, she was merely a larger, heavier replica of the ironclads James Eads was building on the Mississippi for the Federal gunboat fleets.

Henry Davis, a northerner, returning from a flag-of-truce visit to Norfolk (at least a weekly occurrence across the Roads), wrote:

"The *Merrimac* has been transformed into a great battering ram, with a steel nose, for running down vessels. All her internal works are completed, but her plating is only partially effected as yet. . . . her engines are four feet below the water line and her sides slope inward. . . . there is no doubt, if she has a chance, she will do an immense amount of damage to our fleet."

The greatest difficulty—which was not appreciated by those Union officers who should have known—was with the engines which now, as a further complication, would be below the waterline, as Henry Davis had noted. She had been in the yard for cylinder repair, and the southern engineers hadn't been able to do much about them, nor were they willing to experiment with a wholly new set, assuming one could be produced. In other words, upwards of 1,000 tons were being added to a steam frigate's gross, to burden a propulsion system that hadn't been functioning properly to push even her former bulk.

Secretary Mallory knew that this was perhaps a greater weak point even than the *Merrimack*'s excessive draft, severely restricting her theater of operations.

Worry, indeed, remained the order of the day, for North and South. Old Commodore Joseph Smith, aging, troubled, too infirm to travel to New York, maintained a flow of correspondence to Ericsson. For example, even before the final signing of the contract, he wrote, "I am in great trouble from what I have recently learned, that the concussion in the turret will be so great that men cannot remain in it and work the guns after a few fires with shot. . . ."

A younger officer, however, sought to put Ericsson's apprehensions at rest, confiding to him, "The old commodore is fidgety at times and may provoke you by his own anxieties, but he has confidence in you, and he has no confidence in anybody else. So give the old man his tether, and let him fret a little when he feels like it."

Again, Commodore Smith was penning his worries about displacement calculations, wondering if the singular craft would float, and concluding, "I shall be subject to extreme mortification if the vessel does not come up to contract in all respects."

In a few days, another manifestation of his sleepless nights —"Excuse me for being so troublesome, but my great anxiety must plead my excuse"—and within the week, "The more I reflect upon your battery the more I am fearful of her efficiency." Then he wondered if the crew would suffocate and he suggested "a temporary house" on deck . . . would the turret roll her over in a heavy sea . . . and so on and so on.

Finally, on October 25, the keel of the *Monitor* was set in place. By coincidence, Ericsson signed his contract with his partners on the same date.

"... *not the slightest intention of sinking*"

TO: Secretary Welles

Sir:

   . . . I have this day reported for duty for the command of the U.S. Steamer building by Captain Ericsson. . . .

John L. Worden
January 16, 1862

That late fall of 1861 and early winter of '62, John Ericsson was a familiar figure in Greenpoint, night and day, watching, supervising, often raging as workmen fought against time to create his functionally unconventional, ugly brainchild. If Greenpoint, Brooklyn, was not necessarily an "obvious" spawning ground for such a hitherto unknown man-of-war, it was at least industrialized and more or less central to other subcontractors for the *Monitor*.

Its history was very old, Indians having cleared the land for their cornfields, as burial grounds would later bear witness. First called Cherry Point, or the Orchard, the area was settled in the seventeenth century by Huguenots from the Rhine Palatinate and by the Dutch. The land was hospitable for farming, irrigated by two creeks, Newtown and Bushwick. English came over to keep the Germans and Dutch company, and within one hundred years there was sufficient population to merit a major crossroads, known as *het kruis pad,* pretty much the well-known future junction of Bushwick and Flushing avenues. As the nineteenth century moved ahead, the farming character of Greenpoint gave way more and more to commercial: a coal yard, Meserole's storehouse (apparently handling many goods), Poppy Smith's Tavern, Knock's Café, Ferry's Hotel, Metropolitan Hotel, Washington Hall, Valley Forge Engine Company No. 11, several schools, public and private, and a number of churches or religious meeting places.

From Manhattan, Greenpoint was reached, in the late 1850s, via two ferries, from Tenth Street and from Twenty-third Street. Now, "the garden spot of America," at least as those who called it home were wont to refer to it, was accessible to New York City. Until 1852 one had to embark upon a small skiff, after paying the usurious fare of four cents.

Shipbuilding came to the "garden spot" in 1850 when Eckford Webb, who had already founded a naval architecture school, opened a shipyard there, known as Webb & Bell's. The firm's first launch was a small steeamer, the *Honda,* constructed to ply the Magdalene River in South America. Soon, shipwrights were hammering and sawing away in ten shipyards along Greenpoint's river edge, including the Continental Iron Works, on Calyer Street. The smell of pitch was heavy and pungent day and night as all types of vessels, from tiny skiffs on up to majestic schooners, took shape on outside ways or in the big wooden sheds, such as the *Monitor*'s original "nest."

Brooklyn was in the grip of patriotic war fever. Old Glory flew from many buildings and on flagstaffs here and there along the alternately dusty or muddy streets. With all of the rough-tough work gangs necessary to keep shipyards functioning, Brooklyn and Greenpoint would not be touched by the coming draft riots across the East River. Then, upwards of one thousand would die and millions of dollars of property loss sustained.

The nearby Brooklyn Navy Yard—one of nine in the nation—was booming. Its payroll soon soared from $679,000 to nearly $4 million while the workers quadrupled to six thousand. This meant, too, that saloons, springing up like giant's teeth, were doing a barkeep's dream business.

An early scare that southern sympathizers were going to burn down at least the Navy Yard and maybe other ship concerns as well sent one hundred militia plus special police details to guard the area.

Ericsson's work hastened, day and night. The itemized lists scribbled on:

```
    54  oak beams
14,400  linear feet of white pine "streaks"
 7,000  spikes, 10 inches long (9,000 lbs.)
   350  blunt bolts 1⅛ inch diameter, 3 feet long (3,500 lbs.)
 1,400  blunt bolts, 1⅛ inch diameter, 2 feet long (9,380
        lbs.)
```

Tired and tense most of the time, Ericsson could lose his normally mercurial temper at the simplest provocation. Although shifts worked around the clock to ready this warship, the inventor was never quite satisfied with the speed. Once he spoke of a shop foreman who had been guilty of some purported mistake: "too stupid . . . to make a blunder!" Again, of an engineer laboring to install the engines: "a huge sham with bird brains."

Nonetheless, the engineers, with or without "bird brains," got steam up on December 30.

Ericsson manifested his same bad temper—and bad manners—when a seasoned sea dog, Commodore David Dixon Porter (son of the equally illustrious Admiral David Porter), arrived in Ericsson's home at departmental request to survey the progress of the curious iron craft. When Ericsson challenged Porter's mathematical qualifications, the latter replied that he possessed a practical knowledge, knowing at least that "twice two are four." To this Ericsson snapped:

"I don't want practical men sent here, sir! My God, do they take *me* for a fool?"

He paced around the room as if apoplectic, muttering all the while, finally lifting his hands ceilingward in a gesture of desperation. He disclaimed that he was a "school master to teach naval officers!"

Porter, "greatly amused" at the whole performance, goaded the Swede's blood pressure up still further when the pair went over to Greenpoint to inspect the hull itself. Not only did Porter, tongue in cheek, refer to the *Monitor* as an "iron pot," but he alluded to one piece of machinery as a "coffee grinder." It happened to be the turret engine.

Ericsson, at the conclusion of the visit, was wholly unprepared for the naval officer's assessment of his vessel: it could, he asserted, "destroy any ship afloat!"

The inventor exploded, "You are *not* a damned fool!"

Porter returned to Washington to report on a "very powerful" man-of-war, and defend it, further, against remaining critics who still sniffed, it would sink "as soon as it is launched."

And so the first winter of the war moved on, heralded in November by Flag Officer Samuel F. Du Pont's successful amphibious expedition to open up strategic Port Royal Sound, north of Savannah, and thus tighten the blockade from Hatteras to the Gulf.

It was a cold, sometimes snowy, and often sleety winter at Hampton Roads, not a great deal more hospitable ashore than on the many ships at anchor. Tom Selfridge, still attached to the *Cumberland*, though others had come and gone, was aware, like his 267 shipmates, of the "hardship of being allowed no fires on board and of having to keep one watch sleeping at the guns each night . . . yet the spirit of officers and men was maintained at a high level."

As for enemy action, "The rumors of the expected presence of the *Merrimack* were so frequent as to become a standing joke with the ship's company."

Another big sailing man-of-war, the "second-class" fifty-gun frigate *Congress*, 1,867 tons, fresh from the South America station, had joined the North Atlantic Blockading Squadron in the fall. Her complement of some three hundred found her an exceptionally handsome old vessel, with some of her cabins trimmed in solid mahogany and bird's-eye maple.

She was moored near the *Cumberland* a few hundred yards off Camp Butler and Newport News Point to guard the James River against privateers and other blockade runners. Since the mouth of the James was about three miles wide there, the old sailing ships constituted more of a "presence" than an aggressive patrol. Far from the big guns of Fort Monroe and the Rip Raps, they could count on backup protection only from the light field pieces of Camp Butler.

Settled in, the two ships were themselves protected against possible fire rafts (to become more common on the Mississippi) and floating torpedoes (mines) by nets stretched at some length on booms from their sides. According to her surgeon, Dr. Edward Shippen, only a mule was ever snagged by the nets. The monotony from time to time was interrupted by the log-and-earth casemate battery on Pig Point lobbing shells at them, "apparently for practice, since the solid shot fell short," and sometimes, when spent, rolling along the surface of the water and sinking in a very futile and inconsequential sort of way. There was another, and curiously clocklike, diversion, the surgeon would recall:

> Sunday night—or rather Monday morning—was almost always a stirring time for us, for the armed steamers then generally came down before daylight, threatening to run by us, and either get into Norfolk or run the gauntlet of the vessels in Hampton Roads and get to sea, where they could prey upon our commerce. The south side of the river being very shoal, a vessel of any draught must necessarily pass quite close to us. The watch always slept on deck at their guns, where I have often seen them with their blankets and pea-jackets covered with snow; so the battery was always cast loose and ready before the drum had fairly begun to beat to quarters. But the steamers never gave us a chance at them with our broadside.

Dr. Shippen's marine background began with his birth on his father's brig in the West Indies.

The Federal ships also picked up runaway slaves, or "contrabands," from time to time, although the officers' orders remained ambiguous—not to assist them until their little skiffs actually touched the vessels' sides.

Ashore, the some twelve thousand Union troops, in four encampments, almost all of them recently civilians, passed the winter with virtually no shots fired in earnest. They were "generally very good and gallant fellows," by Dr. Shippen's appraisal: "Practical jokes, games and convivial parties occupied fully as much of their thoughts and time as did battalion and skirmish drill."

As far as the *Merrimack* was concerned, Dr. Shippen's sentiments were much as Tom Selfridge's:

". . . as week after week passed and the monster did not appear, we were inclined to regard this one as a myth. At any rate we felt certain that if we could once get her under our broadside we should soon send her to the bottom."

An acting master on the 460-ton gunboat *Mystic* was of mind similar to Dr. Shippen. Rolando F. Coffin found the reports of the *Merrimack*'s alleged appearance on the Elizabeth River so frequent that "we had become used to the canard and paid but little attention to it."

Life—and death—went on much as if the men were home. Private Joshua Lewis, of the 20th Indiana, wrote, "Here the first death in our company occurred. James Custer of Perrysville died of pneumonia and a collection was taken up and his body sent to Perrysville for burial."

Again: "Here we amused ourselves by shooting at ducks in the river. At this point James River was said to be six miles wide; at one time the large steamer *United States* came up the river with 3000 soldiers on board. The rebel battery just across the river fired at the vessel, but the shot fell short by a mile."

To Corporal Thomas Ranson, of the New York Mounted Rifles, stationed at Camp Hamilton, the enemy was rain and mud. He wrote to a friend in Somerville, New Jersey, ". . . weather has for the past two weeks been considerable stormy and wet. So much so that the mud is almost knee deep, and the water in the Horses Stable is up to their knees. . . . we have not drilled for 10 days on account of rain and mud. I am getting tired of this kind of soldiering and wish they would let us fight or send us home . . . for my part, I came here to fight and not to lay idle here in my tent."

"Quiet and monotonous" was the label William E. Rogers, of the 10th New York Regiment, Fort Monroe, stamped on the winter's character. Among his more acutely etched impressions were memories of night picket duty on a lonely stretch of the reservation by a military cemetery, where mostly veterans of the Mexican War were buried: ". . . the wind whistled mournfully through a group of pine trees growing out of the sand dunes . . . rabbits skipped blithely about the old wooden head-boards and I imagined I could see the ghosts of the dead soldiers. . . ."

Bill Rogers would also write home describing his commanding officer, General Wool: "a Mexican War veteran, with snow-white hair. We boys loved him, and his white hair made an impressive figure at all times, especially when he was mounted and surrounded by his staff of young, faithful, energetic officers."

On the other side, rebel soldiers were bored, too, much of the time, and sometimes sick. Lieutenant Charles "Dick" Phelps, stationed at Sewell's Point, apologized to his aunt, Mary Jane Lee, for not having written sooner: ". . . I have been confined to my room for the last ten days with what is called the rheumatism in my limbs and have had the roughest time I have ever experienced. . . ."

He was so weak and stiff that he had to be assisted onto his horse.

Far more cockily, another Confederate soldier, James B. Jones, wrote from Camp Arrington, Pig Point, "I think it would take 300,000 Yankees to take this place . . . there is a great many obstacles in their way to Norfolk of which they are entirely ignorant . . . we are at work erecting rifle pits and masked batteries every day."

If not in the Elizabeth River area, "obstacles" were believed to be in the James—"very powerful submarine batteries . . . connected by hidden wires and remote galvanic batteries," according to a New Yorker, N. Niles, who so advised the navy secretary. Niles, claiming to have reliable southern connections, closed with the suggestion that scows "with iron drags" could be employed to "break all the wires and defeat the purpose of our barbarous enemies."

On January 12, 1862, even as Congress was appropriating $10 million for twenty additional ironclads—partly in response to insistent demands by the press—an ambitious expedition comprised of more than sixty men-of-war, carrying fifteen thousand Federal troops, thumped out of Hampton Roads into stormy seas with the goal of frustrating the "purpose of . . . barbarous enemies." The ships of the line, transports, supply vessels, tugs, and lesser craft—"a most imposing appearance"—were under the joint command of Brigadier General Ambrose E. Burnside and Flag Officer Goldsborough. Their mission was the seizure of strategic Roanoke Island in Pamlico Sound—"the very key," by the estimate of one Confederate general, "of the rear defense of Norfolk and the navy yard."

An army advancing up the often swampy coast could also isolate Norfolk by cutting the Seaboard and Roanoke Railway. The so-called Burnside Expedition honored a general officer who had made one of the few determined stands at Bull Run. At thirty-eight, Burnside, a career railroad man (the Illinois Central) and onetime rifle manufacturer, was a "comer" in Lincoln's new army, with a major generalship on the horizon. Bald, he nonetheless sprouted luxuriant if formidable "sideburns"—his contribution (through reversing his name) to the still adolescent American-English vocabulary.

And as the expedition, bearing Washington's nervous hopes, stirred the muddy, brackish waters of Pamlico Sound, the *Monitor* received a captain: John L. Worden, of Sing Sing, New York, who had spent many of his forty-four years as a naval lieutenant. A lean, solemn, polite man with a long gray beard, Worden could look back on a rather undistinguished if sometimes lucky career. The latter was capped by his transfer from the U.S.S. *Levant* before she sailed, in 1860, from Honolulu—to oblivion. Destined for Panama, she and the nearly two hundred aboard her vanished without trace—another bit of flotsam in the accumulating lore of sea mysteries.

That handsome old sloop of war would become better known, however, as the ship chosen for Edward Everett Hale's piece of fiction, "The Man Without a Country." Philip Nolan, the chief character, was the hapless self-proclaimed expatriot sentenced to cruise on the warship *Levant* the remainder of his life. (When Hale, as an octogenarian, shortly after the turn of the century, was informed that the Navy was mounting a new search for the *Levant*—specifically on a quest for possible uncharted islands—he wryly replied, "If you should find Philip Nolan, I shall adopt him as my grandfather.")

Good fortune continued to be Worden's lot. He was ordered early in April 1861 to Pensacola bearing written instructions to the fleet commander there, Captain H. A. Adams, to reinforce Fort Pickens, which seemed, like Sumter, ready to fall. Riding a southbound train, Worden overheard talk that led him to believe he might himself be captured by the secessionists. In the best cloak-and-dagger tradition, Worden memorized the orders to Captain Adams, tore them into little pieces, and swallowed the lot.

After nearly drowning in a small boat, attempting to reach the flagship *Sabine,* he finally came aboard to advise Adams not only to land troops but that reinforcements were en route from New York as well as Hampton Roads. Fort Pickens held.

Worden's luck ran out on his way home by train when he was arrested in Montgomery, Alabama, on April 13, and he became the first Federal officer prisoner of war. He was transferred between various embryo Confederate prison camps until he reached Norfolk and there was exchanged in late November.

On January 11 fussy Commodore Smith appointed Worden commanding officer of the as yet unlaunched *Monitor.* The old chieftain of the Bureau of Yards and Docks underscored that "this vessel is an experiment," adding, "I believe you are the right sort of officer to put in command of her."

While some believed Worden had asked for such a command, and others, including Ericsson, questioned if he really was the "right sort," he reported for duty on January 16, with the rather oblique remark that he was "induced" to believe in the ironclad's "success." This he at once salted with the reservation that he was "quite willing to be an agent in testing her capabilities."

Just a few days after Worden took command of a ship "still on sticks," by his phraseology, Ericsson sent to Captain Gustavus Fox his nomination for a name, at the assistant secretary of the navy's request:

"The impregnable and aggressive character of this structure will admonish the leaders of the Southern Rebellion that the batteries on the banks of their rivers will no longer present barriers to the entrance of the Union forces.

"The ironclad steamer will thus prove a severe Monitor to those leaders. . . ."

In fighting form, Ericsson closed his letter with broadsides against "Downing Street," alluding to ships being built in England for the Confederacy. Because of his debtor's prison experience in London, the Swedish inventor could not be expected to contemplate Great Britain or the British with affection.

By coincidence, in London, on January 24, 1862, Donald McKay, the builder of Clipper ships, published a letter in the *Times* concerning the iron warships across the Atlantic: "They will not increase much the power of our Navy." While conceding that Ericsson's was the most "ingenious" of the three, he added that it was as well the "most unseaworthy, and incapable of any speed."

During that last week of January, as shipwrights labored to ready

Monitor for launching, considerable conflicting news emanated from Norfolk. For example, the New York *Tribune* reported that the *Merrimack* had "floated out of drydock on Saturday [January 25] and was to make a trial trip on Sunday . . . the people were jubilant in the belief that she could sink the whole fleet at Hampton Roads."

In a dispatch datelined Fort Monroe, the same major United States daily also quoted some black cook deserters from the 3rd Alabama Regiment as reporting that "the last of the iron plates for the *Merrimac* was put on yesterday. . . ."

The Baltimore papers carried much the same intelligence, adding that the *Merrimack* was mounting ten-inch cannon. All in all, the navy's Bureau of Yards and Docks chief was sufficiently concerned to advise Ericsson on January 29:

"The *Merrimac* is out of dock and ready for her trial trip. I think the wrought-iron shot of the Ericsson battery will smash in her 2¼-inch [with the double layers, the thickness was a closer to 4 inches] plates, provided she can get near enough to her, while the 9-inch shot and shells of the *Merrimac* will not upset your turret. Let us have the test as soon as possible for that ship will be a troublesome customer to our vessels in Hampton Roads."

At the same time, indicative of the confusion within the Navy Department, Secretary Welles was ordering the *Congress* up to Boston, feeling that far too much of the fleet was concentrated in southern waters. This was true enough, since not only had the Burnside Expedition gone off to Pamlico Sound with some of the best men-of-war, but tough old Flag Officer David Glasgow Farragut, yet another veteran of the War of 1812, was readying a major squadron to assault New Orleans.

Even so, Captain John Marston, late of the *Cumberland,* now flying his flag from the *Roanoke,* a sister screw frigate of the *Minnesota* and the *Merrimack,* remonstrated. As senior naval officer present in Hampton Roads in the absence of Goldsborough, Marston replied that so long as the *"Merrimack* is held as a rod over us I would by no means recommend that she [the *Congress*] should leave this place."

His advice was taken. As a matter of fact, the addition of the handsome *Roanoke* did not much strengthen the blockading squadron. Her propeller shaft lay in the Brooklyn Navy Yard, awaiting repairs.

Work on the ironclad in the Gosport yard was, in reality, progressing far more tediously than reports trickling across the uncertain, gray waters of the Roads indicated. The Gosport commandant, French Forrest, had advised Major General Benjamin Huger, "We are without oil for the *Merrimack.*" It was needed for lubricating purposes.

A sad-eyed bearded veteran, bearing a remarkable resemblance to Lee, Huger, who commanded ground forces in the Norfolk theater, could never lay hands on enough of anything to satisfy his daily requests—not enough ammunition, guns, shoes, uniforms, flour, bacon, butter, buttons. He had ample cause to regret his leaving the "Federals."

The *Merrimack* alone was possessed of an insatiable hunger. Those precious iron plates—where *were* they?

The frantic Forrest had resorted to such extremes as dispatching officers to scour and sniff around railroad way stations scattered about central, southern, and even western Virginia. At one time, Tredegar reported that a consignment of plates had been lying "on the bank" outside the foundry "for four weeks." They were finally moved to Norfolk all the roundabout way via Weldon, North Carolina.

Machinists, blacksmiths, and other Confederate yard workers were sweating away at Gosport seven days a week. Some volunteered to toil until eight o'clock every evening without extra pay. Still, this did not wholly satisfy the few officers and engineers thus far assigned to the awesome ship, who so passionately wished her afloat.

As January ended, the *Monitor* appeared to be winning the race for first in commission. On Thursday morning, January 30, a sprinkling of spectators, admitted by pass, waited under a cold winter rain in the half-frozen mud and litter of Rowland's shipyard. For two days Brooklyn and Manhattan had shivered and slipped through a snow, sleet, and ice storm. At the height, a fire had razed several buildings on Fulton Street.

Just off the ways, a rowboat idled amid the debris and small ice floes of the East River. It was a precaution just in case this strange vessel should plunge straight down upon launch. In fact, gamblers mingled with the crowd offering odds on this very possibility—an apprehension shared by her builders, since temporary wooden floats had been fastened to the keel. Ericsson, however, as if to demonstrate faith in his creation, stood on board boldly, about twenty feet from the stern.

At 10 A.M. shipwrights knocked away the last chocks, and—anticlimax. The *Monitor,* displaying the United States flag on her bow and stern, took to the water like the "duck" her Swedish parent had imagined her. Spectators cheered, the men waved their hats.

"Notwithstanding the prognostications of many that she would break her back or else swamp," the New York *Times* reporter wrote, "she was launched successfully."

As the reporter for the New York *World* observed, the ironclad "had not the slightest intention of sinking."

The vessel that her creator had predicted would "prove a severe monitor" to "the leaders of the Southern Rebellion" was hauled back to dock, where spectators were soon swarming over her glistening, precarious decks. Ericsson held a telegram from Captain Fox in Washington: "I congratulate you and trust she will be a success. Hurry her for sea, as the *Merrimack* is nearly ready at Norfolk and we wish to send her here."

Presumably the assistant secretary of the navy meant the nation's Capital by "here," and believed it to be so endangered as to merit the *Monitor*'s presence.

However, just what *was* the thrust of Washington's thinking? Would Hampton Roads and the fleet there be sacrificed in an effort to increase the security of Washington?

And the official measure of the *Monitor?* Captain John A. Dahlgren, the designer of wonderful guns and now commandant of the Washington Navy Yard, was alluding to the ironclad in these seemingly deprecatory terms: "a mere speck, like a hat on the surface."

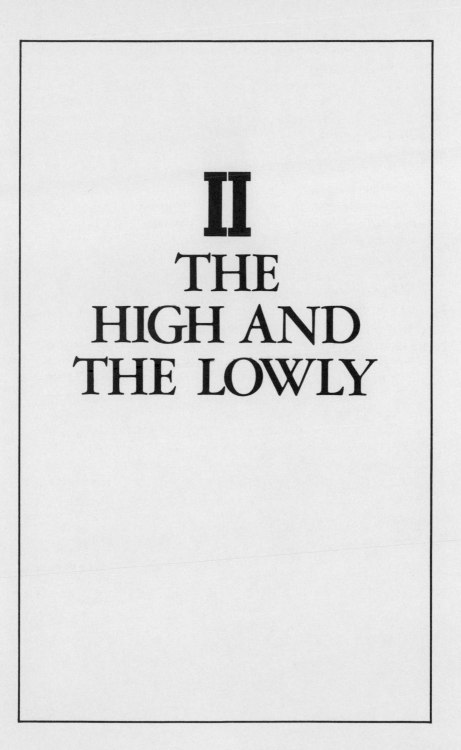

II
THE
HIGH AND
THE LOWLY

" . . . *somebody ought to be hung*"

Headquarters Department of Virginia
Fort Monroe, Va.
February 20, 1862

HON. EDWIN M. STANTON,
Secretary of War

SIR: I hasten to send the copy of the dispatch just received from Norfolk. In five days the *Merrimack* (steamer), in conjunction with the *Yorktown* and *Jamestown,* will attack Newport News, supported by a land force. The attack will be made in the night. We want a larger naval force than we have at present. I will be prepared for them on the land. The Secretary of the Navy ought to be informed.

> I have the honor to be, very respectfully,
> your obedient servant,
> JOHN E. WOOL,
> Major-General.

P.S.—The dispatch alluded to I sent to Cape Charles to be telegraphed. Major Jones, aide-de-camp, who went there with the dispatch, has not yet returned. It being half past 4 p.m., I forward my dispatches by a special messenger. I intended to have done so yesterday, but was prevented by the early departure of the steamer.

> JOHN E. WOOL,
> Major-General

On February 1 Flag Officer Farragut was preparing to depart Hampton Roads the following morning on his way to assume command of the Western Gulf Blockading Squadron and then try an attack upon New Orleans. The opening of the lower Mississippi and denial of the great Louisiana port to the Confederacy was considered by Lincoln as the first really major objective of the war.

The President had in fact confided in November to Commodore Porter, who would command the mortar division under Farragut: "The Mississippi is the backbone of the Rebellion; it is the key to the whole situation."

The same chilly first day of February 1862, aboard the imposing flagship *Hartford* (four years old, newest of a class of five big steam frigates), Fleet Captain Henry H. Bell, Davy Farragut's chief of staff, as tough and almost as senior as his superior, scribbled an informal, gratuitous bit of advice to Goldsborough on the *Philadelphia* at Hatteras Inlet:

"The *Merrimack* is at last anchored off Craney Island. Don't wait for that ironclad to come out. That she won't do; bring out her and the *Germantown* [the sloop abandoned at Gosport and used now as a defensive battery] or sink her there. Two or three gunboats could really do it. Your friends would be charmed; the nation electrified. . . ."

Bell, who thus was the latest of an expanding list of "*Merrimack* experts," closed with a conceivably premature comparison of Goldsborough to "the great Preble." He of course referred to Commodore Edward Preble, of Tripolitan War fame. His *Philadelphia* (predecessor of Goldsborough's) was captured by the Barbary pirates after grounding on a reef; then boarded and burned by Stephen Decatur in one of the most daring feats in United States naval history.

The next day, February 2, Captain Gershon Van Brunt, of the flagship *Minnesota,* also wrote Goldsborough:

"The *Merrimack* is, without doubt, out of dock and almost ready for a move. I am anxiously expecting her and believe I am ready, but I have doubts about her venturing out of Elizabeth River. I understand they have been putting down moorings for her about a mile inside of Sewell's Point and I should not be surprised if she was only used for harbor defense, as I am told she floats with her roofing two feet under water and that, in consequence, she can carry no battery. She is exceedingly crank and would be unsafe if she happened to get across the tides and might turn turtle."

As a postscript, a musing Van Brunt asked his flag officer if he had received the gin he had forwarded, while lamenting that he was missed at the gaming table: "Backgammon does not flourish since you left."

The information repeated by these senior naval officers, while false, was nonetheless typical of the fare regularly served the North. On the day of the *Monitor's* launching, the New York *World* had also reported the *Merrimack* "floating." It observed as well that the length of time of her conversion plus the skill of northern workmen engaged in the task "is enough to create much uneasiness in the public mind, especially as we have as yet no vessel capable of coping with her in a sea flight."

On February 4 the New York *Herald* chimed in, asking for fifty instead of the authorized twenty ironclads, warning "our Navy is just now our most vulnerable point. If we delay we may have cause to repent."

Not only was *Merrimack* hard in dock, however, but the worry of her architects was that she would float too *high,* rather than too *low,* thus exposing her unarmored hull to cannon shot. And still there was difficulty in finding a crew, most available young southerners having already been swept into the army.

On February 7 the Norfolk *Day Book* added to the confusion, perhaps intentionally, with the item, "The calculations in the displacement of the ship was [*sic*] erroneous . . . of considerably more than 200 tons . . . it would be vain to deny that this is a serious injury to the ship . . . her great draught of water will prevent her active operation."

Reprinted widely in the North, it produced its own lulling. In any event there were divided objectives this February in Washington's war strategy—the master plan. Preeminent were the mammoth preparations for marshaling Major General George Brinton McClellan's huge Army of the Potomac, targeted at 155,000 troops in the Hampton area to hurl it up the Peninsula along the James or York with the aim of knocking Richmond out of the war. However, there was also the coming expedition against New Orleans, and this had inspired Fox on February 6 to ask Ericsson, "Can your *Monitor* sail (steam) for the Gulf of Mexico the 12th instant?"

He had only a week previously indicated that the *Monitor* was needed in Washington.

The ironclad, freshly launched, was almost two weeks away from first trials. She did not have even the advantage of a crew, although Worden was engaged in assembling one from the receiving ship *North Carolina* and the frigate *Sabine*. The captain would recall:

". . . after stating fully to the crews of those vessels the probable dangers of the passage to Hampton Roads [even though he was not then sure of his destination] and the certainty of having important service to perform after arriving there, had many more men to volunteer than was required. From them I selected a crew and a better one no naval commander ever had the honor to command."

Her initial total of fifty-eight officers and men was some ten more than the little craft's designed complement. The fifty-eighth at this time was a volunteer, the well-known naval engineer Alban C. Stimers, who had once served as chief engineer of the *Merrimack*. Not until February 19 did Stimers pronounce the *Monitor* ready for a precommissioning test—and it was a disappointing one. The steam cutoff valves had been set primarily for backing, which meant that the engines could receive only partial power, knocking down the *Monitor*'s forward speed to about three and a half knots.

Nor was that all. The blowers broke down, leaving those crewmen belowdeck in a fetid, half-choking atmosphere. There were other problems as well, but not surprising for so new and "radical" a warship. Stimers estimated on the basis of the unsatisfactory trial that the *Monitor*'s speed should be about six knots, although Ericsson thought she could accomplish at least eight of the designed nine knots.

However, as if to compensate for some of the early shortcomings, Ericsson drew from his own savings to make the officers' quarters more "homey"—tapestry rugs and goat's hair mats, black walnut chests of drawers to match the decor of the berths, lace and damask curtains (against no "windows," or portholes, however), and carpeted campstools. Candles were the only means of illumination in these rooms, although there was an oil lamp in the wardroom. Much of the chinaware—both for washing and for dining—was embellished with gilt letters: MONITOR, an artistic touch traceable to the Swedish inventor himself.

The choice of a commanding officer was definitely not Ericsson's, and he did not wholly favor Worden. On the twenty-fourth he wrote Fox, complaining that Worden's "health and energy" did not appear to be "equal to the occasion." He also thought that the technician brought in to "regulate" the compass was far too slow, while the "nice system of doing work in the yard is not calculated to forward matters."

Nonetheless, the next day, February 25, the *Monitor* was placed in commission. The quartermaster wrote across the book, "Log of U.S. Steam Battery *Monitor,*" with the first entry, "Comes in with fine weather," timing it 3 P.M. The first day of commission was closed with "This day ends with clear cold weather."

On the twenty-seventh, delayed one day by lack of ammunition, the *Monitor* steamed out into a snowstorm, under hurried orders to Hampton Roads. Only then was it realized that she did not steer properly. She went back and forth across the East River, from Brooklyn to Manhattan, like "a drunken man," it appeared to Paymaster Keeler. She tied up again at the shipyard, her metal deck inches deep in snow and slush.

Ericsson was infuriated at the suggestion of installing a new rudder, asserting, "The *Monitor* is mine and I say it shall not be done . . . put in a new rudder? They would waste a month in doing that; I will make her steer just as easily in three days!"

During this week of trial and error aboard the *Monitor,* Van Brunt was again advising Goldsborough of the *Merrimack*'s conjectured readiness. On the twenty-third, for example, he had reported anew that the vessel was out of dock "and is everything they expected to make her; in other words a complete success. We are all ready, and the sooner she gives us the opportunity to test her strength the better."

By coincidence, Goldsborough on the same day was communicating to Fox, in Washington:

"I hope the Dept. will be able to send the Ericsson soon to Hampton Roads to grapple with the *Merrimack* and lay her out as cold as a wedge.

"She and another like her would do the work well. What has become of the hundred thousand dollar blowing-up man? Has his scheme collapsed or is the water too cold?"

The writer was referring to one of the several impractical suggestions received by the Navy Department for ridding the *Merrimack* menace. This unnamed individual had claimed, for $100,000, he could slip into the Gosport yard and destroy the big ironclad.

It had been a long, frustrating month at Gosport. The *Merrimack,* an overweight dinosaur trapped inside her big stone graving dock, had not been ready to fight anyone.

Early in February, Captain Franklin Buchanan, head of the Confederate Navy's Office of Orders and Detail in Richmond, who had already established largely ignored recruiting offices in Norfolk and Richmond, lamented to Mallory, "The *Merrimack* has not yet received her crew, notwithstanding all my efforts to procure them from the Army."

"Old Buck" Buchanan, erect, white-haired, balding, distinguished by his Roman nose, in the naval service for nearly half a century, was a somewhat pathetic figure of mixed allegiance which he presumably had not resolved at this late date. A Marylander (even as Dana Greene, of the *Monitor*) and one of eleven children, he could look back on a career that included the establishment of the Naval Academy with himself as the first superintendent, in 1845. Six years later, he had been captain of the U.S.S. *Susquehanna* in Commodore Matthew Perry's historic expedition to "open up" Japan to the West.

In 1861 Buchanan was commandant of the important Washington Navy Yard. And then he made his wrong guess: that his beloved Free State would secede. He resigned his commission—and as quickly asked Gideon Welles to reinstate him when it was apparent that Maryland, if a bit shaky and answerable to Federal armed "persuasion," would persevere under Old Glory. The navy secretary bluntly informed the senior officer that the service did not need irresolute commanders.

Old Buck became emotional. He remonstrated that it was extremists who had "ruined our glorious country" and that he would be "miserable" out of the United States Navy. Welles was content to allow him to remain in such an unhappy state.

As it turned out, Buchanan became bitter, undergoing what some interpreted as a sort of personality change. Before long he went so far as to refer to his erstwhile shipmates as "vile vagabonds"! All of this was especially distressing to his older brother (by two years), McKean, inspector of provisions at Boston Navy Yard, who did *not* believe his allegiance was first to Maryland.

Thus, Old Buck was more than ready when Mallory learned that this capable and experienced officer was out of a job. He welcomed him to his pygmy department, which was so starved for talent, or for any numbers at all.

This being the case, a nucleus of army officers received orders to the *Merrimack* in January. One of them was handsome, serious Lieutenant John Taylor Wood, Louisianan, grandson of President Zachary Taylor and a recent instructor at the U.S. Naval Academy. Thus, he was one of those rare birds who were qualified on land or sea—amphibious fighters.

With the fall of Roanoke Island, on February 7, before the advancing Burnside Expedition (now menacing Norfolk), rebel soldiers as well as sailors from the small gunboat flotilla in North Carolina waters were themselves pushed northward. In the hopes of recruiting some of these dispossessed men, Wood was hastened to General Magruder's headquarters in Yorktown, who was known to have among his command two battalions from New Orleans and possibly some seawise members in this number.

"The general though pressed for want of men," Wood reported, "holding a long line with scarcely a brigade, gave me every facility to secure volunteers. With one of his staff I visited every camp, and the commanding officers were ordered to parade their men, and I explained to them what I wanted. About 200 volunteered and of this number I selected 80 who had had some experience as seamen or gunners. Other commands at Richmond and Petersburg were visited. . . ."

And while Lieutenant Wood was scraping the boondocks for a crew, the citizenry of Norfolk was becoming as anxious as the navy to see the *Merrimack* in commission. For one, Henry Ghiselin wrote to his friend and business partner, "Mac" (Alexander McPheeters), in mid-February that he had gone down to the "whf" (presumably "wharf") in order "to see the *Merrimac* go by and from this whf went down to Sewell's Pt. to see the fight. The newspaper will have informed you that there was no fight. I went down again on Friday. Still no fight. The bad weather for 3 days last week kept one at home which will explain why my letter lay so long unfinished."

Henry then digressed to the preoccupations with daily wartime living: "The butter has not yet come much to my disappointment and I fear it has got lost, if you sent it. . . ."

Tempers at the same time wore thin at the old Federal Navy Yard. The *Merrimack*'s executive and ordnance officer, Lieutenant Catesby ap (Welsh equivalent of "son of") R. Jones, an Alabamian, was so unhappy not only about completion delays but shortages of all components from iron plates and ammunition to oil and caulking that he exploded to his co-workers, "Somebody ought to be hung!"

At best, he found the continuing slowdowns "vexatious," as he decried "the want of skilled labor and lack of proper tools and appliances."

All the more frustrating, there was no one to blame. The South, still unprepared for a major war, whereas the industrial North was finally commencing to tool up, remained desperately short of everything.

Young Jones, a midshipman in 1836, serious, bearded, and highly regarded as an ordnance expert, was among the few officers lost to the secessionist cause whom senior United States naval personages such as Porter or Farragut professed to miss. Old-timers including French Forrest and Buck Buchanan could scarcely be regarded as "comers."

Then, finally, the *Merrimack* was in the water. But the exact date was not logged; if it was, the document was lost. It was probably between February 14, Valentine's Day, and February 17. William R. Cline, one of the crewmen, would recall that only "four marines and a corporal" were aboard at her launching. Stationed in the bow, Cline said she was "then and there christened *Virginia*," adding:

"There were no invitations to governors and other distinguished men, no sponsor nor maid of honor, no bottle of wine, no brass band, no blowing of steam whistles, no great crowds to witness this memorable event. The launching was accomplished quietly, only officers and men stationed at the navy yard witnessing it. . . . there was only one officer of the *Virginia*'s crew who was present at the time the vessel was launched and he was Captain Reuben Thom [in charge of the marines]. . . ."

Cline observed two officers watching the preparations for launching. He heard one ask:

"Are you quite sure after all that when she is put overboard she will not turn over?"

And the other, whom Cline thought to be one of the designers of the ironclad, replied, "You may depend upon her, she is all right."

Bill Cline, too, neglected to note the date of an event much in contrast to the debut of the little *Monitor*.

On the seventeenth, French Forrest ordered the receiving ship, *United States,* whose name remained unchanged from its original ownership, "to hold the crew of the *Virginia* in readiness to go on board that ship with their baggage."

The same day, the flag officer suggested to Major General Huger, commanding the Department of Norfolk, that truce flags between that area and Fort Monroe be suspended, "until the great experiment we have in contemplation has been submitted to the test."

If Forrest thought he was thereby shutting off strategic information to the enemy, he was mistaken. There had been an almost unending stream of informants, especially escaped slaves (even including one who allegedly called on Secretary Welles), workmen, occasionally an officer or a crewman from a foreign warship, and gossipy Norfolk residents. All of them professed to keep the North posted on the progress of the *Merrimack.*

Intelligence that was considered especially reliable had arrived in Fort Monroe from an Irishman who had left Norfolk under a flag of truce. Although he had wished to speak to General Wool, he agreed to confide in the old general's aide-de-camp, Colonel Le Grand Bouton Cannon, forty-six-year-old New Yorker and lifetime friend of the Wools.

Dramatically, the visitor ripped open the sleeve of his coat to produce a communication from a known loyal easterner, who had remained as an iron-finisher at the Gosport Navy Yard. Cannon would recall:

> He said the *Merrimack,* rechristened the *Virginia,* had been launched, but it was found she drew a foot less water than they had intended. She was to receive another coat of mailing, and would be out in a month. Then they were going to attack and destroy the *Cumberland* and the *Congress,* off Newport News, which had been armed especially to meet her. Simultaneously General Magruder was going to come down from Yorktown and attack General Mansfield, at Newport News, and clean out all the Union forces in the neighborhood. The account of the rebel plans was most minute.

This so impressed General Wool that Cannon was hastened to Washington where he spoke with Secretary Stanton—sick in bed —with the President, and with Captain Fox. Although the aide-de-camp, Cannon, found Stanton to be disturbed, he would quote Fox as observing, "Mr. President, you need not give yourself any trouble whatever about that vessel. . . ." Then, to his dismay, the "whole matter was dismissed," and Cannon returned to Fort Monroe, resigned to the fact that "the Washington authorities were lulled into insensibility."

The South, however, had to rely primarily on the Northern press for news of the "Ericsson Battery." And this was reported with virtual blueprint faithfulness. Richmond really did not need any spies, even though some of the so-called Copperheads, sympathetic to the southern cause and in opposition to Lincoln, were thought to be supplying information of military interest to their friends and relatives in the Confederacy.

Further, while alarm, at least in some quarters, was registered in the North over the appearance of the *Merrimack,* there was no parallel evidence that Mallory, Jeff Davis, or the Confederate press—as a presumed echo of opinion—was in any way disturbed about the *Monitor,* whose launching had been so well publicized, or over the nearing completion of the other two formidable ironclads.

Events now accelerated. On February 24, the *Merrimack* at last had a commander, Old Buck Buchanan, not actually a captain in the accepted sense, but a "flag officer" ordered by Secretary Mallory to "hoist your flag" aboard the *Virginia.* At the same time, he took pains to explain to Buchanan that the ship was "a novelty in naval construction, is untried and her powers unknown, and the Department will not give specific orders as to the attack on the enemy."

Mallory then lauded the vessel as a ram: "even without guns . . . formidable." By way of an aside, he continued, "Could you pass Old Point and make a dashing cruise on the Potomac as far as Washington?"

On March 2 Mallory, who had promised "no specific orders" as to operations, indicated that plans "to attack the enemy at Newport News" had now been "agreed upon," possibly verbally.

Buchanan on the same date confided to Major General Magruder, presently commanding the Army of the Peninsula, that the ironclad was "by no means ready for service." He continued:

"She required eighteen thousand two hundred pounds of powder for her battery, howitzers were not fitted and mounted on the upper deck to repel boats and boarders and none of the port shutters are fitted on the ship. Much of the powder has now arrived, and the other matters shall not detain us. You may therefore look out for me at the time named. My plan is to destroy the frigates first, if possible and then turn my attention to the battery on shore. I sincerely hope that acting together we may be successful in destroying many of the enemy."

The next day, from his personal headquarters at the handsome plantation Lee Hall, north of Newport News, "Prince John" Magruder bluntly advised Buchanan, "It is too late to cooperate with my army in any manner . . . for the enemy is very heavily re-enforced both at Newport News and Fort Monroe."

Pointing out that he counted but 4,000 infantry and 450 cavalry in his army, Magruder believed he faced 18,000 Federal forces. Although the present strength of the Fort Monroe complex was not quite 13,000, there *was* a potential of reinforcement. Thus, Magruder was not exaggerating too much.

Buchanan formally replied to Mallory on March 4 aboard the "C.S. Steam Frigate *Virginia*": "Sir, I have the honor to acknowledge the receipt of your order and instructions (received yesterday); appointing me Flag Officer for the command of the Naval Defenses of the James River. Today I assumed command & hoisted my flag on board this ship. The honor conferred upon me, and the confidence reposed in me, by the Department I fully appreciate.

"On Thursday night the 6th instant, I contemplate leaving here to appear before the Enemy's Ships at Newport News, should no accident occur to this ship, when I feel confident that the acts of *Virginia* will give proof of the desire of her officers and crew to meet the views of the Department as far as practicable. From the best and most reliable information I can obtain from experienced pilots it will be impossible to ascend the Potomac in the *Virginia* with the present draft of water, nearly 22 feet.

"None of the port shutters are fitted in the *Virginia*, nor are Howitzers placed on the upper deck, the latter may be ready by Thursday. The shutters for the two bow and quarter ports, I will have temporarily placed there to keep out shot or shells. The last of our powder and shells will be received on board on Wednesday."

He signed himself "Frank Buchanan."

Hastening his plans as workmen still swarmed over the *Merrimack*, Buchanan on March 6, Thursday, wrote to Commander John R. Tucker, of the gunboat *Patrick Henry*, "I am informed by the Hon.

Secretary of the Navy that the *Patrick Henry,* under your command, the *Jamestown,* Lieut Commdg. [Joseph N.] Barney and the *Teaser,* Lt. Commdg. [*sic*] [William A.] Webb, are placed under my command as composing part of my Squadron. It is my intention, if no accident occurs to this ship to prevent it to appear before the enemy off Newport News at daylight on Friday morning next [the seventh], you will, with the *Jamestown* and *Teaser* be prepared to join us. My object is first to destroy the Frigates *Congress* and *Cumberland* if possible and then turn my attention to the destruction of the battery on shore, and the Gun boats. You will, in the absence of signals use your best exertions to injure or destroy the enemy. Much is expected of this ship & those who cooperate with her, by our Countrymen, and I expect and hope that our acts will prove our desire to do our duty, to reflect credit upon the Country and the Navy.

"You will communicate this communication to Lieut. Commdg. Barney & Webb.

"No. 1 signal hoisted under my pennant indicates sink before you surrender."

The three were units of the James River Squadron. The largest was the *Patrick Henry,* fourteen hundred tons, a converted, beautiful side-wheeler, known in more peaceful times as the *Yorktown* on the New York run. She was slightly armed, mounting twelve guns of small caliber. The gunboat *Jamestown* and the tug *Teaser* each carried but two cannon.

On that same March Thursday, Mallory, the usually objective admiralty lawyer, indicated that he was succumbing to his emotions and perhaps overwork, too, as he queried Buchanan:

> I submit for your consideration the attack of New York by the *Virginia*. Can the *Virginia* steam to New York and attack and burn the city? She can, I doubt not, pass Old Point safely, and, in good weather and a smooth sea, could doubtless go to New York. Once in the bay, she could shell and burn the city and the shipping.

Not content with this fantasy about a top-heavy vessel that her own architects admitted would have capsized not far beyond Cape Henry, Mallory continued,

Such an event would eclipse all the glories of the combats of the sea, would place every man in it preeminently high, and would strike a blow from which the enemy could never recover.

Peace would inevitably follow. Bankers would withdraw their capital from the city.

The navy yard and its magazines and all the lower part of the city would be destroyed, and such an event by a single ship would do more to achieve our immediate independence than would the results of many campaigns.

Too occupied with more immediate, as well as more attainable, realities, Buchanan made no attempt to reply for the time being. His "exec.," Jones, at that hour, was advising that the ship was still "too light," that is, "not sufficiently protected below the water." He continued, "Our draft will be a foot less than was intended . . . the eaves of the roof will not be more than six inches immersed, which in smooth water would not be enough; a slight ripple would leave it bare except the one-inch iron that extends some feet below. We are least protected where we most need it. The constructor should have put on six inches where we now have one."

The Thursday night target date was canceled for various reasons, even though the sides had already, according to Jones, been "slushed [greased], supposing that it would increase the tendency of the projectiles to glance." Five pilots were ready to take the untested ironclad, with engines about as bad as when the Union engineers had condemned them two years earlier.

"All preparations were made," Jones continued, "including lights at obstructions. After dark the pilots declared that they could not pilot the ship during the night. They had a high sense of their responsibility . . . it was not easy to pilot a vessel of our great draft under favorable circumstances . . . the difficulties were much increased by the absence of lights, buoys, etc. . . . . to which they had been accustomed.

"The attack was postponed to Saturday. . . ."

He found this strange, cumbersome vessel "badly ventilated, very uncomfortable and very unhealthy." In fact, "There was an average of fifty or sixty at the hospital in addition to the sick list on board."

Emotions ran high as the crew of the Confederacy's largest warship waited, while mechanics still swarmed over her. Captain Charles MacIntosh, at Gosport awaiting orders elsewhere, strolled to the darkened dock to deliver his farewells to the *Merrimack*'s chief engineer, H. Ashton Ramsay.

"Good-bye, Ramsay," he said somberly. "I shall never see you again. She will prove your coffin."

Orders to Hampton

Navy Department
March 7, 1862

Captain John Marston
Senior Naval Officer
Hampton Roads, Virginia

Send the *Lawrence, Congress,* and *Cumberland* into the Potomac River. Let the disposition of the remainder of the vessels at Hampton Roads be made according to your best judgment after consultation with General Wool. Use steam to tow them up. I will also try and send a couple of steamers from Baltimore to assist.

Let there be no delay.

Gideon Welles
Secretary of the Navy

February's days rushed forward, by northern measure, like the sands of a quickened hourglass. Along the East Coast the alarm spread of the *Merrimack*'s conjectured arrival with the potential of laying waste such port cities as Baltimore, New York, Boston, possibly even Portland, Maine—and who or *what* was to stop this floating embodiment of doomsday?

The editors of *Leslie's Illustrated Weekly* declared, "We feel it our duty to utter a cry of warning." At the same time, they sarcastically suggested that the capture of Norfolk, as a checkmate, would not be considered as part of the "profound strategy which develops itself so gloriously on the Potomac."

Charles Ellet, Jr., a well-known Philadelphia engineer—a physical throwback to Thomas Jefferson—who had constructed numerous bridges and dams but had now turned his attention to naval rams, published at his own expense a pamphlet, "Military Incapacity." Distributed to Congress and to the northern press, it warned in part:

> If the *Merrimac* is permitted to escape from Elizabeth river, she will be almost certain to commit great depredations on our armed and unarmed vessels in Hampton Roads; and may even be expected to pass out under the guns of Fortress Monroe, and prey upon our commerce in Chesapeake Bay. Indeed, if the alterations have been skillfully made, and she succeeds in getting to sea, she will not only be a terrible scourge to our commerce, but may prove also to be a most dangerous visitor to our blockading squadrons off the harbors of the southern coasts.
>
> I have attempted to call the attention of the Navy Department and the country so often to this subject during the last seven years, that I almost hesitate to allude to it again; and I would not do so here but that I think the danger from these tremendous engines *is very imminent but not at all appreciated*.

Nowhere, perhaps, was the sense of urgency so acute as in the Navy Department and on most of its war vessels, especially the *Monitor,* where Paymaster Keeler was writing his "Dear Anna" that "all are getting impatient and want to get alongside the *Merrimac*. . . . still I should not be surprised if we met with further delays. . . ."

On March 3, 1862, again in a wet snow squall, the *Monitor* pushed out into the East River to test her rudder and to fire her cannon, using blanks. This time, the helmsman found she steered satisfactorily, while firing the big columbiads only whetted the gunners' taste for real volleys. The deep reports reverberated through the Narrows —between Brooklyn and Staten Island—and sent gulls flapping suddenly seaward.

But southeasterly gales were keeping shipping in port. The *Monitor* could not depart yet.

That night, the quartermaster closed his log with the notation "10 P.M.—Norman McPherson and John Atkins deserted, taking the ship's cutter for parts unknown," then, in curt departure from a log's usual marine banality, postscripted, "So ends the day. . . ."

Tuesday, March 4, Worden was given orders signed by Hiram Paulding, now commandant of the New York (or Brooklyn) Navy Yard: "Sir: When the weather admits you will proceed with the *Monitor* under your command to Hampton Roads and on your arrival report to the senior naval officer there . . . wishing you a safe and successful passage . . ."

Commodore Paulding, who had helped to clinch the contract for the "Ericsson Battery," had remained a staunch supporter of the project, often joining the Swedish inventor in the evening in pushing the workmen along. The aging naval officer had every reason for apprehension, knowing the converted *Merrimack*'s potential.

On Wednesday, March 5, while the ironclad's captain waited for the storm to howl past New York and on to New England, Secretary Welles was starting a curious dispatch to senior officer Marston, on the *Roanoke,* in Hampton Roads, via General Wool and by way of Baltimore. Timed 3:20 P.M., it read, "Direct Lieutenant Commanding [*sic*] John L. Worden of the *Monitor* to proceed immediately to Washington with his vessel. . . ."

Since the Signal Corps faced a few days' work yet to connect the telegraph from Cape Charles underwater to Fort Monroe, this message, as all from Washington to Hampton Roads, was late in arriving. However, Marston replied at once, early on Thursday, the sixth, upon receipt, "The *Monitor* will be sent to Washington immediately on her arrival at this place."

The weather off New Jersey having improved this same Thursday, the *Monitor* cast off her hawsers. Dana Greene would write:

". . . the mechanics worked all night and at 11 A.M. on Thursday we started down the harbor in company with the gunboats *Sachem* and *Currituck.* We went along very nicely and when we arrived at Governor's Island the steamer *Seth Low* came alongside and took us in tow. We went out past the Narrows with a light wind from the west and very smooth water."

Now Worden relayed a message to Welles: "By the pilot I have the honor to report that we passed the bar at 4 P.M. . . . the weather is favorable. In order to reach Hampton Roads as speedily as possible whilst the fine weather lasts, I have been taken in tow by the tug."

As the side-wheel tug *Seth Low* hauled *Monitor* past Sandy Hook, Paulding was still debating what to do about a telegram he had received from Welles, "Let the *Monitor* come direct to Washington, anchoring below Alexandria." There was also another that had tapped in quickly after the first: "Please telegraph as soon as the *Monitor* leaves."

Whether Paulding made an attempt to get these orders to Worden by tugboat remains speculative. His associates believed he did not.

On board the little ironclad, there was some difference of opinion on how the late afternoon and evening went. Engineer Stimers (who had served with Ashton Ramsay on the old *Merrimack*) would note, "As soon as we were outside of Sandy Hook the sea washed over the deck so deeply that it was not considered safe to permit the men to go on deck, the top of the turret only being available."

Paymaster Keeler, however, went onto the turret to enjoy a "moon shining bright," and remarked, "Water smooth and everything seems favorable." He found the sea so calm that the officers lingered at the supper table in the wardroom, with Worden relaxed and reminiscing on his midshipman days.

The quartermaster himself logged "fine weather. At 8:30 made Barnegat Light, bearing S. by W. At 10:15 bore west, at S.S.W. Speed 5¼ knots."

Whatever the weather had been the preceding night, it worsened Friday. At 3 A.M., however, the quartermaster found it "cold and clear," under dazzling stars, with Absecon Light on the New Jersey coast greeting the little convoy only six miles distant.

Absecon Light, bearing west by south, could be seen twenty miles at sea, towering 167 feet above ground level. Erected only five years previously in an effort to reduce shipwrecks off Absecon Island, it was located on the northern limits of Atlantic City. This was a new watering spa, the six-hundred-room United States Hotel sharing honors with the Hygeia at Old Point Comfort as one of the largest resorts in the country.

The ships had steamed about thirty-six miles since passing Barnegat the previous evening.

By 6 A.M. a gray cloud bank rolled in, causing the same quartermaster to log with difficulty, "very heavy sea. Ship making heavy weather."

Waves swept the length of the deck and trickled through the hemp rope stuffed at the base of the turret. It had been placed there in defiance of Ericsson, who had maintained that the bronze ring was itself sufficient seal against the ocean. Nonetheless, the saltwater was soon drenching sailors who had been sleeping in their hammocks in the berth deck below.

Apparently it was worse aboard the two little gunboats, *Sachem* and *Currituck*. Stimers observed that they "rolled so much that when they rolled from us we could see under the bilge and when toward us, could see down the main hatch." While Stimers maintained that the *Monitor,* in spite of her wetting, remained so steady and her motion "so easy and quiet that a glass inkstand stood upon a polished mahogany case in the Captain's cabin . . . without slipping," Worden, along with others, complained of seasickness.

However, as the morning wore on, Stimers had to acknowledge that there was indeed a "tremendous gale," with the seas mounting. Greene, the "exec.," watched the sea "breaking over our decks at a great rate, and coming in our hawse pipes, forward, in perfect floods . . . the water came down under the tower like a waterfall. It would strike the pilot house and go over the tower in most beautiful curves."

It even forced through the narrow eyeholes in the pilot house "with such force as to knock the helmsman completely round from the wheel. . . ."

Nonetheless, "the steady and monotonous clank, clank of the engines" told Keeler and the others aboard that the *Monitor* was continuing to fight her way through the storm. The occasional jerk at the hawser leading from the bow proved that the powerful tug *Seth Low* had the ironclad firmly under control, even if the steam pistons should cease their rhythm.

And while the late winter Atlantic storm mounted in fury this Friday, March 7, both Welles and his assistant, Gustavus Fox, continued priority telegrams addressed to Hampton Roads—following the first to Marston (aboard the still crippled *Roanoke*) —to send the *Congress, Cumberland,* and *St. Lawrence* into the Potomac with "no delay."

The *St. Lawrence* was a sailing frigate mounting fifty-two guns, under the command of a forty-year navy veteran, Captain H. Y. Purviance, a Marylander. Although under sail power solely, she had recently captured and sunk a blockade runner, *Petrel.* The frigate dropped anchor Thursday, in Lynn Haven Bay, on the southern coast, just within Cape Henry.

The telegrams had resulted from a hastily called Cabinet meeting at the White House Thursday night. Lincoln, over Fox's protests, had insisted that the frigates be towed into the Potomac in order to destroy lingering enemy batteries along the banks in advance of McClellan's army, which was nearly ready to move. It was as though the *Merrimack* had been at least temporarily forgotten.

However, Fox returned to the White House early Friday morning, accompanied by a friend, Lucius E. Chittenden, a Vermonter who was an underofficial of the Treasury. At that time Fox advised the President that the Confederate ironclad was not expected to appear in the Roads before Sunday, while he tended to talk down the *Monitor* as "an experiment wholly untried," voicing the gloomy possibility, "She may be already at the bottom of the ocean."

Then, Chittenden would recall, the great phrase-turner President observed, "I am sure that the *Monitor* is still afloat and that she will yet give a good account of herself. Sometimes I think she may be the veritable sling with a stone that shall yet smite the *Merrimac* Philistine in the forehead."

While the brief meeting ended with conflicting opinions as to where the frigates should be, Fox nonetheless followed up the secretary's message with one to Lieutenant F. A. Parker, of the Washington Navy Yard, inquiring, "Is the telegraph to Captain Marston received and understood, and will it go tonight?"

He next asked Francis S. Corkran, naval officer of customs, in Baltimore, "Can you charter and send a couple of steamers to Old Point to assist in towing two or three sailing vessels into the Potomac? Do so, if possible on the best terms." (Corkran, among his diverse duties, was stumbling around East Coast quarries seeking stones for blocking Confederate-held ports.)

At Fort Monroe, the correspondent for the Chicago *Tribune* was closing his generally routine Friday roundup with the note:

"The steamer *Merrimack* was lying near the Navy Yard at Norfolk yesterday morning with flags flying and a crew on board. She draws 23 feet of water and was described as looking like the roof of a sunken house with a smoke stack protruding from the water."

He then posted it for one of the night boats to take to Washington, Baltimore, or Annapolis and thence be put on the telegraph lines to Illinois.

At 4 P.M. conditions aboard the *Monitor* took a dramatic turn for the worse. Water pouring down the smokestacks and blower pipes (six and four feet high respectively) located on the aft decking, caused the belts on the blower wheels to slip, then break.

"The blowers being thus stopped," Worden would explain, "there was no draft for the furnaces, and the engine and fire rooms became immediately filled with gas."

The engineers, led by Isaac Newton (actually the senior engineer on board, since Stimers was in a volunteer observer capacity), "behaved like heroes," in the estimation of Dana Greene, who continued: "They fought with the gas, endeavoring to get the blowers to work, until they dropped down apparently as dead as men ever were.

"I jumped in the engine room with my men as soon as I could and carried them on top of the tower to get fresh air."

Stimers was even more worried, since he believed both firemen and engineers were "so asphyxiated that the lives of some of them were despaired of."

With the crisp wind, the captain was relieved to observe, "they finally revived."

However, with the fires down and no steam, the engines stopped and, as Greene observed, in possible understatement, "times looked rather blue." Worden continued:

". . . the water which was entering the vessel in many places was increasing rapidly. The hand pump was used and men set to work bailing, but with little effect.

"The tug boat having us in tow was ordered to head directly to shore, but being light and of moderate power, she could move us but slowly against wind and sea."

However, by 7 P.M. the ships were in more equable seas, the

engines repaired and moving again. Paymaster Keeler, with some engineering background from his foundry experience, took charge of the engine room.

At 8 P.M. the *Monitor* was logged eight miles off Fenwick Island Light, on the Delaware-Maryland border.

Since Worden had been without sleep for some twenty-four hours, Greene prevailed on him to rest, the latter finding a "smooth sea, clear sky, the moon out and the old tank going along five and six knots very nicely. All I had to do was to keep awake and think over the narrow escape we had in the afternoon."

At midnight, the outlook appeared "so favorable" that his young "exec." told the captain he need not "turn out" for the next watch, that he, Greene, would stand ready for any emergency. However, Worden was scarcely back in his bunk when sudden rough shoal water caused "the most infernal noise" Greene had ever heard.

They were passing Chincoteague Shoals, off Chincoteague Island, Maryland.

John J. N. Webber, of Babylon, New York, one of two acting masters (lieutenants, junior grade) on board, who would recall that "no one slept much," added that the *Monitor* was "broadside to seas rolling over and over in all kinds of ways."

Water and air rushed through the hawse pipe leading to the *Monitor*'s novel bonus of a protected anchor, not only drenching the berth deck and wardroom but causing a sound Dana Greene likened to "the death groans of twenty men—the most dismal, awful sound I ever heard."

Worden attempted to hail the tug. Since the ironclad had not been equipped with a steam whistle, the *Seth Low*'s crew could not hear anything above the howl of the wind. In moments, the wheel ropes slipped off the helm, causing the *Monitor* to sheer and yaw "at an awful rate," which in turn threatened to split the hawser. Greene continued:

"In the course of half an hour we fixed the wheel ropes and now our blowers were the only difficulty. About 3 o'clock on Saturday morning the sea became a little smoother, though still rough and going down our blowers to some extent, and the never failing answer from the engine room, 'blowers going slowly, but can't go much longer.' "

From 4 A.M. till daylight Greene described as "the longest hour and a half I ever spent. I certainly thought Old Sol had stopped in China and never intended to pay us another visit."

Even though conditions were generally drenched, soggy, and cold below, sailing became smoother with dawn of Saturday, March 8, in coastal waters. The quartermaster logged "fine weather and clear sky."

At the same hour Gideon Welles, extremely concerned for the safety of McClellan's impending expedition and the existing fleet in Hampton Roads, scribbled another message while still in his night attire. He hastened it by an aide to the signal room where, he mused, Lincoln himself may have been at this very hour. Addressed again to Marston, it read:

"The Assistant Secretary will be at Old Point by the Baltimore boat of this eve. Do not move the ships until further orders, which he will carry."

Fox himself was advising Corkran, again in Baltimore, "Wait further instructions. I go to Old Point in the 3 P.M. train."

There was, however, *no* train to the Norfolk area. There was not even a direct rail to Richmond from Washington, nor had there ever been one. Fox had a choice of a Fort Monroe boat from Washington, Baltimore, or Annapolis. He could conceivably entrain to Wilmington, transferring in Baltimore (from the Washington Railroad to the Philadelphia, Wilmington, and Baltimore Railroad) and then shunting off in Wilmington onto a freight line down the eastern shore to Princess Anne, and attempt ferry connections across the lower reaches of the bay to Fort Monroe. But this circuitous route might have required a day or more.

Whatever his route, Fox, while hastily packing, was endeavoring to decide whether he should keep *all* the frigates where they were. He knew time was running out. But he had no way of ascertaining if the *Merrimack* would appear this Sunday as he had speculated on Friday to Lincoln. And he had also asserted, as quoted by Chittenden:

> I think you do not take into account all the possibilities of the *Merrimac*. True, she may break down, she may accomplish nothing, she may not be shot proof, but she will be commanded by a skilled naval officer. The engineers who have had charge of her construction are as competent as any in their profession. If they risk her in action, you may be sure she will do good work.

All it revealed was Gustavus Fox's own uncertainty. If only he *knew* . . .

The sun was bright and the temperature nearly fifty degrees that Saturday as the *Monitor* continued down the low coastline. However, she still rolled, making it impossible for the men to warm and dry themselves on deck. About noon, Cape Charles was sighted.

At 2:45 the hawser parted, but was secured rather quickly.

At 3 P.M. Cape Henry Light was picked up. At the same time, clouds of smoke were made out hanging in the direction of Fort Monroe. As Keeler noted:

". . . little black spots could occasionally be seen suddenly springing into the air, remaining stationary for a moment or two and then gradually expanding into a large white cloud. . . ."

Worden, assuming these indicated "an engagement," concluded it "to be with the *Merrimac*." While it was now obvious that they were too late, the captain ordered "the vessel stripped of her sea rig, turret keyed up and in every way to be prepared for action."

Saturday Morning, March 8

[Telegram]

Newport News
March 8, 1862

Major-General Wool,
Commanding.

The *Merrimack* is being towed down by two steamers past Craney Island toward Sewell's Point, so reported to me from the *Cumberland*.

Mansfield
Brigadier-General

Saturday morning along the tidewater of Virginia was one of those late winter days rich with a hint of spring—"beautiful . . . mild, bright and clear," it appeared to Tom Selfridge, of the *Cumberland*. The harshness of a bleak, cold winter, suggested by sleet squalls of but twenty-four hours before, seemed suddenly long past as the sun rose over Cape Henry and the marsh birds flapped out above the unusually calm Hampton Roads—their cries mingling with the dying, brassy matins from many buglers.

Soon, the smoke of breakfast fires from the opposing encampments mingled with a woody and familiar pungency over the flat gray waters.

It was a great and welcome day aboard the frigates *Cumberland* and *Congress*, anchored about a quarter of a mile off Newport News, with little or no heat belowdecks for drying clothes and bedding. Lines were strung across the decks, soon heavy with pants, shirts, socks, and underwear, while topsides the sails were loosened from the yardarms to absorb the warming rays. Small boats bobbed from lines securing them to swung-out booms in anticipation of shore leave.

Officers, including Dr. Shippen of the *Congress*, after an ample breakfast, were "pacing the poop," as they watched the gulls "scream and fight" for garbage just thrown overboard by the cooks. The surgeon had, as a matter of fact, just finished reading the latest copy of the Norfolk *Day Book* printing a "violent diatribe" against the Confederate naval authorities for their "bad management in fitting out the *Merrimack*," declaring the iron plating to be "a failure," and, further, that she nearly sank when brought out of dock. The writers professed to see no use for her "except to be moored in the harbor as a floating battery."

The *Congress* this week had, in effect, two captains, both named Smith, but of no relationship. Commander W. B. Smith had been detached a few days previously and was awaiting passage south for another command. He had been relieved by the youthful Lieutenant Joseph B. Smith, son of old Commodore Smith in Washington. As a matter of fact, Commander Smith was packed and ready to go ashore in the afternoon.

Also on board was the former provisions inspector of the Boston Navy Yard, McKean Buchanan, now paymaster of the *Congress*. While he of course knew his brother, Franklin, was in Richmond, he had not yet learned of his recent appointment to the *Merrimack*.

Crew-wise, it had been feast or famine on the old *Congress*. Most of her former complement had been paid off during the winter. They had set out noisily, seabags over shoulders, for their homes primarily in the East. Worried that there would be none to man her guns, General Wool sent aboard a detachment from the 99th New York Infantry, also known as the Union Coast Guard—89 officers and men. The enlistments picked up and soon ship's company counted 270—meaning that nearly 400 called *Congress* "home," of a sort.

The *Cumberland,* a quarter of a mile south of the *Congress,* while still under command of capable old Captain William Radford, nonetheless answered to her youthful "exec.," Lieutenant George U. Morris. Radford was aboard the *Roanoke,* anchored closer to Fort Monroe, as president of a court martial. The *Roanoke* remained dead in the water, a frustration to her engineers. While mounting forty-four guns, as powerful as the *Minnesota,* she continued a helpless giant, her shaft and other parts yet to be returned from Brooklyn. Thus stripped of power except for her canvas, she was no more maneuverable than the *Congress* or *Cumberland.*

There were more than sixty vessels in the Hampton Roads area operated by the navy or the Quartermaster Corps of the army, chartered by or in some manner supporting the two military services—a wide diversity in type, size, and function, from supply and transport vessels, mostly under sail, to the innumerable small tugs, which also doubled as lightly armed gunboats. Among the latter was the *Whitehall,* one of an increasing number of New York ferry boats that, unbelievably enough, had nailed down their passenger and cart ramps and tooted defiantly off to war.

In the evaluation of Marston, the senior officer present, the four most important warships were his own *Roanoke,* in spite of her disabled condition, and—anchored southward off shallow shores from Fort Monroe from about a quarter to half a mile respectively —the *Minnesota* (the flagship of Goldsborough still in Hatteras Inlet), under Captain Van Brunt, the *Congress,* and the *Cumberland.* The sailing frigate *St. Lawrence* remained newly anchored closest to Fort Monroe, actually just inside Chesapeake Bay.

A routine morning was being logged by the *Minnesota*'s quartermaster, D. A. Campbell. About dawn, noting "moderate breeze and clear weather," he also wrote, "Several schooners passed out." The temperature was fifty degrees.

At 8 A.M. "mail boat arrived."

At 9 A.M. "a steamer came in from New York."

At 11 A.M. "steamer *Sewanee* sailed," while a working party was sent ashore with the master and "returned at 12."

Also by noon, it was chow time on most if not all Union ships. Acting Master Rolando Coffin, aboard the little gunboat *Mystic,* still anchored off Fort Monroe, recalled that the crew of a tug had tarried for dinner, "our rations being superior to the Army rations on shore." The tug had been assisting the gunboat in clearing twisted anchor chains in the hawse pipes.

Ashore, inside Fort Monroe, certain high officers found themselves all at once concerned about matters other than food and the mild weather. The previous day "three or four" officers from the French side-wheeler sloop of war *Gassendi* (named after the seventeenth-century French philosopher Pierre Gassendi) had gone to Norfolk under a flag of truce, a common practice among visiting foreign navies. In this particular case, the communication was even more routine, since France maintained consular offices in the Confederate-held major seaport.

General Wool's staff, attempting to elicit information from the Frenchmen about the *Merrimack,* met with little success, leaving the question unresolved as to whether the officers were withholding something or merely had no intelligence to convey.

However, about midmorning the Fort Monroe signal tower reported the little *Gassendi* (mounting but six guns) was coaling up as if subsequently to shift anchorage. She lay between the fort and the Rip Raps. Colonel Cannon, Wool's aide-de-camp, checked the daybook and found no notice had been logged of the *Gassendi*'s departure —which would have been routine for a foreign man-of-war's intention of getting under way. This would entitle her to a salute, keeping both nations correct in their protocol.

According to Cannon, this slight nuance "excited a suspicion that the *Merrimack* was coming out and the Frenchmen, knowing it, were prepared to move, as they were at anchor in the line of fire."

Wool at once telegraphed Brigadier General Joseph K. Mansfield, commanding Camp Butler and Newport News Point, to "keep a sharp lookout."

White-haired and conventionally bearded, the Connecticut-born patriarch Mansfield had been wounded and decorated in the Mexican

War. J. M. Doubleday, of the 20th Indiana, for one, thought of him as a "very strict but considerate elderly West Pointer."

A good soldier, Mansfield kept his own alert patrols and his eight-inch howitzers and heavier columbiads ever aimed at the mouth of the Elizabeth River as well as across the far closer mouth of the broad James.

However, as the newspaper correspondents quartered at Fort Monroe put it, the "dullness" of Hampton Roads duty was master. It was not easy to arouse soldier and sailor alike from the apathy that had settled in from long, dreary months of inaction.

Across the waters, a reporter for the Norfolk *Day Book,* hastening from his home for a special assignment, momentarily paused, impressed by a certain quality of this Saturday: ". . . the morning was still as that of a Sabbath."

He went on toward the docks where the small tugboat, *Harmony,* was waiting.

At the Gosport Navy Yard, Franklin Buchanan was preparing to haul to sea what his own officers and others versed in ships and navigation were in agreement had to be history's most ill-prepared and unlikely warship. Her "exec." and ordnance officer, Catesby Jones, minced no words:

"The lower part of the shield forward was only immersed a few inches instead of two feet as was intended, and there was but one inch of iron on the hull. The port-shutters, etc. were unfinished. The *Virginia* was unseaworthy; her engines were unreliable, and her draft, over 22 feet, prevented her from going to Washington. . . . there was no regular concerted movement with the Army."

Even at this late hour, with bone-weary workmen still shuffling off of her from their all-night labors, "not a gun had been fired, hardly a revolution of the engines had been made," according to Lieutenant Wood.

Her surgeon, Dinwiddie Phillips, would postscript, "Many of those who watched us predicted failure, and others pleasantly suggested that the *Virginia* was an enormous metallic burial case, and that we were conducting our own funeral, and saving our friends and undertakers the trouble."

To H. Ashton Ramsay, acting chief engineer, there was a desperation about Buchanan as, shortly after 10:30, he ordered everyone off the ship except for the crew of about 350 and her four pilots. In fact, even then, although Old Buck had briefed the captains of his James River escorts, the *Patrick Henry, Jamestown,* and *Teaser,* his immediate officers were uncertain of the captain's exact plan of action.

All Ramsay knew for certain was that "we were off at last." Buchanan, "the veteran sailor, the beau ideal of a naval officer of the old school, with his tall form, harsh features and clear, piercing eyes, was pacing the deck with a stride I found it difficult to match, although he was then over 60 and I but 24." He asked Ramsay:

"What would happen to your engines and boilers if there should be a collision?"

The engineer assured the commanding officer that although the boilers were fourteen feet high, they were "braced tight." Then Buchanan belatedly confided to his subordinate:

"I am going to ram the *Cumberland.* I am told she has the new rifled guns, the only ones in their whole fleet we have cause to fear. The moment we are in the Roads I'm going to make right for her and ram her."

Then he questioned Ramsay about the engines, speculating as to whether they should first be tested "by a trial trip."

Ramsay expressed the belief that the *Merrimack*'s ten-mile run down the river would probably be sufficient. That seemed all the assurance Buchanan needed. At 11 A.M. when the tide was at its "last half flood," he hoisted his flag officer's red ensign, a Navy Yard signal gun was fired, and lines were cast off. The gun proved the clarion the townspeople were awaiting, at least "a signal for something," according to a soldier in the area, James Keenan, who wrote:

"In an instant the whole city was in an uproar, women, children, men on horseback and on foot running down towards the river from every conceivable direction, shouting, '*Merrimac* is going down."

At five to six knots top speed and far less than that in the narrow channel of the Elizabeth River, the ironclad, drawing at least her calculated twenty-two feet of water, afforded the curious ample time to watch her departure. They had never before seen anything like her.

To Phillips there was "an unusually large number of persons" on both shores, but for the most part constrained. A crew member, Virginius Newton, would write, "As we passed the wharves of Portsmouth and Norfolk we discovered the landings to be well crowded with men, women and children who gave us salutation, but seemed too deeply moved by the gravity of the moment to break into cheers."

Lieutenant William H. Parker, of the tug *Beaufort,* thought the crowd was even more vast: "nearly every man, woman and child in the two cities of Norfolk and Portsmouth" were traveling "by land . . . and by water" to locations such as Sewell's Point and Craney Island. . . .

"All the batteries were manned; all work was suspended in public and private yards, and those who were forced to remain behind were offering up prayers for our success. A great stillness came over the land. . . .

"Everything that would float, from the army tugboat to the oysterman's skiff, was on its way to the same point, loaded to the water's edge with spectators."

He added that the *Merrimack* was "saluted by the waving of caps and handkerchiefs; but no voice broke the silence of the scene; all hearts were too full for utterance . . . there were many who thought that as soon as the *Merrimack* rammed a vessel she would sink with all hands enclosed in an iron-plated coffin."

On board, William F. Drake, one of a volunteer detachment of eighty men from the United Artillery, a Norfolk company, would write: "The men were standing at their guns, a bright sun overhead; all quiet save an occasional order and the throbbing of the machinery below; passing between the two cities we beheld what seemed to be the entire population, and from wharves, balconies, windows and even housetops ten thousand waving handkerchiefs told us that in their hearts they were bidding us 'Godspeed!' "

The *Day Book* correspondent, trailing behind in the little *Harmony,* carrying also Flag Officer Forrest and other officers, wrote, "It was a gallant sight to see the ironclad leviathan gliding noiselessly through the water flying the red pennant of her commander at the fore flag staff and the gay Confederate ensign aft . . . past the wharves thronged with eager citizens, past the batteries whose parapets were dark with soldiers. . . ."

All hands at this point were "piped to dinner," according to Bill Cline, who had been present at the launching.

Now Ramsay asked one of the pilots how fast the ironclad was going. When he replied, "Eight or nine knots," the engineer officer reported to Buchanan, "The machinery is all right."

But she did not *steer* "all right." Her accompanying tugs *Raleigh* and *Beaufort* had to guide her in the channel—in fact, the *Beaufort* at one time passed her a line to keep her head straight.

The word of her coming preceded her along the Elizabeth River. Rebel gunners left their batteries to race to the water's edge. They were waiting for her at Sewell's Point. Lieutenant Phelps, who had been suffering from rheumatism, was helped onto his horse so he could gallop to the beach. John Cary, a soldier stationed there, was quietly "mending my pants" when he heard the cry, "The *Merrimack* is coming!"

It echoed from mouth to mouth farther up the James where Brigadier General R. E. Colston also lifted himself onto his horse to gallop twelve miles to Ragged Island for a frontline view of whatever was going to happen.

The James River squadron, led by the *Patrick Henry,* with the *Merrimack* in sight, was getting under way. Aboard the side-wheeler flagship, Lieutenant James H. Rochelle would rhapsodize over the ironclad, "grand and strong and confident, a Hercules of the waters, she moved straight upon the enemy."

Soon, Ramsay and other officers were watching the batteries "and white tents of Newport News, together with the *Congress* and *Cumberland,* tall and stately, with every line and spar clearly defined against the blue March sky. . . . the rigging of the *Cumberland* was gay with the red, white and blue of sailors' garments hung out to dry."

To the *Day Book* writer the two old sailing ships were "rising like prodigious castles above the placid water."

Dr. Phillips, however, interpreted the peaceful washday scene, accompanied by the "glassy" water, as a trick. Since neither vessel seemed "to take any active interest in our movements, I concluded that the rumors concerning torpedoes in the channel . . . were true, and that they were simply awaiting our approach to the proper spot before firing them and sending us broadcast into the air and afterward returning us as food for the fishes of the sea."

Actually, the signal station at Newport News Point, being able to look down much of the length of the Elizabeth River, had spotted the telltale smoke not long after 11 A.M., when the slow-moving ironclad was plowing down the narrow channel. This inspired General Mansfield to telegraph Fort Monroe, "The *Merrimack* is close at hand."

Long expected, her coming nonetheless took many by surprise in addition to those sailors washing their clothes. Josh Lewis at Camp Butler, who had amused himself during the winter by shooting ducks, was absently watching "three or four vessels steamen [*sic*] up the mouth of the river, yet with no thought that they might be the enemy." In fact, he contemplated their approach with "some eagerness" when he heard the "long roll" sounded.

This sent him and his companions of the 20th Indiana, including Erasmus C. Gilbreath, scrambling up to high ground "to see."

An aging quartermaster on watch aboard the *Congress,* John Leroy, studying the channel to Norfolk for some time through his long glass, finally reported, "I believe *that thing* is a-coming down at last, sir!"

Tom Selfridge, as officer of the deck of the *Cumberland,* reported that the *Merrimack* "had just hove in sight, a long distance off in the direction of Norfolk. Owing to the mirage, her movements were much obscured and her progress was so slow that at first it seemed doubtful if she was really coming out. But surmises were dispelled as the large, low hull came in view abreast of Craney Island, heading for the mouth of the Elizabeth River."

The ominous drumbeat to quarters then reverberated through the handsome old sloop-of-war. A pilot aboard the same ship, A. B. Smith, could have sworn he was looking at "a half-submerged crocodile." The frigate at once fired signal guns.

The Newport News tug-picket boat *Zouave,* which had towed ships under the grain elevators in Albany, was tied to a wharf after having brought "mail and fresh provisions" to the *Congress* and *Cumberland.* When her acting master, Henry Reaney, noticed "black smoke in the Elizabeth River," he cast loose and steamed to the side of the *Cumberland,* whose officer of the deck ordered him to hurry down to Pig Point and find out what was happening.

In moments, the little tug was churning toward the point. As Reaney would report, "It did not take us long to find out for we had not gone over two miles when we saw what to all appearances looked like the roof of a very big barn belching forth smoke as from a chimney fire."

Reaney fired six rounds from the *Zouave*'s thirty-pound Parrott gun toward the "very big barn," then turned back toward the two frigates for which the tug acted as tender and guardian terrier. Although the light rounds were largely in the nature of a warning signal, the master would claim he actually fired the first shots at the enemy that Saturday.

The *Minnesota* logged, "At 12:45 P.M. saw three steamers off Sewell's Point standing towards Newport News; one of these was supposed to be the *Merrimack* from the size of her smokestack. We immediately slipped chain with buoy and rope attached at the 15-fathom shackle and steamed towards Newport News."

The prearranged emergency signal "551" was flag-messaged from ship to ship. The disabled *Roanoke*, bearing the senior officer Marston, called "with every exertion" for the tugs *Dragon* and *Young America* to take her in tow. Not sure that all ships understood the hoist "551," she then hauled another onto her lofty halyards: "1218."

At the same time, William Radford, captain of the *Cumberland*, hurriedly recessed his court martial on the *Roanoke* and embarked on a small boat for shore where his horse was tethered.

Another armed steamer, the small *Mount Vernon*, also with engines disassembled, which had been coaling, signaled for other tugs. After Captain O. S. Glisson hoisted signal "551" without answer (and apparently not understanding "1218") she fired "a shotted gun in the direction of the enemy."

The long "drum roll" had awakened William Rogers, of the 10th New York, inside Fort Monroe. By the time he arrived at his gun station on the "flagstaff bastion" he saw General Wool, "mounted on his white horse," galloping up and down the sloping ramparts, ordering messages sent to Newport News.

In comparison to the mounting furor in the fort and encampments and, certainly, aboard ship, the French *Gassendi* settled down with objective anticipation to watch what her captain, Ange Simon Gautier, fully expected to be a first-class naval engagement—or, as he would later observe, a "study" that was *"très intéressante."*

Gautier likened the distant appearance of the *Merrimack* to "a barracks roof surmounted by a large funnel." In fact, the roof analogy—a house or a barn—was the most general. Even at this moment, the correspondent for the New York *Herald* was starting his story:

". . . a suspicious looking vessel, supposed to be the *Merrimack*, looking like a submerged house, with the roof only above water, was moving down from Norfolk by the channel in front of the Sewell's Point batteries. . . ."

As the *Merrimack* emerged from the mouth of the Elizabeth, her officers realized that the big, squat presence was known. Ramsay watched "the white-winged sailing craft that sprinkled the bay and long lines of tugs and small boats [that] scurried to the far shore like chickens on the approach of a hovering hawk."

Next he observed the *Minnesota* getting up steam and the *Congress* as she "shook out her topsails. Down came the clothesline on the *Cumberland* and boats were lowered and dropped astern." Then Buchanan summoned most of his crew to the gun deck to deliver a Nelson-like exhortation:

"Sailors, in a few minutes you will have the long-looked-for opportunity of showing your devotion to our cause. Remember that you are about to strike for your country and your homes. The Confederacy expects every man to do his duty. Beat to quarters!"

According to Bill Cline, "not one of her crew" had "suspected" the nature of this mission. He also thought the commanding officer had added, "The eyes of the whole world are upon you this day, and in the good old name of Virginia let every man do his duty!"

As Buchanan finished, the mess caterer touched the chief engineer's elbow and whispered, "Better get your lunch now, Mr. Ramsay. It will be your last chance. The galley fires must be put out when the magazines are opened."

On his way to lunch, Ramsay saw the assistant surgeon, Algernon S. Garnett, at a table laying out lint and surgical implements. This shrank the appetite of the thin-skinned Ramsay, who satisfied himself with a bite of cold tongue and a cup of coffee. He then passed along the gun deck where he observed "the pale and determined countenances of the guns' crews, as they stood motionless at their posts, with set lips unsmiling, contrasting with the careless expression of sailors when practised at 'fighting quarters,' on a man-of-war. This was the real thing. . . ."

Will Drake would add, "The strictest discipline was in force on our gun deck, no one at the guns was allowed to talk, not even to whisper. Everything was ready, guns loaded and run out for action. . . ."

And still trailing well in the van aboard the *Harmony*, the *Day Book* correspondent wrote at what he timed 1:20 P.M., "the heavy boom of a gun from beyond Sewell's Point . . . another gun . . . steadily with grim and ominous silence the *Virginia* glides through the water . . . with a defiant valor the *Beaufort* and *Raleigh* followed where she led."

About the same time, as the *Minnesota* was already steaming southward toward Newport News, guns manned, the *Roanoke* was still attempting to get under way with the help of the tugs *Dragon* and *Young America.* The former tug already had secured a hawser to her bow. Captain Glisson, of the equally helpless *Mount Vernon,* finding the navy tugs otherwise busy, asked the army quartermaster at Fort Monroe if he could scare up an extra one.

Coffin, of the small gunboat *Mystic,* also trying to clear for action, observed, "It was a sorry fleet to attack a vessel like the *Merrimack. . . .*"

As if in line with this seemingly Gilbert and Sullivan navy (lacking only H.M.S. *Pinafore*), the newly arrived frigate *St. Lawrence* started toward Newport News under tow of the gunboat *Cambridge.*

Smith, as captain of the *Congress,* quickly assembled his men to reassure them, as he was quoted, "My hearties, you see before you the great southern bugaboo, got up to fright us out of our wits. Stand to your guns and let me assure you that one good broadside from our gallant frigate and she is ours!"

Seaman Frederick H. Curtis, who shared a mutual hometown —Hanover, Massachusetts—with the *Congress*'s youthful captain, then reported of the ensuing moments:

"Not a word was spoken, and the silence that prevailed was awful."

Gautier, on the *Gassendi,* with rapt attention, watched the *Merrimack* executing "several evolutions . . . doubtless to assure herself of the good working of her machinery," appearing "for an instant to turn back towards Norfolk, but then aim once more for Newport News Point." For a ship requiring nearly thirty minutes to turn in her length, what were normal maneuvers appeared exaggerated as well as misleading.

He also observed the *Minnesota* and *Roanoke* struggling heroically to reach Sewell's Point, the latter under tow from the *Dragon.* The *Minnesota* arrived there first, a few minutes before 2 P.M., and exchanged shots with the enemy batteries. One ball hit the main mast, necessitating emergency procedures to secure the flopping lines and broken spars.

A *Harper's Weekly* artist saw the *Monitor* loss like this. The U.S.S. *Rhode Island* was a typical rather large side-wheeler of the times. Note the *Monitor's* single telescopic smokestack aft, which had been substituted for the twin boxlike ones, similar to the twin air intakes just aft. While the men, in fair weather or foul, used the top of the turret as a "roost," the vulnerable pilot house, with sloping sides, located forward, was not replaced on the turret until subsequent monitors. *Courtesy of Naval History Division, Navy Department*

Reoccupation of the Gosport Navy Yard, May 1862, following its successive destructions by Union and Confederate forces. Some of the tugs shown at right doubtless took part in the March battles with the *Merrimack*. *Courtesy of U. S. Army Military History Research Collection, Carlisle Barracks, Pa.*

This panoramic view of Hampton Roads during the Civil War shows, among other points of interest: Rip Raps (5), with the Elizabeth River, Norfolk, and Portsmouth above (9, 10, 11), and Newport News at the right (17). *Courtesy of Fort Monroe Casemate Museum, Fort Monroe, Virginia*

John Ericsson was a difficult, stubborn, often arrogant genius. Like so many inventors, his contribution lay in his ability to combine and make workable the ideas and prior inventions of others. The screw or "rotary" propeller was first perceived by Archimedes two centuries before Christ; the idea for iron-plating could be traced back to the warriors who held their shields against the sides of the earliest galleys; the turret, steam engines, and, of course, the 11-inch cannon were previous inventions. *Official U.S. Navy Photograph*

Gideon Welles, Lincoln's Secretary of the Navy, was a familiar and commanding sight in wartime Washington, with his generous white beard and immense gray wig that fooled none. *U.S. Signal Corps Photo*

A contemporary artist's conception of the conversion of the *Merrimack* in the Gosport Navy Yard stone drydock. No photographic negative of the Confederate ironclad has ever been located, despite the most meticulous search in past decades by students of the War Between the States in the Norfolk-Newport News area. *Official U.S. Navy Photograph*

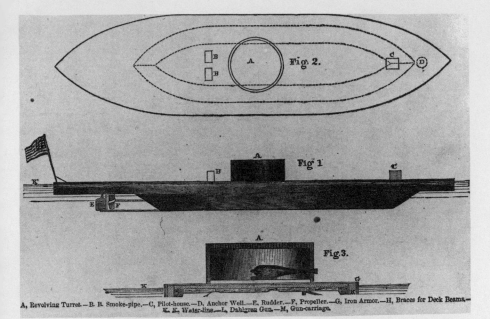

A, Revolving Turret.—B. B. Smoke-pipe.—C, Pilot-house.—D. Anchor Well.—E, Rudder.—F, Propeller.—G, Iron Armor.—H, Braces for Deck Beams.—K. K, Water-line.—L, Dahlgren Gun.—M, Gun-carriage.

Sketch of the U.S.S. Monitor copied from *Harper's Weekly*, January 1863. *Official U.S. Navy Photograph*

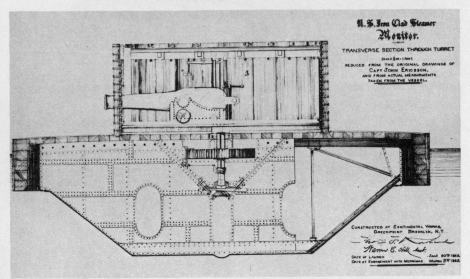

U.S.S. *Monitor* (1862) transverse section through the turret, engraving from the original drawings of John Ericsson. *Official U.S. Navy Photograph*

Harper's Weekly, faithful chronicler of the *Monitor*'s fortunes, depicted the launch of the ironclad, January 30, 1862, at the Continental Iron Works, Brooklyn. A sprinkling of spectators waited in a cold winter rain as gamblers offered odds on whether the novel craft would sink. To underscore his faith in his creation, Ericsson himself, standing about twenty feet from the stern, rode her down. As a *New York World* reporter wrote, the *Monitor* had "not the slightest intention of sinking." *Official U.S. Navy Photograph*

Monitor turret. *Harper's Weekly*, which published many *Monitor* sketches, produced this generally accurate concept of the turret and the twin 11-inch Dahlgren cannon. With a 20-foot inside diameter and 9-foot height, the 120-ton revolving turret carried 8 inches of armor. The reinforcing railroad bars, or beams, are clearly depicted. *Official U.S. Navy Photograph*

The sinking of the *Cumberland* from an engraving that appeared in *Leslie's Illustrated. Official U.S. Navy Photograph*

Leslie's Illustrated Weekly's rendition of the *Monitor* and *Merrimack*. The *Merrimack,* somewhat too large, is also floating too high in the water, which would have exposed her wooden, unarmored hull to enemy fire. The artist unquestionably never saw the Confederate ironclad, although first-hand drawings of the *Monitor*—oversimplified here—were plentiful. *Naval History Photograph*

John L. Worden was a 44-year-old lieutenant when he was ordered to command the *Monitor,* as yet unlaunched. Fresh out of Confederate prison, he held the dubious distinction of being the South's first Federal officer POW. *U.S. Signal Corps Photo*

Chow time on deck. "Probably no ship was ever devised which was so uncomfortable for her crew," her Executive Officer declared. There are about as many "action" expressions on these faces as can be found in any of the long exposures of the day. Apparently, the sailor on the barrel decided he'd just keep his eyes closed through the tedium. Note the black man, foreground. *Courtesy of Naval History Division, Navy Department.*

Commodore Josiah Tattnall, CSN, who took command of the *Merrimack* after her battle with *Monitor*. *Official U.S. Navy Photograph*

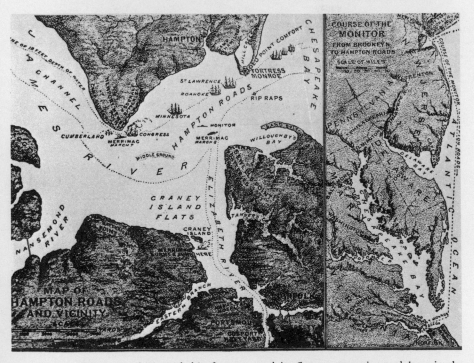

This map, which probably first appeared in *Century* magazine and later in the periodical's compilation, *Battles and Leaders of the Civil War,* positions the combatants in the two-day Battle of Hampton Roads reasonably well. However, the two dates are in error: March 7 should be the 8th, and March 8, the 9th. The waters were a nightmare of shallows and ill-suited to a vessel with the *Merrimack*'s draft.

Then, up the flagstaff of the *Merrimack* streamed the signals spelling out: "Close Action!"

Parker, on the *Beaufort,* steaming on the port bow of the *Merrimack,* wrote that his little ship, in obedience, fired the first shot of Buchanan's little squadron about 2 P.M., while hoisting the same battle flag she had flown at the losing battle of Roanoke Island, when overwhelmed by the Burnside Expedition.

Josh Lewis, of the 20th Indiana, from his vantage point at Camp Butler watched the *Beaufort*'s shot fall short of the *Congress,* then the *Merrimack* take the lead toward the anchored frigate.

According to Dr. Shippen, the *Congress* waited until the enemy's "plating and ports" could be easily discerned, then "tried her with a solid shot from one of our stern guns, the projectile glancing off her forward casement like a drop of water from a duck's back . . . this opened our eyes."

The ironclad fired a volley of grape, "killing and wounding quite a number on board the *Congress."* However, the latter replied with a broadside of some thirty-two guns—"a tremendous roar"—which, it was apparent both on the *Congress* and on shore to those such as Josh Lewis, "rattled on the armored *Merrimack* without the least injury;" as the horrified pilot, Smith, of the *Cumberland,* observed, "like India-rubber balls."

It was an analogy employed as well by Lieutenant Samuel R. Franklin, a passenger on the *Roanoke* waiting for the arrival of the screw sloop *Dacotah* to become her "exec." He was given charge of the forward pivot gun.

Ashore, Bill Rogers thought the Union fire against the ironclad was "as harmless as marbles."

The *Merrimack,* now only three hundred yards off—point-blank range—returned the broadside, the results of which Dr. Shippen found "simply terrible." He would report:

> One of her shells dismounted an eight-inch gun and either killed or wounded every one of the gun's crew, while the slaughter at the other guns was fearful. There were comparatively few wounded, the fragments of the huge shells she threw killing outright as a general thing. Our clean and handsome gun-deck was in an instant changed into a slaughter-pen, with lopped-off legs and arms and bleeding, blackened bodies scattered about by the shells. . . . One poor fellow had his chest

transfixed by a splinter of oak as thick as the wrist, but the shell-wounds were even worse. The quartermaster who had first discovered the approach of the iron-clad—an old man-of-war's man, named John Leroy—was taken below with both legs off. The gallant fellow died in a few minutes, but cheered and exhorted the men to stand by the ship almost with his last breath.

Frederick Curtis, captain of No. 8 gun, "felt something warm, and the next instant I found myself lying on the deck beside a number of my shipmates."

One shell made a direct hit on No. 7 cannon beside him, "dismounting the gun and sweeping the men about it back into a heap, bruised and bleeding. The shell struck right back of me and took my left-hand man."

Curtis and others had the impression the *Merrimack* was preparing to send a boarding party.

Especially appalled—and perhaps disbelieving—of the carnage was Paymaster McKean Buchanan, brother of his adversary, temporarily in charge of the powder-passing division.

The *Merrimack,* however, did not turn to deliver a broadside from her port battery, or approach to board, keeping on toward the point and the *Cumberland,* "severely," according to J. Tyler Jobson, of the Portsmouth Rifle Company, at Pig Point. This somehow led the survivors of the *Congress* to believe the battle was over and they waved their caps and cheered. Most did not realize that the *Congress* was already afire from hot shot, in the sick bay, in the main hold, and under the wardroom, near the after magazine. Pumps were started.

Lieutenant Smith, the commander, knew the *Congress* was doomed. He ordered topsails and jib set, the anchors slipped, and called for the tug *Zouave* to help him ground on the seventeen-foot shoals offshore. At least, then she could not be sunk and she could renew the battle—seemingly—like any fort.

Lewis, "sure that the *Cumberland*—no mean frigate—and the land battery would sink her . . . ran up the river to be in at the death."

Selfridge himself possessed much the same assurance, even though with the turn of the tide, the *Cumberland*'s crew was having trouble with anchors and "spring" lines to place the old sailing vessel in position for a broadside. It was because of "slack water" at this phase of the tide, and was just as the enemy had calculated. Indeed,

Buchanan's concern for the *Cumberland*'s "new rifled guns" was much exaggerated, since the latter carried but one 6-inch rifled cannon, on her stern.

The *Merrimack* steamed across the *Cumberland*'s bow, within three hundred yards, obviously getting in position to ram. The gun crews moved from battery to battery, trying to find angles that would afford a good clean shot at the big black enemy. The rigging obstructed the 10-inch forecastle pivot gun.

Finally, as the *Merrimack* closed, the *Cumberland* was able to open fire with "a few forward 9-inch guns" as well as the big pivot. The Confederate replied, aiming both at the shore and at the frigate. One passed through the starboard hammock netting, killing and wounding nine marines. As Selfridge noted:

"These men, the first to fall, were promptly carried below, and their groans were something new to us and served as an introduction to a scene of carnage unparalleled in the war."

One ball crashed onto a wharf, as Camp Butler's many artillery pieces opened wildly against the *Merrimack.* Yet another rattled over Josh Lewis's head, "bursting with an awful report a short distance from me." He fell to the ground, "almost senseless," but quickly recovered when he realized he had not been scratched.

Mansfield at the same time was telegraphing General Wool: "The *Merrimack* is engaging the *Cumberland* at close quarters."

In reply, Wool started mounted detachments from Camp Hamilton galloping southward, firmly believing that General Magruder was pounding the trails by land to join in the assault.

Gautier, on the *Gassendi,* who at times could see only the masts of the Union vessels, nonetheless was "able to estimate the force of the fire which, during a quarter of an hour, particularly, was of the hottest.

"We could see the entrance of the river constantly swept in all directions by the shot that ricochetted, and the strength of the detonations indicated to us that they were guns of the heaviest calibre which were testing the armor of the *Merrimack.*"

Now the ironclad raked the *Cumberland* with broadsides as she had the *Congress,* "a situation," according to Selfridge, "to shake the highest courage and the best discipline." Like Buchanan's own brother, Selfridge could not understand the hate manifested by this old officer whose career had been so closely linked with the growth of the Federal Navy. Tom Selfridge watched a whole gun crew wiped out, with the lone exception of the powder boy, a gun captain who lost both arms but "managed a smile" as he died. He continued:

> The dead were thrown to the disengaged side of the deck; the wounded carried below. No one flinched, but everyone went on rapidly loading and firing; the places of the killed and wounded being taken promptly by others, in accordance with previous drill and training. The carnage was frightful.
>
> Great splinters torn from the ship's side and decks caused more casualties than the enemy's shell. Every first and second captain of the guns of the first division was killed or wounded, and with a box of cannon primers in my pocket, I went from gun to gun firing them as fast as the decimated crews could load.

Then, on board the *Merrimack,* Bill Drake listened to the word passed along the noisy, smoke-filled gun deck, "Stand fast!" In the next instant, "We are going to run into her!"

Firing ceased.

Below, Ramsay heard two gongs, the signal to stop. He sensed his ship was already plowing toward the starboard beam of the *Cumberland,* "relentless as fate," the captain figuring on her momentum to carry her the rest of the short distance. Then:

". . . three [bells] the signal to reverse. There was an ominous pause, then a crash, shaking us all off our feet. The engines labored. . . ."

To Catesby Jones, the ordnance and executive officer, the noise of the "crashing timbers," compounded by the *Merrimack*'s ram first going through the torpedo net spars, "was distinctly heard above the din of battle."

The ships momentarily stayed together even though the blow had completely broken off the heavy ram.

Ramsay, noting that the *Merrimack* had been "shaken in every fiber" (but denied by Lieutenant Taylor Wood, who reported the blow "hardly perceptible," and "slight," according to Jones), continued, "Our bow was visibly depressed. We seemed to be bearing down with a weight on our prow. Thud, thud, thud, came the rain of shot on our shield from the double-decked battery of the *Congress.* . . ."

With the ships so close that the muzzles, according to Surgeon

Phillips, were "so near touching," the *Cumberland* got off "three solid broadsides in quick succession," Selfridge would report, causing the ironclad to "fairly reel." The muzzles of two of the 9-inch Dahlgrens on the *Merrimack* were shattered, the smokestack was riddled, and the flag shot down. Torn off again, it was finally fastened "to a rent in the stack."

A "terrible crash in the fire room" at first caused Ramsay to believe that a boiler had burst. He was then informed it was the concussion from the shell hitting the stack.

> Cheer upon cheer went up from the *Cumberland* [Selfridge wrote], only to be followed by exclamations of rage and despair as the enemy slowly moved away . . . the water was rising rapidly, the *Cumberland* going down by the bows. The forward magazine was flooded, but the powder tanks had been whipped out and carried aft, whence the supply of powder to the forward guns had been subsequently maintained. As the water gained the berth deck, which by this time was filled with the badly wounded, heart-rending cries above the din of combat could be heard from the poor fellows as they realized their helplessness to escape slow death from drowning.

Only then, too late, could Selfridge speculate what might have happened had Morris, in command, linked the two warships by grapples.

The gunners of the *Merrimack,* it appeared to Ramsay, "were fighting like demons," as though, somehow, there was a danger the *Cumberland* might actually possess the capability of sinking them.

"Sponge, load, fire! Pass along the cartridges! More powder! A shell for number six . . . a wet wad for the hotshot gun!"

If her engineer officer thought the gunners fought "like demons," a view from shore tended to complement this analogy. Erasmus C. Gilbreath, of the 20th Indiana, observed, "The rebel vessel's smoke stack was often pierced by shot from our batteries, and as the smoke and flames poured out of these openings she looked more demoniacal than before."

A shell ripped into the *Cumberland*'s sick bay, exploded, and killed four of the wounded. The latter had to be evacuated and placed atop mess chests and other high places on other decks as the water cascaded through a hole Taylor Wood believed wide enough to admit "a horse and cart."

From across the mouth of the James, on his vantage point, Ragged Island, General Colston "could hardly believe" his "senses" when he watched the masts of the *Cumberland* "begin to sway wildly." Colston was among the "great numbers of people," residents and soldiers, watching the engagement. Although the cannonade was "visibly raging with redoubled intensity . . . to our amazement not a sound was heard by us . . . a strong March wind was blowing direct from us toward Newport News. We could see every flash of the guns and the clouds of white smoke, but not a single report was audible."

Momentarily, the *Merrimack* paused, and a figure, possibly Buchanan, appeared on the grating deck to demand the *Cumberland*'s surrender. Lieutenant Morris called back:

"Never! We will sink alongside with our colors flying."

The broadsides from the ironclad resumed. The slaughter continued. The gun deck, Selfridge wrote, "was covered with the dead and wounded and slippery with blood. Some guns were left run in from their last shot; rammers and sponges, broken and powder-blackened, lay in every direction; the large galley was demolished and its scattered contents added to the general blood-spattered confusion."

Then, "for some reason which I have never understood," the *Merrimack* rammed the sinking *Cumberland* a second time. Gautier on the French *Gassendi* thought it "unnecessary." Morris passed the order, given only in extremis, "Every man look out for himself!"

The time was a bit after 3 P.M.

And yet those guns with crews kept firing, one of the last shots hitting a bow gunport of the enemy, killing two outright and wounding others. The stubbornness of her adversary evoked the admiration of all aboard the *Merrimack,* referring to the "gallantry" and "bravery" of the crew.

"No braver heroes ever lived," thought Bill Cline.

Even the *Day Book* reporter, on the *Harmony* hove to just off Craney Island, would write, "A gallant man fought that ship—a man worthy to have maintained a better cause. Gun after gun he fired; lower and lower sunk his ship; his last discharge comes from his pivot gun, the ship lurches to starboard, now to port, his flag streams out wildly. . . ."

"Game to the last," J. Tyler Jobson, of the Portsmouth Rifle Company, on Pig Point, put it.

Josh Lewis, on the banks, watched the men leaping into the water.

Some made it to the boats—a small freight steamer, tugs, and launches—some swam, others clung to the masts, yardarms, and rigging jutting at a cant grotesquely above water, trying to decide whether to jump. The first survivors ashore were greeted by soldiers who embraced them, offered them "whiskey flasks," or even shoved plugs of tobacco into their sodden pockets—"They cried and cheered and cursed."

Selfridge, among the last to leave, found the wardroom hatch ladder "blocked by our fat drummer, Joselyn, struggling up with his drum." The lieutenant then stripped off his coat and sword and squeezed through a gunport. He almost made it when his boot jammed on the sill. Finally, the heel came off and he went through, "into the icy water encumbered by boots and clothing."

He swam until picked up by a launch. Nearby was the "fat drummer." For a life raft he was hanging onto the drum.

From the decks of the *Congress,* the final plunge of the *Cumberland* appeared to be abrupt. One seaman would write, "We saw her give one lurch, and then she went down like a bar of iron, but her flag still flew at her mast head; all was lost except honor."

". . . and now the *Cumberland* goes down on her beam ends," the *Day Book* correspondent continued, "at once a monument and an epitaph to the gallant men who fought her."

The diehard secessionist Charles "Dick" Phelps, who had to be helped onto his horse, would write his aunt, Mrs. Mary Jane Lee, that he had "the pleasure of seeing her [the *Cumberland*] go down with all hands on board except some 20 or 30. . . ."

Because of either the distance across Hampton Roads from Sewell's Point or the myopia of his zeal, the young lieutenant wove a fantasy of "a large transport steamer lying at the wharf" blown up along with "all the guns in the Battery [Camp Butler], destroying all their breastworks, burning up all their quarters and killing and wounding a great many," while all the time the *Merrimack* remained "perfectly indifferent—although their shot and shell were falling on her and sounded like hail falling on a tin roof."

All in all, Phelps confided that "this was an exciting time."

To some other Confederates, it was as well a giddy, exhilarating time.

Captain Benjamin Sloan, a West Pointer and ordnance officer on the staff of General Huger, who had been following the battle on a tugboat, was in his "youthful exuberance of spirits . . . dancing a jig on the deck to a paraphrased rendition of the old negro refrain . . . 'such a getting up of sails I never did see.' "

This was inspired by the sight of all the smaller craft under canvas "scudding away to a safer haven."

Out of some 376 aboard the *Cumberland* that morning—taking into consideration badly kept muster rolls and constant shore leave—upwards of 121 perished. Among them was the first navy chaplain to die in combat, John T. Lenhart, last seen entering his cabin. There were not many more than a dozen chaplains in the entire naval service (and even that modest number represented "more . . . than can be used," according to Assistant Secretary Fox).

Thus while the loss on the frigate was some 30 percent below Phelps's estimate, it was bad enough.

The enemy's shelling continued, although it was not certain whether it was intended for the sunken ship, the survivors, or the very shore. One shell of doubtful origin "knocked to pieces" the end of a wharf, toward which some sailors were stroking. Another, according to Colonel Cannon, "demolished General Mansfield's headquarters, half burying the general under the debris."

The general's assistant adjutant, W. D. Whipple, quickly got off a telegram to General Wool: "General Mansfield has gone to visit the pickets. A shot from the *Congress* has just struck the upper wharf."

Residents of the area who had come down to the banks to watch the fight began to scurry for safer ground. For, according to Corporal Thomas Ranson, of the New York Mounted Rifles, at Camp Hamilton (who had during the winter watched the horses standing in water "almost knee deep"), "it was indeed a trying time."

With the *Cumberland* gone and the *Merrimack* now reloading, other ships were nearing the scene of battle. The *Roanoke*, under tow of the *Dragon*, had passed Sewell's Point under "a brisk fire," and been hit in the sails and rigging some five times. Her return fire, as the *Minnesota*'s, had proved ineffectual, to the pleasure of the many spectators, young and old, who had been watching, in holiday mood, since morning.

The *St. Lawrence*, under hawser of the *Cambridge*, was nearing. The *Mystic*, towed by the steamer *Kingston*, was attempting to get into action, while the *Mount Vernon* was still awaiting her engine parts.

Ashore, opposite the exposed, slanting masts of the sunken

Cumberland, her captain, William Radford, had just arrived following his dash by horseback. He dismounted, and his steed, frothing, rolled over dead.

As Tom Selfridge, still soaked and shivering, started to speak to his commanding officer, he was suddenly "impelled to tears" and "sobbed like a child."

Aboard the Confederate ironclad, grief was not the foremost of emotions. Now, even though additional support appeared unnecessary, the James River Squadron had arrived under "that gallant officer," as Buchanan thought him, Commander John R. Tucker, on the flagship *Patrick Henry.* They were, Buchanan would add, "standing down James River under full steam, accompanied by the *Jamestown* and *Teaser.* They were all nobly into action, and were soon exposed to heavy fire of the shore batteries."

The *Patrick Henry* passed the shore batteries at considerably less range than that for which her guns were elevated. Lieutenant Rochelle would write:

> And now the hush which precedes the shock of battle settled alike on Federal and Confederate. Glimpses could be caught of the men at their guns through the embrasures of the enemy's batteries, but not a sound came from them. As the *Patrick Henry* ranged up abreast of the first battery she delivered her fire, and the flash from her guns had hardly vanished when the Federal works were wrapped in smoke and their projectiles came hissing through the air. The first shots from the *Patrick Henry* went over the batteries, her guns having been elevated for a range of 800 yards; consequently she was passing the batteries at less than that distance, and to this circumstance is to be attributed her not having been sunk or disabled by them.
>
> The enemy supposed she would pass as far from them as the channel would allow and had elevated their guns for that range. The vessel passing closer than they thought she would, their shot for the most part passed over her. She was struck, however, several times during the passage. One shot passed through the crew of No. 3 gun, wounding two men and killing one. Poor fellow, he was an humble hero; his last words as he fell were "Never mind me, boys."

Buchanan continued:

> Their escape was miraculous as they were under a galling fire

of solid shot, shells, grape and canister a number of which passed through the vessels without doing any serious injury, except to the *Patrick Henry*. . . .

Having sunk the *Cumberland*, I turned my attention to the *Congress*. . . .

Saturday Afternoon, March 8

THE GREAT NAVAL VICTORY
FULL PARTICULARS

Departure of the Fleet—The Enemy Surprised—Terrible
Cannonade—The *Cumberland* and *Congress* Destroyed—Incidents
of the Fight, etc., etc.

Weekly Dispatch, Richmond
March 14, 1862, Friday

Other ships were still struggling to the aid of the *Congress* which, to any observer, was the next target. Having passed Sewell's Point sustaining but minor damage, the *Minnesota* steamed "without difficulty" to within one and a half miles of Newport News Point.

However, since the *Minnesota* drew twenty-three feet of water, about the same as the *Merrimack,* she went hard aground on the seventeen-foot shoal line. Sails were set and engines thrown into hard reverse. The big frigate would not move. Knowing the tide was on the ebb, and the *Merrimack* nearing, Captain Van Brunt fully appreciated the hopelessness of his situation.

The gunboat *Mystic,* under tow, was nearing Sewell's Point. Her gunners were impatient.

"With our smooth 32s," Master Rolando Coffin would write, "I suppose we were able to throw a shot about half way to the shore; but then we were able to make a great noise and considerable smoke, and we loaded and fired as rapidly as possible.

However, since the *Mystic* was firing over the deck of the consort army tug, the blasts "succeeded in breaking every pane of glass in the windows of his [the tug's] pilot and deck houses and in smashing all the crockery in the steward's pantry. . . . the only damage inflicted by our fire."

At this point Captain Arnold called a council of his masters and other officers on board.

The *Roanoke,* in the meanwhile, had been towed out of range, under the guns of Fort Monroe.

On the *Merrimack,* Buchanan continued to court trouble in maneuvering his ship, which remained, as Taylor Wood pronounced, "as unwieldly as Noah's Ark."

The flag officer found, "We were some time in getting our proper position in consequence of the shoalness of the water and the great difficulty of managing the ship when in or near the mud. To succeed in my object I was obliged to run the ship a short distance above the batteries of James River in order to wind her. During all the time her keel was in the mud; of course she moved but slowly.

"Thus we were subjected twice to the heavy guns of all the batteries in passing up and down the river, but it could not be avoided."

Smith on the *Congress,* already with too many dead and dying aboard his shattered vessel, still afire, had observed with cold horror

118

the death of the *Cumberland*. But he had succeeded with the aid of the staunch little *Zouave* in grounding his command. Dr. Shippen noted:

"Here the vessel heeled over as the tide continued to fall, leaving us only two guns which could be fought, those in the stern posts."

About 150 yards astern of the *Congress,* the *Merrimack* hove to and resumed the attack, aimed, as Buchanan aptly enough described, at causing "carnage, havoc and dismay." According to Dr. Shippen:

"She deliberately raked us with eighty-pounder shell, while the steamers we had so long kept up the river and those who had come out with the ironclad from Norfolk all concentrated the fire of their small rifled guns upon us."

Officers fell beside the men they had commanded. They died from grapeshot, from shell fragments, from wood splinters and bolts and other parts of the stricken frigate torn loose by the constant broadsides from the enemy. As gun after gun was knocked out of action, rifles and carbines were taken in hand by the desperate defenders "to try to pick off some of the *Merrimack*'s crew when her ports were opened to fire," by the report of Dr. Shippen. He continued:

"Men were being killed and maimed every minute, those faring best whose duty kept them on the spardeck. Just before our stern guns were disabled there were repeated calls for powder for them, and none appearing, I took a look upon the berth deck to learn the cause. After my eyes had become a little accustomed to the darkness and the sharp smoke from burning oak, I saw that the line of cooks and wardroom servants stationed to pass 'full boxes' had been raked by a shell, and the whole of them killed or wounded—a sufficient reason why there was a delay with the powder.

"The shells searched the vessel everywhere."

Wounded, many of them "dreadfully" died, even as the ship's surgeon was attempting under these most difficult conditions to treat them, or were killed while waiting for him. And all the while, those men not serving such guns as were yet in action were throwing water on the decks to keep the fire from the burning ship away from the magazines—"or the whole of us would go into the air together."

In the wardroom and other living areas, bulkheads had been knocked down with axes to make way for bucket and hose parties, producing, as Dr. Shippen would write, "a scene of perfect ruin and desolation." He amplified: "Clothing, books, glass, china, photographs, chairs, bedding and tables were all mixed in one confused heap."

Unknown to most of the surviving crew, the *Congress* had lost its captain, Joseph B. Smith. The young lieutenant was instantly killed by a shell splinter driven into his head as he walked down an after ladder of the gun deck. Dr. Shippen, seeing that he could do nothing for his commander, removed the dead officer's watch, chain, and one shoulder strap (the other having been torn off) with the intent of sending them to his father, old Commodore Smith, of the Navy Department.

"So," a sailor on the *Congress* would write, "we stood and worked in blood, smoke, noise and stench . . . we carried the wounded below to the berth deck . . . never was there such murder!"

Frederick Curtis, himself wounded, watched "one little powder boy, a lad of only thirteen years of age . . . bring us ammunition, with the tears streaming down his cheeks. . . ."

After nearly an hour of slaughter with "no prospect of assistance from any quarter," by the appraisal of Dr. Shippen, and with all guns now silenced, the executive officer, Lieutenant Austin Pendergrast, who had succeeded to command, conferred with Commander William Smith, the previous captain, and quickly resolved to strike the frigate's colors.

A white sheet was run up one of the masts. Then another.

The *Merrimack* acknowledged with the order "Cease fire!" Someone cried out within the ironclad's gun deck:

"The *Congress* has surrendered! Look out of the port. See, she has run up white flags. The officers are waving their handkerchiefs!"

However, as some of the crew started toward the hatches to see for themselves, Jones, the "exec.," in what Ramsay would describe as "his stentorian voice," shouted:

"Stand by your guns and, lieutenants, be ready to resume firing at the word. See that your guns are well supplied with ammunition. . . . Dr. [Algernon S.] Garnett, see how those poor fellows yonder are coming. . . . call away the cutter's crew and have them in readiness. . . ."

Joining Flag Officer Buchanan on the grating of the "promenade," Ramsay observed:

"The whole scene was changed. A pall of black smoke hung about the ships and obscured the clean-cut outlines of the shore. Down the river were the three frigates *St. Lawrence, Roanoke* and *Minnesota,* also enveloped in the clouds of battle that now and then reflected the crimson lightnings of the god of war.

"The masts of the *Cumberland* were protruding above the water. The *Congress* presented a terrible scene of carnage."

A small boat from the *Merrimack* was the first beside the *Congress.* According to Dr. Shippen, the Confederate officer from her did nothing but "gaze about a little and pick up a carbine and cutlass—I presume as trophies."

However, he departed when another officer, from the *Beaufort,* arrived at the surrendered warship. The former's captain, Parker, was under orders to take off "officers and wounded men prisoners and permit the others to escape, and to burn the ship."

Captain Smith and Lieutenant Pendergrast then formally surrendered the *Congress* to Parker's representative, "and delivered up their arms." Now the *Raleigh,* too, came alongside.

"Just then," as Parker would recall, "a tremendous fire was opened on us from the shore."

At Camp Butler, as close a participant as a shore installation could be to a sea engagement, General Mansfield had made the decision that *he* had not surrendered. He ordered two rifle companies of the 20th Indiana, various cannon and howitzers—some already manned by *Cumberland* crewmen—to open bombardment on the two Confederate steamers, *Raleigh* and *Beaufort,* beside the *Congress.*

"We had them at about 800 yards to advantage," Mansfield would report.

To a colonel of the 20th, he underscored, "I would rather his [Lieutenant Smith's] ship go down like the *Cumberland* with the flag flying. Colonel, send down marksmen and do not permit them to board the *Congress.*"

John Doubleday, of Caldwell, Kansas, with the 20th, thought there "could not have been more than 45 present" who advanced to the beach in the first skirmish line and opened fire on the two vessels that had reached the *Congress.* In moments the Confederate tug *Teáser* neared the beach "and opened fire with canister."

This was returned by the soldiers, taking aim at those crewmen visible on deck. However, at this juncture, according to Josh Lewis, "the officer of the day came, he being a young lieutenant and ordered us to cease firing, making some threats, so we separated, I going toward our quarters. But just as I got up the bank I came to face with General Mansfield, who was looking at the ill-fated frigate through his glass.

"He asked me to stop, and enquired what kind of gun I had. A rifle, I answered. He said, 'look, do you see that rebel officer with our flag getting down off the *Congress?*' and if I could hit him. I answered that I saw him and could hit him, but the officer of the day had ordered us away.

"He simply said, 'I say, shoot!'

"I did so the instant, and he and some other soldiers who had come up said, 'you got him!' "

Confusion, however, was not limited to the shore. On the *Congress,* Curtis found Paymaster McKean Buchanan wandering about, "his sword in his hand," and "much excited," while giving orders to the men to go below, even though the flames were mounting inside and the smoke was dense.

Nonetheless, the frigate's cutters were going ashore, filled with wounded, many of them critically burned.

Now Captain Parker, whose *Beaufort* remained alongside the *Congress,* advised Dr. Shippen, "You must make haste: those scoundrels on shore are firing at me now!" The surgeon had to agree since "rifle balls were pinging about very briskly, scarring the rusty black sides of the poor old frigate."

A suggestion that the *Beaufort* also fly a white flag temporarily to bring a halt to the fusillade was refused by Parker. With some prisoners on board, he found that bullets were going through his own cabin "like hail—I would not have put a dog there," while "the sides and masts of the *Beaufort* resembled the top of a pepper box, from the bullets which went in one side of her, and out at the other."

He blew the steam whistle and ran over to the tug *Harmony* still carrying Flag Officer Forrest and the *Day Book* correspondent. He disembarked his prisoners onto the little craft.

Lieutenant W. A. Webb, of the *Teaser,* which had been under such concentrated shore fire, now boarded the *Congress.* Curtis found him "smoking a cigar, and seemed to be very cool." He looked about him and observed, aghast, "My God, this is terrible. I wish the war was over."

He left after taking a few prisoners.

Now the *Patrick Henry,* under fire from the grounded *Minnesota,* which had never been wholly out of action, attempted herself to silence the shore batteries. The result was disastrous. Rochelle would write:

"Several shots struck the hull; a piece was shot out of the walking beam [the exposed upper part of the piston machinery] . . . a rifle shot from the field batteries penetrated the steam chest; the engine room and fire room were filled with steam; five or six of the firemen were scalded to death; the engineers were driven upon deck, and the engine stopped working.

"The vessel was enveloped in a cloud of escaped steam, and the enemy, seeing that some disaster to the boiler had occurred, increased his fire."

The side-wheeler would have drifted ashore to face certain capture had not the *Jamestown,* under heavy bombardment, towed her back into the Roads.

By now concerned over the damage being sustained by his consorts, Buchanan remained, fully open to the shore fire, on the top decking, shouting orders. According to Surgeon Phillips (but no other member, on record, of the *Merrimack*'s complement), Buchanan at the time was wielding a carbine in a manner foreign to a high commanding officer and firing wildly at the *Congress.* His luck ran out. One of the 20th Indiana's marksmen shot him in the groin, knocking him down onto the grating.

Carried below, he ordered his "exec.," Catesby Jones, "Plug hot shot into her and don't leave her until she's afire! That ship must be burned! They must look after their own wounded, since they won't let us!"

Ramsay noted, "We had kept two furnaces for the purpose of heating shot. They were rolled into the flames on a grating, rolled out into iron buckets, hoisted to the gun deck, and rolled into the guns, which had been prepared with wads of wet hemp. Then the gun would be touched off quickly and the shot sent on its errand of destruction."

After a few of the hot cannonballs were hurled into the sides of a ship flying white flags and already burning, the *Merrimack* backed off and started for the *Minnesota.* This afforded opportunity for more of the survivors of the *Congress* to come ashore. Those who did not wait for the boats swam. Some made it, others drowned, others were rescued, gasping, by the soldiers of the 20th. The wounded were piled onto cots in the little log hospital built by the Indiana regiment.

Dr. Shippen managed to bring the body of Lieutenant Smith ashore by explaining to the seamen that he was "wounded." He did not believe that the remaining crewmen, so "gallied" by the action of the past hours, would have consented to move a corpse off the burning ship.

Although, as Lieutenant Wood, on the *Merrimack,* noted, the *Minnesota* "was aground and at our mercy," the tide was fast ebbing and the pilots would not guide the ironclad in close enough for accurate gunnery. It was after 5 P.M., shadows were long, and it was time for the Confederate squadron to return for Sewell's Point.

Even the little *Harmony* during the closing action had come under the fire of the *Minnesota,* as the *Day Book* reporter would write, "sizz comes a shell ahead; presently another astern; finally a third, with a clear, sharp whizz just over head, to the great delight of the commodore who appreciated the compliment of those good shots which were the last of six directed at the *Harmony.*"

Under sporadic fire from Sewell's Point, the gunboat *Mystic,* "still full of fight," according to Rolando Coffin, remained the scene of a continuing council of war. All but one said, "Go ahead!" and join battle with the *Merrimack.* Then "an old acting-master" aboard spoke up:

"If I were you, I would get just as far away from here as the Lord would let me."

"I think you are right," replied the captain. "Hard-a-port the helm!"

The little *Mystic* set course for Fort Monroe—and out of history.

The day's shooting, however, had not quite echoed into silence —or history.

The *St. Lawrence,* which had passed Sewell's Point with negligible damage, grounded not far from the *Minnesota* and came under notice of the withdrawing *Merrimack.* Captain Purviance would report:

"Taking advantage of these portentous circumstances, the *Merrimack* directed her attention to firing several projectiles of formidable dimensions, one of which, an 80-pound shell, penetrated the starboard quarter about 4 inches above the water line, passed through the pantry of the wardroom and into the stateroom of the assistant surgeon on the port side, completely demolishing the bulkhead, and there struck against a strong iron bar, which secured the bull's-eye of the port; it returned into the wardroom expended. It fortunately did not explode, and no person was injured. The damages done by this one shot proved the power of the projectiles which she employed, and readily explained the quick destruction of our wooden and antiquated frigates.

"Our position at this time was one of some anxiety. Being aground, the tug *Young America* came alongside and got us off, after which a powerful broadside from the spar and gun decks of the *St. Lawrence*, then distant about half a mile, thrown into the *Merrimack* induced her to withdraw, whether from necessity or discretion, is not known; certainly no serious damage could have been done. . . ."

The gunboat *Cambridge* then towed the "antiquated" frigate to an anchorage under the protection of Fort Monroe.

The *Zouave*, which had been bathed with blood flowing from the *Congress*'s scuppers "like water on a washdeck morning," according to her master, lost her rudder post and a propeller blade to a wild shot from the ironclad. Henry Reaney, a literal man, could only repeat the understatement he had made several times that chaotic day; the gunboat was "in rather a bad plight."

Luckily, the *Whitehall* towed him to the now quiet but shaken *Minnesota*, damaged, aground, counting some five killed, twenty wounded.

The long-range Sawyer gun on the Rip Raps had itself been barking defiance at the invaders and the Confederate shore. One shell smashed onto a battery on Sewell's Point, mortally wounding Private William H. Warden, of the Jackson Greys, Norfolk's "own," and critically injuring others, thus bringing war home to a community that thus far had experienced only its veneer—its dazzle and excitement.

During this waning afternoon, a distraught General Mansfield had been scribbling off dispatches one after the other to General Wool:

"We want powder by the barrel, we want blankets sent up tonight for the crews of the *Cumberland* and the *Congress*. The *Merrimack* has it all her own way this side of Signal Point. . . ."

"We have no more ammunition . . . send us cartridges and shells for 8-inch columbiads and howitzers by land."

"The *Congress* is now burning. The enemy's steamers have hauled off toward Pig Point. . . . we should have another light battery to resist attack by land if they come."

Wool himself, bending over his desk in a casemate of Fort Monroe by kerosene lantern, hurried word, somewhat behind the events, to Secretary Stanton, in Washington, of the day's debacle:

". . . the *Congress* surrendered. The *Minnesota* is aground and attacked by the *Jamestown, Yorktown,* and *Merrimack.* The *St. Lawrence* just arrived and going to assist. The *Minnesota* is aground. Probably both will be taken. That is the opinion of Captain Marston and his officers. The *Roanoke* is under our guns.

"It is thought the *Merrimack, Jamestown,* and *Yorktown* will pass the fort to-night."

There was little time left to make the evening boat to Baltimore, the *Adelaide,* under Captain Cameron, which would leave Old Point at 8 P.M. In Baltimore all of the dispatches would be telegraphed to Washington. These fragile side-wheelers, under the bristling protection of Fort Monroe, hauled in from and put out into Chesapeake Bay as though there were no war.

Wool's fear, however, that the *Merrimack* could pass his stronghold headed for the bay and, presumably, the national Capital, was unfounded. She was well battered, Ramsay attested, and in no condition to pass any fort even if her draft permitted. Likewise, Mansfield's concern over an "attack by land" was of gossamer.

General Magruder, with light advance units, had ridden to within a mile of Newport News, until farthest opposing pickets could easily discern or theoretically call to one another. There, what he could not see of the afternoon's engagement he heard and concluded, "as I anticipated, that the naval attack produced no effect upon the fort."

He ordered all his forces to withdraw by dusk.

The usually canny "Prince John," had miscalculated this time. He did not realize—or estimate, from the volume of cannonading—that Camp Butler was out of ammunition. He could readily have seized Newport News Point and possibly even held it for a time.

Even as the *Merrimack* steamed in the ebbing tide for Craney Island—carrying two dead, some twenty wounded, minus her ram and several guns, many of her plates loose, a number of her beams split and her stack riddled—the spectators, adults and children, started for their homes in the early March evening's gloom. They quit

Ragged Island, Pig Point, Sewell's Point, and other vantage outjuts, weary, chilled, but still in holiday mood, heady from the day's martial sounds, the spectacle of motion, the bloodletting. . . .

The Forum grew cold, and empty, if not entirely silent.

Dick Phelps, exhausted both from his ailments and from excitement, was assisted off his horse and to his cot, "suffering as much as if I had been in the engagement and had both legs shot off."

Colston, however, lingered on Ragged Island to watch the moon "in her second quarter . . . rising over the waters," and the mounting conflagration of the doomed *Congress* burning so brightly that she seemed very close to the island. He wrote:

"As the flames crept up the rigging, every mast, spar, and rope glittered against the dark sky in dazzling lines of fire. The hull, aground upon the shoal, was plainly visible, and upon its black surface each port-hole seemed the mouth of a fiery furnace."

And it burned on, "with hardly a perceptible change in the wondrous picture. . . ."

To Rogers, in Fort Monroe, the same scene was like filmy "spiders' webs traced against the dark sky."

At the Hygeia, a visitor wrote, "Oh! what a night that was! The heavens were aflame with the burning *Congress*. The hotel was crowded with fugitives . . . there was nothing to dispute the empire of the seas with the *Merrimack*. . . ."

"Helpless, burning charnel house!" penned an Englishman of the pyre that was the *Congress*.

On the Federal shores, it had to be the gloomiest evening of the war, after in some respects a more stunning defeat than Bull Run. It was the navy's worst day in history, its greatest humiliation since the U.S.S. *Chesapeake*, in 1813, struck to H.M.S. *Shannon*.

Never had there been such human toll in one United States naval action—some 250 killed outright, by best estimates (the deaths on the *Congress* being almost exactly equal to those on the *Cumberland*), at least one hundred injured in varying degrees of severity.

The Confederate casualties were disproportionate, although statistics would not be officially forthcoming. Parker, of the *Beaufort*, estimated that "our total loss, however, did not exceed 60," presumably in killed and wounded.

At 8:30 P.M. Wool wrote another telegram to Stanton:

"No firing for last two hours. Newport News camp is uninjured. We are towing transports out to sea to keep clear if the *Merrimack* comes down to the fort. *Minnesota* and *St. Lawrence* still aground. The tide will not float them for three hours."

However, the side-wheeler *Adelaide* was already thumping up the darkened bay for Baltimore. And he was in error, anyhow, relative the *St. Lawrence.*

The commanding general had come to the conclusion that no Federal guns could claim the ability to repulse the enemy ironclad. As Colonel Cannon, his aide-de-camp, wrote:

"Our magazines were shot-proof only from the sea side; the parade in the fort was filled with quartermaster and commissary stores, with slight protection from the weather; the barracks were of wood; there were no means of extinguishing fire, and outside the fort an immense quantity of naval ammunition for the coast fleets, all utterly unprotected and with no means of removal to meet the emergency."

He believed that if the *Merrimack* could obtain sufficient elevation to her guns, "she had the ability to shell and destroy the vast stores in and about the fort without the least power on our part to resist her."

Assistant Secretary of the Navy Fox, who had just arrived from Washington, was in agreement with Captain Van Brunt, of the *Minnesota,* that some of the crew of that grounded frigate should be landed ("to save unnecessary slaughter") and that while she should "fight . . . to the last," she should nonetheless be blown up "in an emergency."

It was an equally "dismal crowd" at the mess table of the *Mystic,* where orders had been received, likewise, to destroy her if operations were resumed in the morning and capture appeared imminent. Under similar "ultimate" instructions were the captains of the *Roanoke, St. Lawrence, Mount Vernon,* other greater and lesser vessels of the navy, including supply ships, which neither General Wool nor Captain Fox desired to see become prizes of war.

To Gautier aboard the *Gassendi,* the mood of Hampton Roads that Saturday night transcended gloom or despair—"Panic appeared to take possession of everyone." He elaborated:

"Several vessels changed their anchorage, and all held themselves in readiness to stand out to sea at the first movement of the enemy. Everything was in confusion at Fort Monroe; ferryboats, gunboats and tugboats were coming and going in all directions; drums and bugles beat and sounded with unusual spirit.

"Fort Monroe and the batteries of the Rip Raps exchanged night signals without intermission."

The garrisons, augmented by survivors from the *Cumberland* and *Congress,* were throwing up strengthened earthworks and stronger barricades around the magazines and stores.

Then, about 9 P.M. the signal tower at Fort Monroe received the news that the *Monitor* had arrived and was anchoring at a shoal area known as the Horseshoe or Tail of the Horseshoe, in the middle of Chesapeake Bay about ten miles east of the fort. General Wool at once ordered Colonel Cannon "to take an armed tug and report to her commander the result of the day's conflict and the perilous condition of the *Minnesota.*"

Cannon, however, would not be the first to greet John Worden. Word that the little ironclad—like Federal cavalry coming to the relief of legendary Fort Defiance, besieged by Indians—was en route had somehow spread through Hampton Roads. Wool himself had to know this, but apparently her presence afforded him little comfort.

Lieutenant N. Goodwin, commanding the navy bark *Amanda,* newly arrived from blockade duty before Wilmington, North Carolina, had been waiting beside the inner lightship, at the Horseshoe. Now denuded of much of his own crew, he had sent officers and men aboard the tug *America* to aid, in turn, the *Roanoke* and *Minnesota.*

Worden would be grateful for Goodwin's presence. He found it was not easy to obtain a pilot. There were several factors involved: Many of this group of harbor specialists were Baltimoreans and suspect of southern sympathies; the dangers of further attack inherent that night and the distrust of so radical a craft as the *Monitor* augmented their unwillingness.

However, Acting Master Samuel Howard, of the *Amanda,* a Hartford, Connecticut, citizen, not only volunteered "earnestly," according to Worden, but reiterated his familiarity with the channels. The *Monitor* called first on the *Roanoke.*

There, he was welcomed by Marston, who "immediately" ordered the *Monitor* to the *Minnesota,* "hoping that she would be able to keep off an attack on the *Minnesota* till we had got her afloat again." Worden also left a dispatch for Secretary Welles:

"Sir: I have the honor to report that I arrived at this anchorage at 9 o'clock this evening, and am ordered to proceed immediately to the assistance of the *Minnesota,* aground near Newport News."

En route to the big, helpless steam frigate, Worden sat down by the flickering yellow light from his cabin's kerosene lamp to write another message, to his "darling wife," that he had "arrived here an hour since and am going immediately to the assistance of the *Minnesota* near Newport News. She is aground. The *Merrimack* has caused sad work amongst our vessels. She cannot hurt us. God bless you and our little ones. . . ."

He timed it 10 P.M.

Colonel Cannon now arrived on board the *Monitor,* to be immediately impressed with the "overworked crew from her perilous passage." While he discussed with her commanding officer in more detail the events of the day, Lieutenant Greene took the ironclad's cutter over the the *Minnesota.* He formally reported to Van Brunt and inquired of his prospects of moving the frigate off. Greene wrote:

"He said he should try to get afloat at 2 A.M. when it was high water. I asked him if we could render him any assistance, to which he replied no. I then told him we should do all in our power to protect him from the attacks of the *Merrimack.* He thanked me kindly and wished us success.

"Just as I arrived back to the *Monitor* the *Congress* blew up, and certainly a grander sight was never seen, but it went straight to the marrow of our bones. Not a word was said. . . ."

It was a spectacle that would never be forgotten by those who were witness. Lieutenant Franklin, aboard the *Roanoke,* would write:

". . . like a tremendous bombshell, and with a roar that could be heard for miles around, the *Congress* went up into the air with a fearful explosion."

James B. Jones, of Camp Arrington, Pig Point, wrote to his sister Bettie (Mrs. Hayes, of Richmond) of "such an explosion I never saw before, an enormous column of fire ascended apparently a mile high, with the most terrific report I ever heard."

The soldiers at Newport News Point had already been brought back from the beach, since the ship's loaded guns, as they heated, had been firing "up or down the river," according to Gilbreath, of the 20th Indiana. He added, "They seemed like signals of distress or that the noble vessel was firing her own death knell."

All along the shores, as he and others would note, "were cast bolts, nails or burning bits of timber. In our camp for a thousand men there was scarcely a tent but was riddled."

To Josh Lewis, "the whole country around" was "lit up."

Rogers, at Fort Monroe, watched "flaming timbers . . . thrown high in the air."

It was just as visible in Norfolk. "A column of fire ascended in the darkness," Rochelle described.

Colston, at Ragged Island, entranced by the spectacle all evening, saw in disbelief "a monstrous sheaf of flame" rising "to an immense height."

Captain Marston, of the *Roanoke,* obtained at least the "melancholy satisfaction" that the *Congress* had not "fallen into the hands of the enemy."

Mansfield would pronounce his own doleful amen, that the explosion was followed by "the stillness of death."

However, as the Confederates celebrated this night of victory and applauded the flaming end of the *Congress*—the "grandest sight ever witnessed," in Dick Phelps's opinion—there were some very few, those who had soberly questioned Virginia's secession, who could well wonder if this was a triumphant, final drum roll to a day's battle, or the fiery portent of a most uncertain tomorrow.

Sunday, March 9, Washington

EXCITEMENT AT WASHINGTON

Washington, March 9—The excitement at the hotels and elsewhere all day has been most intense consequent on the news from Fortress Monroe.

Special to the Baltimore *Sun*

Washington, March 9—This has been a day of alternate gloom and sunshine. . . .

—The New York *Herald*

Sunday dawned warm and clear in Washington even as it had been and, in fact, was balmily continuing to be in tidewater Virginia—and just a week before it had snowed. Not only was the forsythia yellow, but snowdrops and crocuses were blooming.

Within the cold white corridors and formally upholstered parlors of the White House there was cause equally for satisfaction and sorrow.

Federal troops and ships were scoring victories. Consolidating the capture of Roanoke Island, North Carolina, the Burnside Expedition hammered closer to New Bern, which would bring the forces to the Weldon Railroad and, ultimately, Norfolk. On February 6 Fort Henry, on the Tennessee River, had surrendered to a Federal gunboat flotilla. On the sixteenth Fort Donelson, twelve miles to the east, on the Cumberland River, fell to Brigadier General Ulysses S. Grant, both precipitating the loss of Nashville and setting "Unconditional Surrender" Grant on the road to destiny.

The only remaining southerner in the U.S. Senate, a former tailor from Tennessee, Andrew Johnson, was hastily assigned the rank of brigadier general of volunteers and ordered to Nashville as military governor of Tennessee.

Only the day before, Saturday, March 8, the campaign of Pea Ridge, Arkansas (also known by the Confederacy as the Battle of Elkhorn Tavern) had been concluded. What marked "the last effort of the South to carry the war into the State of Missouri," according to Major General Franz Sigel, who had commanded the first and second divisions, was halted by Federal forces who gained this "first clear and decisive victory . . . in a pitched battle west of the Mississippi River" at a cost of about two hundred killed, one fourth of the enemy losses.

The same Saturday Confederate batteries had been driven for the moment from Aquia Creek, forty-five miles below Washington, terminus of the Richmond and Fredericksburg Railroad, where they had been a continuing harassment to the Union's traffic along the Potomac River. A supporting steamer, the *George Page,* was scuttled. Leesburg, Virginia, thirty miles west of Washington, had been captured while other Federal troops were advancing from their base at Lovettsville on Manassas and Centreville, Virginia, both southwest of the Capital. Manassas, since the Bull Run battle, had often been a no-man's land for advance picket skirmishes or fast cavalry raids.

Washington itself reflected the vigor and buoyant expectations of the Army of the Potomac. The great, superbly organized force was ready any day to embark on its considerable mission—to take Richmond and end the war. Generals were clomping around everywhere, and those closest to the thirty-six-year-old elegant "Little Mac" McClellan (barely recovered from typhoid fever) naturally adopted his own spit and polish. Many were already known from the Mexican War or lesser expeditions or as leaders in the realm of business, especially railroading. If general officers' combined military records, their enthusiasm, plus their epaulets and immaculate uniforms could win a war, McClellan was in luck.

Nevertheless, they had paused, on February 24, in their staff work and their preening to attend somber ceremonies in the East Room of the White House—last rites for twelve-year-old Willie Lincoln, the President's second son. The little boy had died four days previously from an illness "of a typhoid character."

The executive mansion's black seamstress, Mrs. Elizabeth Keckley, who had washed and dressed the lifeless body, would recall Willie's father murmuring, as he looked at him, "My poor boy, he was too good for this earth . . . it is hard, hard to have him die. Why? Why?"

She could not forget that "great sobs choked his utterance." There wasn't much, either, that Lincoln's friend and pastor of the New York Avenue Presbyterian Church, the Reverend Phineas Densmore Gurley, could do to console the President.

Elizabeth Keckley was herself no stranger to grief. Her own son had been killed fighting for the Union in Missouri.

Sunday morning moved on. At 9:30 A.M. the steamer *Adelaide,* bearing passengers bursting to recount what they'd seen yesterday in Hampton Roads, docked in Baltimore. Mail was posted and telegrams tapped onto the lines. In surprisingly few minutes David Bates, in the War Department telegraph room, though well accustomed to momentous dispatches, blinked as he read, and then transcribed General Wool's report to Secretary Stanton. Even as a Baltimore *Sun* staffer would observe of Baltimoreans' reactions to the passengers' stories, this particular dispatch "created quite a sensation."

Stanton, who lived on Franklin Square near the White House, received the telegram in his office. Since the entire Cabinet had known of the *Merrimack*'s existence and conjectured intentions for months, Wool's news, while blatantly unpleasant, should not have come as a shock. But it did.

The emotional Stanton, holding the telegram, dashed from the signal room to the White House. It was not quite ten o'clock but, for a man of Abraham Lincoln's frontiersman's early-rising habits, the day was well on.

As invariably happened, Lincoln thought first of Illinois Senator Orville Browning, who at the moment was dressing at his lodgings at Mrs. Carter's on Capitol Hill for the Reverend Gurley's morning services. The senator would write:

> At 10 o'clock A.M. the President sent his carriage down for Mrs. Browning, Emma [his daughter by tacit adoption] and myself. We went up.
> I went directly to the President's and found the Secretary of War, with a telegram in his hand from Fortress Monroe giving information the Rebel Iron Clad steamer had come down from Norfolk and sunk the *Cumberland* and captured the *Congress*.
> Mr. [William H.] Seward [secretary of state] and General McClelland [*sic*] soon came in. They all seemed a good deal excited but Mr. Seward said nothing.
> There were apprehensions that the *Merrimack* might come here & destroy the Town, but none of the persons present knew her draft of water. It was also apprehended that she might get out to sea and destroy all our transports now on their way to Annapolis with supplies, and also Annapolis with all our accumulations of stores etc.
> The President and myself got in his carriage and drove to the Navy yard to see Capt. Dahlgren.

John Dahlgren would confide to his diary that he was "sitting in my office at 10½ in the morning when I should have been in church" when "bang comes the blow from a clear sky and on a beautiful warm Sunday." The circumstance of the President of the United States being "announced at the door" was not in itself cause for surprise. Lincoln, who attached much weight to Dahlgren's judgment, was apt to be a weekly caller at his Navy Yard office. Regarding lesser affinities, Dahlgren, a big man, was one of his few close associates with whom Lincoln could converse on approximately the same eye level. It was relaxing to the lofty Commander in Chief's neck muscles.

The latter and Senator Browning were bearers of what Dahlgren considered "frightful news," which seemed to be accentuated by Lincoln's very appearance. "Poor gentleman, how thin and wasted he is!" the captain wrote as an aside, continuing:

"The President didn't know whether we might not have a visit here which would indeed cap the climax! I could give but little comfort. Such a thing might be *prevented* but not met."

As the three drove in the carriage back to the White House Lincoln talked of blocking the Potomac, which Dahlgren agreed "was about all which could be done at present."

According to Browning, Dahlgren did not stop there: "He said there was nothing to prevent the *Merrimac* from coming here as she drew only 21 feet of water, and any vessel drawing not more than 22 feet could come here. He also said she could go to New York, lie off the City, and levy contributions at will."

Nonetheless, to the navy captain, the President "was not at all stunned at the news but was in his usual suggestive mood."

Once in the executive mansion, Browning excused himself, determined to make Dr. Gurley's service. However, if his reactions were similar to Lucius Chittenden's—many of Government being parishoners at the New York Avenue Presbyterian Church—he would wish he had stayed at the White House. The sermon, according to the underofficial of the treasury, would prove "very gloomy."

In Lincoln's absence, his Cabinet had assembled, and it was a group as acrimonious and mutually contemptuous as had yet counselled a Chief Executive.

Present now, in addition to McClellan and Seward, were Gideon Welles (who, along with Seward, lived on Lafayette Square across from the White House), the politically ambitious secretary of the treasury, Salmon P. Chase; Brigadier General Montgomery Meigs, quartermaster general of the army; Assistant Secretary of War Peter Watson, until recently a little-known Washington attorney of Scottish descent; and John G. Nicolay, Lincoln's secretary. The latter was as assiduous in maintaining his own day-by-day diary as he was in keeping up with his master's voluminous correspondence and other paper work.

At once in this "private room" (possibly the War Office) where they had gathered, there ensued "a hasty and promiscuous emission of opinions from every one," according to Dahlgren, "without much regard to rank and some inter-talking which rather confused. Meigs looked desponding and was silent. McClellan was concerned about the troops at Newport News. Seward was composed."

There were, however, strong, conflicting, and persistent currents responsible for this "emission." The distrusting Welles approved of no one in the administration with the conceivable exception of Lincoln. He thought of Chase, the abolitionist, dour son of New Hampshire, who had moved to Ohio and become governor, as "selfish, vain, ambitious . . . irresolute, wavering," a "sycophant." And as a matter of fact Lincoln himself had allowed that Chase was "a little insane" on the subject of the presidency.

Seward, the polished, genial, former governor of New York, was, by the navy secretary's measure, "sometimes victim of his own vanity and conceit . . . a very emphatic opponent of any proposition that was made." But Welles saved his prime invective for Stanton, whom he disliked obsessively: "frightened . . . fond of power . . . ungracious and rough . . . bearish . . . little moral courage nor much self-reliance . . . glorified in his extravagance!"

Welles had already crossed verbal swords with Meigs, the engineer of the half-completed Capitol dome and the Washington aqueduct, believing that he was overly ambitious and that he trespassed unforgivably on naval prerogatives. Nor was he ready to give much credit even to his own deputy, John Dahlgren, "much of a courtier," whom he lumped in one unenviable package with Meigs, "by nature and training cautious, not to say timid." Besides, Dahlgren's rapport with the President, thus bypassing the secretary of the navy, was a continuing irritant to the latter.

Chase regarded Welles as "slow and incompetent." This was the acid treasury secretary at perhaps his most generous. His dislike and obvious jealousy was focused equally on Seward and Lincoln and upon Stanton if only because the secretary of state had championed the new war secretary as Simon Cameron's successor. Faithless, Chase, who had helped promote McClellan as leader of the Army of the Potomac, would soon be reviling him as "a little Napoleon . . . an imbecile, a coward," and even "a traitor."

Seward spoke of Stanton as the "Carnot of the War," recalling Lazare Nicolas Carnot, Napoleon's minister of war and French Revolution figure, sometimes as "Stanton the Divine." But Welles

Monitor vs. *Merrimack*. This much-reproduced artist's conception of the famous fight of March 9, 1862, appeared in *Century* magazine and then its outgrowth, *Battles and Leaders of the Civil War*. From the many accounts by participants, the details appear generally authentic, although the decks of the *Merrimack* were never quite this much awash—this was a *desideratum* never fully attained by her frustrated designers and officers: the lower she could float in the water, the less of her "tender" hull would be exposed to enemy fire. *U.S. Signal Corps Photo*

Apparently Franklin D. Roosevelt, a great sea and naval buff, liked this version of the *Monitor* encounter. The artist is identified as W. F. Halsall. *Official U.S. Navy Photograph*

The Battle as depicted by an unidentified artist. The *Monitor* is not especially true to life, and the stack on the *Merrimack* is too far forward. The *Minnesota*, in the foreground, appears to be the best rendition of the three. All are probably too close together. *Courtesy of Naval History Division, Navy Department*

Lieutenant Thomas Catesby ap R. Jones. *Naval History Photograph*

Lieutenant Samuel Dana Greene. *Naval History Photograph*

Franklin Buchanan in uniform of a U. S. Navy Captain, 1861. Shortly after this photo was taken, he resigned the Union Navy and entered the Confederate Navy. *Naval History Photograph*

This photograph of the *Monitor* is remarkable in a number of respects. It shows the dents in her turret remaining from the memorable battle, the big rivets used in plating, and the pilot house above the turret; the latter originally was a separate structure closer to the bow. The officer standing in the foreground with binoculars (instead of the more common telescope or "long glass") is identified as Lieutenant William Flye. The only other subject named is the seated officer, Second Assistant Engineer Albert B. Campbell, of the ironclad's original complement. Flye, who came aboard later, is definitely wearing a "non-reg" broad-brimmed hat. If it were protection against summer sun (as also the awning over the pilot house seems), then why are they in winter blues and obviously heavy coats? The stretching shadows testify that the photograph was made in early morning or late afternoon, a difficult time of day for always-prolonged exposures on slow-emulsion glass negatives. *Courtesy of Naval History Division, Navy Department*

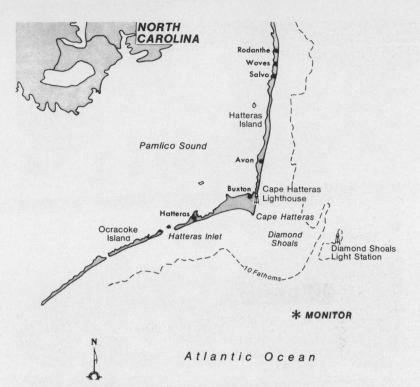

Here lies the U.S.S. *Monitor*. The old ironclad's location was long concealed by the many wrecks off Hatteras and lack of scientific knowhow. According to the National Oceanic and Atmospheric Administration of the U. S. Department of Commerce, the wreck lies "about 16.10 miles south-southeast of the Cape Hatteras Light," upside-down in 220 feet of water. While within skin divers' depth potential, the location is extremely hazardous because of currents.

Eastward, the 117-foot Duke University exploration vessel, but two thirds the length of the little *Monitor* whose location she sought off Hatteras. *Eastward* was mother hen to a small search fleet, the largest of which was the 243-foot *Alcoa Seaprobe,* one of the world's most scientifically advanced exploration and recovery ships.

Monitor Turret. This is a mosaic of photographs of the upside-down *Monitor* made from the exploration vessel *Alcoa Seaprobe* zeroing in on her distinctive turret, which obviously tore off as the ironclad plunged down. The wreck came to rest on top of it. The bottom plates of what was known as the "lower hull" are completely missing, although ribs show. There is no clue in this or in other photographs as to where the two 11-inch cannon lie. Note the marine growth and the fish. *Duke University Print*

The four scientists principally involved in locating the wreck of the *Monitor*, from left: John G. Newton, marine superintendent of the oceanographic program at Duke Marine Laboratory; Dr. Harold Edgerton of M.I.T., inventor of the strobe light for photography, airport approach systems, and other uses and, as well, developer of side-scan sonar; Dr. Robert Sheridan of the University of Delaware; and Gordon P. Watts, Jr., underwater archaeologist for the State of North Carolina. *Duke University Print*

This mosaic of undersea photos shows the *Monitor* lying upside down off Cape Hatteras. The turret, having fallen off as the vessel sank, rests partly under the stern at the upper right. Other features include the armor belt around the hull and the anchor well at the bow. *Photographs by Glen Tillman, Alcoa Marine Corporation; Photomosaic by U. S. Navy*

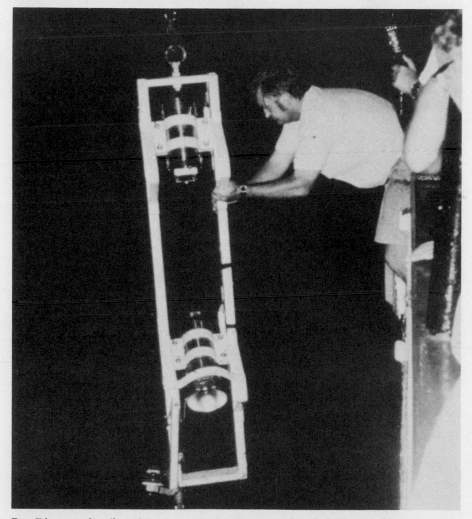

Dr. Edgerton describes this apparatus, worth thousands of dollars, as his "camera-strobe system." On its second descent it became snarled in the *Monitor* wreck, and there it still lies with its undeveloped film. *Photograph by Ed Jaeckel*

Cathie Newton, daughter of John Newton, at the depth finder aboard the *Eastward*. Cathie, a senior at Duke University, and Dorothy Nicholson, of the National Geographic Society, were the only two women on the exploration ship. *Photograph by Ed Jaeckel*

The boom over the side of the *Eastward*, by which cameras, grapples, buoys, and other gear were lowered. *Photograph by Ed Jaeckel*

dismissed these characterizations as "mere fulsome adulation from an old politician."

McClellan would soon feel betrayed by them all. Having early in the war driven Confederate forces out of northwestern Virginia, he was brought to Washington to command forces there and bring order after Bull Run. His star continued to rise when he succeeded Scott, in November 1861, as general in chief of all the armies. Although Stanton, as incoming secretary of war, had assured the young general, "now we two will save the country," soon McClellan was unable to see his superior "even for the transaction of ordinary business." His relations with Lincoln also deteriorated.

And so it went, seeming to confirm an outburst by Francis Preston Blair, Jr., soldier-statesman from Missouri: "I never since I was born imagined that such a lot of poltroons and apes could be gathered together from the four quarters of the Globe as Old Abe has succeeded in bringing together in his Cabinet."

As Nicolay would record that morning:

> . . . the hasty meeting of the Cabinet and other officials . . . was perhaps the most excited and impressive of the whole war. Stanton, unable to control his strong emotion, walked up and down the room like a caged lion. McClellan was dumbfounded and silent. Lincoln was, as usual in trying moments, composed but eagerly inquisitive, critically scanning the dispatches, interrogating the officers, joining scrap to scrap of information, applying his searching analysis and clear logic to read the danger and find the remedy; Chase impatient and ready to utter blame; Seward and Welles hopeful, yet without encouraging reasons to justify their hope. The possibilities of the hour were indeed sufficiently portentous to create consternation. What might not this new and irresistible leviathan of the deep accomplish?

Nicolay would later write, "Mr. Welles . . . was in the habit of coldly noting in his deadly diary all the indiscretions of his colleagues. . . ."

While testifying to his own equanimity in an atmosphere of emotion and turmoil, Welles would concede that the day "and its incidents were among the most unpleasant and uncomfortable" in his life. When Captain Dahlgren suggested that Port Royal be alerted and vessels be readied for blocking the Potomac, the navy secretary's professedly calm facade was severely tested.

Had *he* and McClellan not been laboring for weeks to prepare a clear waterway of that river for the great Army of the Peninsula? Thus, "the inability of Dahlgren to advise" or to advise properly "seemed to increase the panic."

Welles exceeded Nicolay's assessment of Stanton: "The most frightened man on that gloomy day . . . was the Secretary of War . . . at times almost frantic, and as he walked the room with his eyes fixed on me, I saw well the estimation in which he held me with my unmoved and unexcited manner and conversation."

The *Merrimack,* the secretary of war asserted, according to Welles,

> could lay every city on the coast under contribution, could take Fortress Monroe; McClellan's mistaken purpose to advance by the Peninsula must be abandoned, and Burnside would inevitably be captured. Likely the first movement of the *Merrimac* would be to come up the Potomac and disperse Congress, destroy the Capitol and public buildings; or she might go to New York and Boston and destroy those cities, or levy from them contributions sufficient to carry on the War. He asked what vessel or means we had to resist or prevent her from doing whatever she pleased.
>
> I stated our vessels were not as powerful or in numbers as extensive as I wished. It was certain, however, the *Merrimac* could not come to Washington and go to New York at the same time. I had no apprehension of her visiting either, and wished she were then in the Potomac, for if so we could take efficient measures to dispose of her. That Burnside and the force in the Sounds were safe from her, because her draft of water was such she could not approach them. That the *Monitor* was in Hampton Roads, and I had confidence in her power to resist, and, I hoped, to overcome the *Merrimac.* She should have been there sooner to have destroyed the *Merrimac,* but the contractors had disappointed us.
>
> Mr. Seward, who had been desponding, contrary to his usual temperament and custom, rendered more timid by the opinion and alarm of Stanton, said my remark in relation to the draft of water of the *Merrimac* gave him the first moment's relief he had experienced.
>
> Stanton made some sneering inquiry about this new vessel the *Monitor,* of which he admitted he knew little or nothing. I described her, and [said] that it had been our intention, had she been completed within contract time, to have sent her up to

Norfolk to destroy the *Merrimac* before she came out of dry dock. Stanton asked about her armament, and when I mentioned she had two guns, his mingled look of incredulity and contempt cannot be described; and the tone of his voice, as he asked if my reliance was on that craft with her two guns, is equally indescribable.

Stanton (who did not write his own version of that emotional Cabinet session) was further described by Welles as running from room to room, sitting down, jumping up after writing a few words . . . "swung his arms, scolded and raved."

It was true and generally conceded by his few friends that Edwin McMasters Stanton had never been the same man since the death, in childbirth, of his first wife two long decades earlier. While he would prove an adequate administrator and supporter of the President, his emotional stability remained precarious. This day, sharing Lincoln's own morbidly exaggerated fears for the safety of the national Capital, Stanton was exceptionally unnerved. In fact, Nicolay would note, "Mr. Stanton closed his list of sinister prophecies by predicting that a shell or a cannon shot from the *Merrimac* would probably land in the Cabinet room before they separated."

All present confirmed that it was some time before Stanton could in any measure be placated.

The President, whom Welles found to be "as uncomfortable as any of us," joined Stanton "repeatedly" at the window "and looked down the Potomac—the view being uninterrupted for miles—to see if the *Merrimack* was not coming to Washington." The navy secretary continued:

> It was asked what we could do if she were now in sight. I told the President she could not, if in the river, with her heavy armor, cross the Kettle Bottom Shoals. This was a relief. Dahlgren was consulted. He thought it doubtful if she could reach Washington, if she entered the river.
>
> Stanton asked what we could do for the defense and protection of New York and other cities. I knew of nothing. Our information of the *Merrimac*—for we had had every few days report of her condition—was that she could not, with her heavy and ill-adjusted armor, penetrate the river nor venture outside, and was to be used in Hampton Roads and the Chesapeake. I stated these facts, and they with other matters had a good effect upon the President.

By now the morning was wearing on. The churchgoers were returning. Chittenden, seeking out his "boss," Secretary Chase, stumbled into the War Office just as he heard someone saying, "Would it not be fortunate if the *Monitor* should sink her?" He then thought Lincoln himself "calmly" replied:

"It would be nothing more than I have expected. If she does not something else will. Many providential things are happening in this war, and this may be one of them."

The meeting commenced to disband. Welles was the first to leave. As though this were a signal to act in his absence and put into effect the very measures all present knew he opposed, Lincoln directed McClellan, Meigs, and Dahlgren to arrange as fast as they possibly could the blocking of the Potomac. Stanton went further. He dictated telegrams to governors of the coastal states north of Washington and mayors of the principal ports warning of the approach of the *Merrimack* and "to prepare," as Nicolay would report, "all possible resources of their own for defense." These included "rafts of timber and other obstructions" to be placed at harbor mouths.

McClellan sent dispatches to commanding officers of forts in Delaware, New York, Connecticut, Rhode Island, and Portland, Maine, advising:

> The rebel iron-clad steamer *Merrimac* has destroyed two of our frigates near Fort Monroe and finally retired last night to Craney Island. She may succeed passing the batteries and go to sea. It is necessary that you at once place your post in the best possible condition for defense, and do your best to stop her should she endeavor to run by. Anything that can be effected in the way of temporary batteries should be done at once.

Paulding, at the New York Navy Yard, was asked to charter the 355-foot *Vanderbilt* at once, fill her bow with timbers for use as a ram and plate her sides with iron—then send her to Hampton Roads with orders to seek out "at whatever risk" and smash the *Merrimack,* hopefully, like an eggshell. At 5,000 tons she had been the largest steamship in transatlantic service until the giant *Great Eastern* had been launched. Owned by Commodore Cornelius Vanderbilt, she had been offering service out of New York every forty days.

Assistant Secretary of War Peter Watson was himself not idle. He wrote to Henry B. Renwick, in New York, an engineer and patent expert on steam engines and related marine components, promising that "the whole wealth and power of the United States" would be "at command" for destroying the *Merrimack,* which was threatening "to sweep one whole flotilla from Chesapeake Bay." He continued:

> The Secretary of War desires you quietly to call a meeting of from three to nine persons, at your discretion, of the best judgment in naval engineering and warfare, to meet immediately at your father's house or some other convenient and suitable place, and to sit as a committee to devise the best plan of speedily accomplishing the capture or destruction of the *Merrimac.* I would suggest the name of Abram S. Hewitt [foundry owner who had supplied some of the steel for the *Monitor*] as a member of the committee. You will bear in mind that every hour's delay to destroy the *Merrimac* may result in incalculable damage to the United States, and that the plan or plans for her destruction should be submitted at the earliest hour practicable for the approval of this Department, to the end that their execution may not be unnecessarily delayed a moment. To enable you to communicate hourly with this Department, the telegraphic company is directed to transmit all messages from you at the expense of the Government.
>
> Acknowledge this dispatch the moment you receive it. Spare no pains or expense to get the committee together immediately. Act with the utmost energy. You and each member of the committee will consider this whole matter confidential.

Encountering Orville Browning, just back from church, in the hall outside the President's office, Stanton confided that he would seek the construction of another "iron clad boat with a powerful engine . . . at whatever cost, to run down and sink the *Merrimack.*" The secretary of war obviously did not know or, if he did, had forgotten that the *Galena* and *New Ironsides* would soon be commissioned. Browning, who conversed privately "for some time" with Stanton, added:

> He also had sent a steamer down the Potomac to give notice of the approach of the *Merrimac* if she should attempt to come up, and had 30 canal boats loading with stone to be sunk in the Channel of the River about 40 miles below the City, in the event of the *Merrimac* attempting to ascend the River.
>
> He spoke in terms which clearly indicated his want of confidence in McClellan.

In fact, he planned to "try" one general after another until he found one "equal to the emergency."

Stanton, when he had finished talking with Browning, took it upon himself to give Dahlgren "the most ample authority for men and cannon" and "to lay hands on the river boats." The commandant of the Navy Yard then accompanied Stanton and Seward on a river steamer to survey the approaches to Washington. In midafternoon, upon his return, Dahlgren sent a telegram to "His Excellency the President of the United States":

> I beg leave to inform you that upon consultation with such pilots as I have in the yard, I find them to be of opinion that a vessel drawing 22 feet water can pass up the Potomac within a hundred yards of the arsenal.
>
> As far as the light house on Blakiston Island, some 30 miles, there is abundant water for any ship.
>
> About 5 miles higher up is the first obstacle—the Kettle Bottoms. The channel passes among these shoals for 5 miles and the pilot says 24 feet can be had, which I doubt; the narrowest part about 300 yards wide.
>
> From this the channel continues good until just below Aquia, where it shoals so that 23 feet is considered the best water at common high tide.
>
> Having passed this the water deepens, passing the batteries and shoals about Mattawoman Creek, where the depth at common high tide is 22 feet. This obstruction is less than a mile in extent, after which the channel deepens several feet; though it narrows, it runs deep very nearly to the arsenal and perhaps some 3 miles from the capital.
>
> The actual blocking of the river is only to be resorted to when the exigency arises, the means being at hand.
>
> There are three points where it can be done—the Kettle Bottoms, below Smith's Point, and at Mattawoman.
>
> I would advise that some heavy ordnance he got ready for placing at the arsenal, at Giesboro Point, and at Buzzard Point. Fort Washington should also have suitable cannon. I have telegraphed to the flotilla for some steamers to tow down the blocking vessels as soon as General Meigs has them ready. It happens, unfortunately, that the only two good steamers belonging to the yard are at Fortress Monroe.

(The "arsenal" referred to was within the city limits of the nation's Capital. Today named Fort McNair, it was the site of the execution of

Mary Surratt and the "Lincoln Conspirators." Buzzard Point was immediately adjacent and Giesboro Point directly across the mouth of the then Eastern Branch, now Anacostia River, as it empties into the Potomac in southwest Washington. Fort Washington is about twelve miles below the city proper, and its surrender during the War of 1812 presented Washington to the British for burning. Blakistone Island is about seventy miles downriver from the city. The Kettle Bottoms Shoals begin a few miles above Blakistone and extend for twice the distance given by Dahlgren. They were as shallow as fifteen feet, and Mattawoman Shoals, twenty-five miles downriver from Washington, was certain only for nineteen and a half feet depth, with a one-mile river width, opposite the present-day marine base at Quantico. Smith Point is at the mouth of the Potomac, opposite Point Lookout, which is on the Maryland shore.)

Dahlgren, all energy, advised McClellan at about the same time that he had already placed an eleven-inch gun and some ten-inch mortars at Giesboro Point, "which will command at short range the nearest point that a vessel drawing 22 feet can approach the capital; the channel passes within 50 yards of this position."

While Captain Dahlgren had not yet been informed that the *Merrimack* consumed a half hour in executing a complete turn, he should have recalled that the steam frigate even in her original incarnation would have experienced slow and painful maneuvering in the torturous narrow channel before Washington. Riflemen on the banks could leisurely have taken aim through her gunports. Even strong little boys with big rocks might have contributed a modicum of annoyance.

Having departed this far from his nautical role and duties, he then requested "some assistance from the neighboring regiments."

He paused, belatedly, in his flurry of activity to bang off telegrams to his superior, Secretary Welles, advising that he had secured a number of boats which were now being loaded with stone and gravel, while suggesting "authority to charter or hire one or two of the best steamers in the river, if necessary, without consent of the owner."

He asked Welles, as an aside, if he was acting "in conformity" with the secretary's orders. Without waiting for a reply, Dahlgren continued his assembling of what Lincoln would ultimately refer to as "Stanton's Navy."

Montgomery Meigs was himself not idle. He prepared a letter to his representative in Annapolis, outlining what he thought should be done in the event the *Merrimack* arrived at that historic capital of Maryland:

> . . . it is believed that the best defense would be an attack by a number of swift steamers, full of men who should board her by a sudden rush, fire down through her hatches or grated deck, and throw cartridges, grenades, or shells down her smoke pipes; sacrifice the steamers in order to take the *Merrimack*.
>
> If an overwhelming force can be thus thrown on board, there will be little loss of life, though the steam transports may be destroyed. Of course the steamers should be provided with ladders, planks, grapplers, and other means to board with. The *Merrimack* has iron sides sloping above water to a deck about 9 feet wide; said to be an iron grated deck.
>
> Promotion, ample reward, awaits whoever takes or destroys her.

"Stanton's Navy" was weighing anchor by late afternoon. Colonel D. H. Rucker, one of Meigs's deputies, advised Dahlgren that the steamer *Sophia* was leaving the G Street wharf towing eight canal boats, "loaded with sufficient stone to sink them." Another steamer, shepherding eight more, would depart "in the course of the night." The captain of the *Sophia* carried a letter to the "officer in command of the flotilla" stating that "the boats are to be sunk if necessary."

None except Welles apparently paused long enough to realize what should have been obvious: if the river were blocked so that the *Merrimack* couldn't steam up, then the Federal Navy, like caged seabirds, couldn't steam *down*.

The crisis was rather upsetting to some civilians. Senator William Pitt Fessenden, of Maine, chairman of the Senate Finance Committee (who had risen to legislative prominence in spite of the illegitimacy of his birth), sat down to supper at Mrs. Shipman's boardinghouse on Seventh Street, halfway between the Capitol and the White House, then quickly slippered off to his room. He would write:

"I confess I was so frightened . . . that I could not eat my dinner."

Fessenden was not a happy or a well man. Like Stanton, he mourned his first love, who had died before their wedding. Now recently widowed, he was the father of four sons, a daughter having died in infancy. The war and his onerous responsibilities toward its funding had drained him. Even as the popular Reverend Gurley, he suffered from some not adequately diagnosed stomach ailment, or ailments.

Hardest hit, perhaps, was old Commodore Smith. When he learned of the *Congress*'s surrender, he was heard to observe, "Joe's dead."

In other words, he could not believe that *his* son would have surrendered his frigate.

About nine o'clock, Dahlgren sent word to Lincoln that measures were "in progress and ready for use." Shortly thereafter, Welles opened Dahlgren's telegram to be dumbfounded.

Within the hour, preparing for bed, the navy secretary received another telegram—all the way from Fort Monroe. At 4 P.M. the final telegraph link had been connected across the bay to the fort. This one, to take advantage of the direct communications link, was signed, "Fox."

In some excitement, Welles dressed again. Clutching the telegram, he started across the street, under the flickering gaslights, for the White House.

Sunday, March 9, Hampton Roads

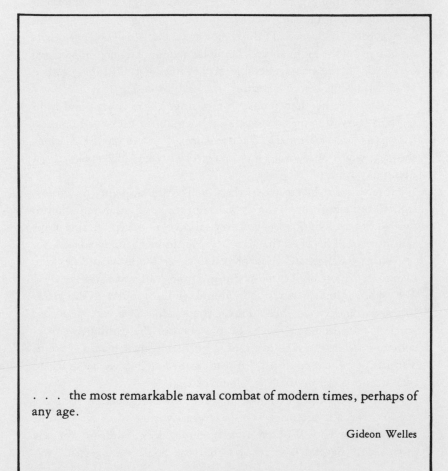

. . . the most remarkable naval combat of modern times, perhaps of any age.

Gideon Welles

The burning, exploding *Congress,* as Josh Lewis observed, had amply "lit up" the whole area, including the many ships at anchor. On board the *Merrimack,* licking her wounds, Catesby Jones, the acting commander, would report:

"One of the pilots chanced . . . to be looking in the direction of the *Congress* when there passed a strange-looking craft, brought out in bold relief by the brilliant light of the burning ship, which he at once proclaimed to be the *Ericsson.*"

However, Lieutenant Jones did not take all of the officers into his confidence. John Taylor Wood, for example, wrote, "Commodore Buchanan and the other wounded were sent to the Naval Hospital; and after making preparations for the next day's fight, we slept at our guns, dreaming of other victories in the morning."

According to Surgeon Phillips, however, Buchanan and the others spent most of the night aboard, being landed, apparently, in predawn darkness. In the one serviceable boat remaining, Phillips "pulled around the ship before boarding" to survey the damage:

"I found all her stanchions, iron railings, boat davits, and light work of every description swept away, her smokestack cut to pieces, two guns without muzzles, and 98 indentations on her plating, showing where heavy solid shot had struck, but glanced off without doing any injury."

He returned to be greeted by the aroma of breakfast and the sounds, sights, and smells of a man-of-war coming alive in anticipation of renewed battle. Curiously, however, almost all except Acting Captain Jones still believed the *Minnesota* would be the only adversary.

Aboard the *Monitor,* whose arrival Gideon Welles would describe blandly as "most opportune and important," all was activity. By 1 A.M. she was anchored virtually alongside the grounded *Minnesota,* like some undersized sheep dog in the shadow of a very large but partially incapacitated ram. The presence of the diminutive newcomer, nonetheless, was heartening to the steam frigate's captain, Van Brunt, who would pen, "All on board felt that we had a friend that would stand by us in our hour of trial."

While the men cleaned and loaded the guns and generally straightened up the ship after her wet, hazardous voyage from New York, Dana Greene and Worden remained on deck "waiting for the *Merrimack.*" Several false reports that the South's juggernaut was

150

indeed returning for the kill kept all hands at quarters most of the tense, remaining early morning hours. None slept.

The "exec." wrote:

"At three A.M. we thought the *Minnesota* was afloat and coming down on us, so we got under weigh as soon as possible and stood out of the channel. After backing and filling about for an hour, we found we were mistaken and anchored again."

About dawn, when Worden could confirm the silhouettes of the *Merrimack* "with several consorts" at anchor off Sewell's Point, he returned by small boat to the *Minnesota,* which was still "in a helpless condition." He wanted to assure Van Brunt "that I would develop all the qualities, offensive and defensive possessed by the 'Battery' under my command to protect his vessel from the attack of the *Merrimack,* should he come out again, and that I had great faith in her capabilities."

By now, the *Minnesota* was surrounded by tugs and barges into which, according to Paymaster Keeler on the *Monitor,* "were being tumbled the bags and hammocks of the men and barrels and bags of provisions some of which went into the boats and some into the water, which was covered with barrels of rice, whiskey, flour, beans, sugar, which were thrown overboard to lighten the ship."

Taken ashore, too, was about $100,000 from the paymaster's safe.

William Rogers, at Fort Monroe, expressed the view of many around him in noting that the *Minnesota,* in spite of these heroic efforts to float and haul her off the mud and sand banks, "seemed to be doomed to destruction like her companions of the previous day."

He also watched a sobering spectacle: "Members of the crews of these two vessels [the *Cumberland* and *Congress*] with bloody bandages and many wounds, arrived at the Fort after a weary tramp from Newport News of eight or ten miles overland."

Those unable to shoulder a rifle or who were unfamiliar with land warfare were moved away from Camp Butler, since it was still believed that Magruder was advancing on Newport News. In fact, General Wool was working on a request to McClellan for "two additional light batteries," following a telegram to him from Mansfield advising:

I have just completed my arrangements for battle in the morning. The enemy is 1½ miles on the river road beyond my brick house pickets. A large body of cavalry, some infantry, and artillery are as above posted, yet they may simply be there to reconnoiter and wait the result of the *Merrimack*'s operations.

The telegram had barely cleared his desk before the seventy-eight-year-old general was preparing a far more desperate one:

> I want for immediate defense, to be sent as soon as possible, 2,000 regular infantry and 8,000 volunteer infantry; five batteries of light artillery, regulars if possible; 1,100 horses to furnish the five batteries, to complete the batteries I have here, and for the unmounted cavalry.
>
> The rebels are threatening Newport News. Scouts report they have appeared in large force within 5 miles of that port. With this force I can evacuate Newport News by land if necessary. You can probably best determine, from a knowledge of the enemy's movements near you, what additional force I may require. I want three quartermasters, the chief of whom should be a superior man, and four brigadier-generals, with an efficient staff.

It was quite a dawn. Dr. Shippen, late of the *Congress,* now in Camp Butler, would write that Sunday "dawned fine and spring-like, a haze hanging over the broad waters, through which the sun as he rose looked red and angry; but it soon cleared off . . ." and was replaced by a "singular transparency of the atmosphere," according to Colonel Cannon.

Simultaneously the appearance of the *Monitor* was revealed to most shores of Hampton Roads. Aboard the *Patrick Henry,* Lieutenant Rochelle observed:

> The *Minnesota* was discovered in her old position but the *Minnesota* was not the only thing to attract attention. Close alongside of her there lay such a craft as the eyes of a seaman never looked upon before—an immense shingle floating on the water, with a gigantic cheese box rising from its center; no sails, no wheels, no smokestack, no guns. What could it be? On board the *Patrick Henry* many were the surmises as to the strange craft. Some thought it a water tank sent to supply the *Minnesota* with water; others were of opinion that it was a floating magazine replenishing her exhausted stock of ammunition; a few visionary characters feebly intimated that it might be the

Monitor which the Northern papers had been boasting about for a long time.

All doubts about the stranger were soon dispelled.

Dilatory as he was in spreading the word to his command, at least to his staff of officers, Jones, now in the breaking dawn on the top deck of the *Merrimack,* confided in one of his lieutenants, Hunter Davidson. According to the latter, the executive officer expressed "determination to attack and ram her [the *Monitor*] and to keep vigorously at her until the contest was decided."

Jones "left the impression" on Davidson that "the engagement could only end in the overthrow of either the enemy or ourselves."

After what Bill Cline described as a "hearty breakfast," topped off by "two jiggers of whiskey," the *Merrimack* was under way just before eight o'clock, accompanied by the *Patrick Henry, Jamestown,* the tug *Teaser,* and gunboat *Raleigh.*

According to Ramsay, she "steamed across and up stream toward the *Minnesota* thinking to make short work of her and soon return with her colors trailing under ours. We approached her slowly, feeling our way cautiously along the edge of the channel. . . ."

Van Brunt, on the *Minnesota,* however, thought it was closer to 6 A.M. when he saw "the enemy again . . . coming down from Craney Island. I beat to quarters."

Since the big ironclad was well across the Roads and heading, seemingly, for the Rip Raps, Van Brunt instructed the bugler to sound retreat "to allow my men to get something to eat."

Worden then called up to the captain of the towering flagship, asking him what he intended to do. The latter replied, "If I cannot lighten my ship off I shall destroy her."

Worden reaffirmed, "I will stand by you to the last if I can help you." Some aboard thought they heard Van Brunt shout down a reply to the effect that he did not think the little *Monitor* could help him at all.

This belief, or fear, was prevalent on shore, voiced for many others by Frederick Curtis, the former gunner of the *Congress:* "To tell the truth, we did not have much faith in the *Monitor;* we all expected to see the *Merrimack* destroy her."

To Dr. Shippen "she seemed so small and trifling that we feared she would only constitute additional prey for the leviathan."

Rogers, at Fort Monroe, concluded that the Ericsson invention was "a queer looking little craft which seemed to be neither ship nor anything resembling a ship—something which the soldiers quickly dubbed 'cheese box on a raft.' "

At best, the Baltimore American correspondent sniffed that the *Monitor* was "the reverse of formidable."

Soon, it was apparent to Van Brunt that the *Merrimack* was not going to test the Rip Raps' big guns. She turned and headed down channel for the *Minnesota*. The captain wrote:

"Again all hands were called to quarters and when she approached within a mile of us I opened upon her with my stern guns. . . ."

There was some dispute as to which ship fired the first shot. Keeler, of the *Monitor,* observed a puff of smoke from the direction of the *Merrimack* as a "shell howled over our heads and crashed into the side of the *Minnesota."* Thereupon, Worden, "more sternly" than he had been heard to speak previously, ordered, "Gentlemen, that is the *Merrimack,* you had better go below."

They did, securing the iron hatch even as the gunners were lifting solid shot, weighing somewhere between 175 and 185 pounds, into the twin muzzles. The captain pointed to one of the big spheres with the remark, "Send them that with our compliments. . . ."

In the pilot house, with its narrow, frustrating eyeslits, were Worden, Samuel Howard, the pilot, and Peter Williams, the quartermaster, at the wheel. Greene was in command of the turret, accompanied by Acting Master Louis N. Stodder and "sixteen brawny men," eight to a gun to load and clean them. Stimers and First Assistant Engineer Isaac Newton were at their customary stations in the engine room. Acting Master John Webber was in charge of the powder division at its normal battle station, the berth deck.

Now, although it appeared wholly unnecessary, Van Brunt "made signal to the *Monitor* to attack the enemy," then recorded:

"She immediately ran down in my wake, right within the range of the *Merrimack,* completely covering my ship as far as was possible with her dimensions, and, much to my astonishment, laid herself right alongside of the *Merrimack* and the contrast was that of a pigmy to a giant."

Worden would assert, "I got underway as soon as possible and stood directly for her, with crew at quarters, in order to meet and engage her as far away from the *Minnesota* as possible."

On board the *Merrimack* there was confusion and, in some minds, surprise. As she approached the *Minnesota* "slowly," according to Ramsay, "feeling our way cautiously along the edge of the channel . . . suddenly to our astonishment a black object that looked like . . . 'a barrelhead afloat with a cheesebox on top of it' moved slowly out from under the *Minnesota* and boldly confronted us . . . both ships were queer-looking craft."

Jones, the acting commander of the *Merrimack,* would observe with evident displeasure, "The pilots were to have placed us half a mile from her [the *Minnesota*], but we were not at any time nearer than a mile."

Bill Drake, bearing out Ramsay's "astonishment," wrote, "As the gun deck was already vibrating and smoky from the opening attack on the *Minnesota,* no one knew that the *Monitor* was lying by her . . . the *Minnesota* had been hit by several shots when the *Monitor* came from behind her and started toward the *Merrimack,* and at the same time notice was given to the gunners to look out for an ironclad that was bearing down on us."

James Stephens, of Company K, 20th Indiana, from a vantage point at Newport News, was making mental notes for a graphic letter about the events of this early morning:

"After gazing for some time on the intruder, she [the *Merrimack*] was evidently convinced that it was nothing but a Yankee trick to cheat her of a noble prize. She proposed to ignore the trick and secure the prize. Without further delay she bore down again upon the *Minnesota.*"

Inside the "buttoned-up" *Monitor* the crew waited. Keeler, experiencing "a peculiar sensation" that he nonetheless was not prepared to admit was "fear," listened to the "infernal howl" of the shells crossing above the little ironclad toward the *Minnesota.* Nervously, Greene called:

"Paymaster, ask the captain if I shall fire!"

There was a speaking tube connecting turret and pilot house forward, but it had temporarily broken down. Keeler and the captain's clerk, Daniel Toffey, relayed commands the short distance.

The reply came back from the commanding officer, "Tell Mr. Greene *not* to fire till I give the word, to be cool and deliberate, to take sure aim and not waste a shot."

Worden continued, "As I approached the enemy, her wooden

consorts turned and stood back in the direction from which they had come. . . ."

Gautier, on the *Gassendi*, raptly fascinated as he had been the previous day, chronicled the same withdrawal: "The little black mass [the *Monitor*] had put itself in motion. . . . they [the gunboats] were then seen to abandon the attack and retire under the batteries of Sewell's leaving the *Merrimack* to defend alone the honor of their young flag."

Worden: ". . . she turned her head upstream against the tide remaining nearly stationary and commenced firing. At this time about 8 oc AM I was approaching her on her starboard bow, on a course nearly at right angles with her line of keel, saving my fire until near enough that every shot might take effect. I continued to so approach until within very short range [a third of a mile, Jones on the *Merrimack* estimated] when I altered my course parallel with hers but with bows in opposite directions, stopped the engine and commenced firing."

As Greene would describe, "I triced up the port [lashed open the metal gunport shutter], ran out the gun, and, taking deliberate aim, pulled the lockstring."

The report, according to Keeler, "jarred our vessel," but it was also welcome "music."

The fight had begun.

Stephens, ashore, thought the *Monitor*'s "maiden shot" had struck the enemy "plump on the waterline," and in so doing "crowned the *Monitor* our accepted champion." He continued:

". . . it aroused the fury of the *Merrimack*. She turned and belched an angry volume of fire and shot upon her little rival as though she would blow her out of the water at once."

Dr. Shippen obtained the "impression of a big, hulking bully suddenly attacked by a plucky, determined little man."

It was, according to Greene, "a rattling broadside . . . the turret and other parts of the ship were heavily struck, but the shots did not penetrate; the tower was intact, and it continued to revolve.

"A look of confidence passed over the men's faces, and we believed the *Merrimack* would not repeat the work she had accomplished the day before."

Keeler noted that the enemy's shots "rattled on our iron decks like hailstones." He saw one of the gunners thrust his head through an open port and quickly draw back with a "broad grin" as he observed, "The damned fools are firing canister at us."

Worden would report:

"I passed slowly by her, within a few yards, delivering fire as rapidly as possible and receiving from her a rapid fire in return both from her great guns and musketry—the latter aimed at the pilot house, hoping undoubtedly to penetrate it through the lookout holes and to disable the commanding officer and helmsman.

"At this period I felt some anxiety about the turret machinery, it having been predicted by many persons that a heavy shot with great initial velocity striking the turret would so derange it as to stop its working; but finding that it had been twice struck and still revolved as freely as ever, I turned back with renewed confidence and hope and continued the engagement at close quarters; every shot from our guns taking effect upon the high sides of our adversary, stripping off the iron freely."

Worden was already finding it not so simple to adhere to his own initial strategy of keeping "the *Monitor* moving in a circle just large enough to give time for loading the guns." He had hoped to fire at the point "where the circle impinged upon the *Merrimack*," then curve away to reload.

Van Brunt, whose flagship's broadsides kept up an almost "continuous sheet of flame," according to one witness, added, "Gun after gun was fired by the *Monitor* which was returned with whole broadsides by the rebels with no more effect, apparently, than so many pebblestones thrown by a child.

"After a while they commenced maneuvering, and we could see the little battery point her bow for the rebels, with the intention, as I thought, of sending a shot through her bow porthole; then she would shoot by her and rake her through her stern.

"In the meantime, the rebel was pouring broadside after broadside, but almost all her shot flew over the little submerged propeller, and when they struck the bombproof tower the shot glanced off without producing any effect."

It was especially frustrating to Jones, on the *Merrimack,* who would write, "She and her turret appeared to be under perfect control. Her light draft enabled her to move about us at pleasure. She once took position for a short time where we could not bring a gun to bear on her."

The engineering officer, Ramsay, recorded in more flamboyant manner, "We hovered about each other in spirals, gradually contracting the circuits until we were within point-blank range, but our shell glanced from the *Monitor*'s turret just as hers did from our sloping sides. . . . the cannonade continued without perceptible damage to either of the combatants.

"On our gun deck all was bustle, smoke, grimy figures and stern commands, while down in the engine and boiler rooms the sixteen furnaces were belching out fire and smoke, and the firemen standing in front of them like so many gladiators, tugged away with devil's claw and slice-bar, inducing by their exertions more and more intense combustion and heat. The noise of the crackling, roaring fires, escaping steam, and the loud and labored pulsations of the engines, together with the roar of battle above and the thud and vibration of the huge masses of iron which were hurled against us produced a scene and sound to be compared only with the poet's picture of the lower regions."

As Bill Cline, who had been with the *Merrimack* since her launching, observed, "Every officer and gunner on board the *Virginia* was puzzled to know how to disable the curious little craft. The truth, however, was that we could do nothing with her just then."

All in all, it was "a thrilling scene," by James Stephens's measure. "In the foreground lay a magnificent ship, an alluring stake in the contest. Immense volumes of smoke rolled away from her decks as she rained ponderous balls upon her would-be captor. To the left was the Fortress Monroe and in the background Sewell's Point, their parapets and beach crowded with interested spectators. Hovering on the outskirts at a safe distance were numbers of Union and rebel vessels.

"In the center the attraction of all eyes were the two ironclads grappling as in a life and death struggle, the one maneuvering for position to rake the strange ship, the other rushing in to make her change position and defeat the project."

It was becoming increasingly apparent ashore that the mighty *Merrimack* had met her match. In fact, Captain Jim Byers, with his tug *J. B. White* (the Buffalo native who had been caught in Norfolk at the Confederate take-over) now hovering off Sewell's Point, heard other officers who had steamed somewhat closer to the scene of action observe that:

". . . the unknown craft was a 'wicked thing,' and that we better not get too near her." One of the shots "came skipping over the water very near us."

General Colston himself, who enjoyed a grandstand view the day before at Ragged Island, had this morning commandeered a barge to be closer. He reported, "I was now within three-quarters of a mile of them, and more than once stray shots came near enough to dash the spray over my barge, but the grandeur of the spectacle was so fascinating that they passed by unheeded."

The ailing Dick Phelps, on Sewell's Point, proved to be more dismayed at the reversal of events from the preceding day than fascinated. "The Ericsson battery," he wrote, "commenced an attack on the *Merrimack* in the most ferocious manner."

Bill Rogers, at Fort Monroe, being reminded of David and Goliath, feared,

> truly this odd little craft was no match for the great monster. They closed in, however, and a curtain of smoke settled down over the scene with the Confederate batteries on Sewell's Point, Pig Point and Craney Island in the fray. With breathless suspense we listened to this firing, but could see nothing for the clouds of smoke. We heard the whistle of the shells and the shot, and we could recognize the shots of the *Monitor*. One takes no note of time under such circumstances. How long that first round lasted before the firing ceased I have no idea.
>
> When the thunder ceased, oh! We thought, the 'cheese box' had gone to the bottom. Gradually the smoke lifted and there lay the two antagonists, backing, filling and jockeying for position, then at it again, and again the cloud of smoke which settled over their struggle hid them from view.

The "suspense" of those moments when the combatants were completely obscured was "dreadful," according to James Stephens. At one point, he was certain that the little ironclad had been sunk by "the sheer weight of metal hurled upon her at so short a distance."

Then the smoke cleared to reveal the *Monitor*, "blithe and nimble as ever, apparently rubbing her tiny sides against the huge flanks of her adversary . . . like a duck hunting for the weak spots and angles and pounding her. . . ."

Those aboard the *Monitor* also bore witness to the smoke, compounded, according to Stodder, by the desultory firing from opposing shore batteries and even from the remaining wreckage of the *Congress*.

In fact, the acting master thought the visibility was so bad at one time that Worden himself stepped outside of the pilot house to take a look around and assess damages. He would refer to the *Merrimack*'s musketry fire as "thick as hailstones in a storm."

All in all, Acting Master John Webber thought Worden "as cool as a man playing a game of chess."

Stodder, working the little steam engine that turned the turret, was leaning against the latter when it was struck by a shot. Stunned, he was sent below and replaced by the jack-of-all-trades Stimers.

At best, the turret presented problems, its operation, as Greene would report, "not altogether satisfactory." It was difficult not only to start revolving but to stop once started. Stimers, "an active muscular man," accomplished miracles in keeping it moving at all. Greene would write:

> My only view of the world outside of the tower was over the muzzles of the guns, which cleared the ports by only a few inches. When the guns were run in, the portholes were covered by heavy iron pendulums, pierced with small holes to allow the iron rammer and sponge handles to protrude while they were in use. To hoist these pendulums required the entire gun's crew and vastly increased the work inside the turret.
>
> The effect upon one shut up in a revolving drum is perplexing, and it is not a simple matter to keep the bearings. White marks had been placed upon the stationary deck immediately below the turret to indicate the direction of the starboard and port sides, and the bow and stern; but these marks were obliterated early in the action. I would continually ask the captain, "How does the *Merrimac* bear?" He replied, "On the starboard-beam," or "On the port-quarter," as the case might be. Then the difficulty was to determine the direction of the starboard-beam, or port-quarter, or any other bearing. It finally resulted, that when a gun was ready for firing, the turret would be started on its revolving journey in search of the target, and when found it was taken "on the fly," because the turret could not be accurately controlled.

The men, stripped to the waist and sweating profusely, worked in smoke and semidark. In spite of their herculean labors it required at least eight minutes between rounds. Breechloaders were very rare. Keeler would record, in one of his many letters to "Dear Anna," the crosscurrent of commands and remarks:

"Tell Mr. Greene that I am going to bring him on our Starboard beam close alongside."

"That was a good shot, went through her waterline."

"That last shot brought the iron from her sides."

"They're going to board us, put in a round of canister."

"Can't do it, both guns have solid shot."

"You've made a hole through her, quick give her the other."

"Why don't you fire?"

"Can't do it, the cartridge is not rammed home."

"Depress the gun and let the shot roll overboard."

"A splendid shot, you raked them. . . ."

It now occurred to Worden that he could break the *Merrimack*'s rudder or propeller by running close to her stern. He missed, the captain estimated, by no more than two feet.

Jones himself believed that the *Merrimack* could "have been easily disabled" by this maneuver. He wrote of his continuing frustration:

"We could only see her guns when they were discharged; immediately afterward the turret revolved rapidly, and the guns were not again seen until they were again fired. We wondered how proper aim could be taken in the very short time the guns were in sight.

"The *Virginia,* however, was a large target, and generally so near that the *Monitor*'s shots did not often miss. It did not appear to us that our shells had any effect upon the *Monitor.* We had no solid shot. Musketry was fired at the lookout holes. In spite of all the cares of our pilots we ran ashore."

Less charitable, Dr. Phillips believed "the pilot purposely ran us aground nearly two miles off" from the *Minnesota,* fearing that frigate's "terrible broadside."

Whether the grounding was intentional or not, the *Monitor* took advantage of her opponent's plight, moving in close "where none of our guns could be brought to bear," according to the surgeon, and "she directed a succession of shots at the same section of our vessel, and some of them striking close together, started the timbers and drove them perceptibly in. . . ."

Ramsay added, "In she came and began to sound every chink in our armor—every one but that which was actually vulnerable, had she known it."

While he struggled to get up emergency "bursting" steam pressure, Jones wandered down to the spar deck to check on the gunnery.

Noting a division standing "at ease," he inquired of its captain, Lieutenant J. R. Eggleston:

"Why are you not firing, Mr. Eggleston?"

"Why our powder is very precious," came the reply, "and after two hours' incessant firing I find that I can do her about as much damage by snapping my thumb at her every two minutes and a half."

"Our situation was critical," wrote Ramsay. "The coal consumption of the two days' fight had lightened our prow until our unprotected submerged deck was almost awash. The armor on our sides below the waterline had been extended but about three feet, owing to our hasty departure before the work was finished. Lightened as we were, those exposed portions rendered us no longer an ironclad, and the *Monitor* might have pierced us between wind and water had she depressed her guns."

Jones hoisted signal flags to recall his wooden consorts. Tucker on the *Patrick Henry* saw them. According to his lieutenant, James Rochelle, "apprehensions were entertained" that she was indeed aground or her machinery disabled but as the flags fouled on their lines the numbers could not be read. Rochelle added:

> At length he [the signal officer] reported the signal to be "Disabled my propeller is." No wooden vessel could have floated twenty minutes under the fire that the *Virginia* was undergoing, but if her propeller was disabled it was necessary to attempt to tow her back to the cover of our batteries, so the *Patrick Henry* and *Jamestown* started to make the attempt.

Ramsay continued:

> Fearing that she might discover our vulnerable "heel of Achilles," we had to take all chances. We lashed down the safety valves, heaped quick-burning combustibles into the already raging fires, and brought the boilers to a pressure that would have been unsafe under ordinary circumstances.
>
> The propeller churned the mud and water furiously, but the ship did not stir. We piled on oiled cotton waste, splints of wood, anything that would burn faster than coal. It seemed impossible that the boilers could stand the pressure we were crowding upon them.

Jones added, "The *Monitor* and *Minnesota* were in full play on us. A small rifle-gun on board the *Minnesota* or on the steamer alongside her [one of the tugs] was fired with remarkable precision."

Then, Ramsay reported, "just as we were beginning to despair, there was a perceptible movement, and the *Merrimack* slowly dragged herself off the shoal by main strength.

"We were saved!"

In undisguised relief Rochelle on the *Patrick Henry* realized the "sacrifice [of his ship] was not necessary."

The *Merrimack*'s acting captain continued:

". . . when we saw that our fire made no impression on the *Monitor* we determined to ram her if possible. We found it a very difficult feat to do. Our great length and draft in a comparatively narrow channel, with but little water to spare, made us sluggish in our movement and hard to steer and turn."

According to Taylor Wood, "nearly an hour" was consumed in this basic maneuver:

"Now 'go ahead!' Now 'stop!' Now 'astern!' "

Lieutenant Wood could only repeat what he had observed already: "The ship was as unwieldly as Noah's Ark."

Van Brunt, understandably perplexed by the elephantine efforts of the *Merrimack* to swing into position to ram, would log that he observed "the little battery chasing her with all speed."

However, the *Merrimack* was driving in. Worden relayed the order to the turret:

"Look out now they're going to run us down, give them both guns!"

"This," according to Keeler, was "a moment of terrible suspense."

Jones, however, fearing a full-speed collision because his ram was in the sunken *Cumberland,* ordered reverse engines well before the moment of impact. At the same time, Worden set the helm of the *Monitor* "hard a-port!"

As a result, the hulking Confederate struck only a glancing blow on her opponent's starboard quarter—so lightly that Ramsay did not feel "the slightest shock down in the engine room." On the *Monitor,* however, there was a "heavy jar" and some were thrown off balance.

Aided by a long glass, the reporter for the Baltimore *American* watched as the *Monitor* "spun around like a top and, as she got her bearing again, sent one of her formidable missiles into her huge opponent."

Both contestants, as a matter of fact, got off rounds during this moment of meeting. The *Merrimack,* according to the ship's carpenter, had sprung a leak forward because of the collision. Ramsay dismissed any cause for worry, observing, "with the two large Worth-ington pumps besides the bilge injections, we could keep her afloat for hours, even with a 10-inch shell in her hull."

Less sanguine, Jones considered the leak "alarming."

Again, the vessels touched. Apparently it resulted from Worden's maneuvering this time, as each desperately tried to sink or at least disable the other. Keeler found "the sounds of the conflict . . . terrible," the concussion coming from not only the *Merrimack*'s shells against the turret but at least two strays from the *Minnesota*. Two men leaning against the turret, as Stodder had been, were knocked "sense-less" and had to be carried below.

On the *Merrimack,* Taylor Wood thought some of the armor plate, aft, had been forced in "bodily two or three inches," adding, "All the crews of the after guns were knocked over by the consussion and bled from the nose or ears."

Boarders—something Worden had already feared but wasn't at all sure how to repulse—were called. As they prepared to leap onto their antagonist, the *Monitor* dropped astern. She had reason to move away—her turret was bare of ammunition. More had to be hoisted up from the berth deck.

The sharp-eyed Gautier, on the *Gassendi,* then noticed that the *Merrimack*'s flagstaff had been shot away, while "the tops in the Roads [mast tops of Federal ships?] as well as the ramparts of the fortress saluted this accident with frantic hurrahs as a victory.

"But soon a sailor appeared on the gratings, showing at the end of a staff the flag which had for an instant disappeared."

Leaving the *Monitor* "unscathed," according to Ramsay, the *Merrimack* sought to "get between her and the *Minnesota*," already damaged at the waterline, and resume fire on the latter. Van Brunt would log:

> . . . and now, on her second approach, I opened upon her with all my broadside guns and 10-inch pivot a broadside which would have blown out of water any timber-built ship in the world. She returned my fire with her rifled bow gun with a shell, which passed through the chief engineer's stateroom, through the engineer's mess room, amidships, and burst in the boatswain's room, tearing four rooms all into one in its passage, exploding two charges of powder, which set the ship on fire, but it was promptly extinguished by a party headed by my first lieutenant; her second round went through the boiler of the

tugboat *Dragon,* exploding it and causing some consternation on board my ship for the moment, until the matter was explained. This time I had concentrated upon her an incessant fire from my gun deck, spar deck, and forecastle pivot guns, and was informed by my marine officer, who was stationed on the poop, that at least fifty solid shot struck her on her slanting side without producing any apparent effect. By the time she had fired her third shell the little *Monitor* had come down upon her, placing herself between us, and compelled her to change her position.

It was now about noon.

Generously, Ramsay would write in praise, "The *Monitor* gallantly rushed to her rescue, passing so close under our submerged stern that she almost snapped off our propeller. As she was passing, so near that we could have leaped aboard her, Lieutenant Wood trained the stern gun on her when she was only 20 yards from its muzzle and delivered a rifle-pointed shell which dislodged the iron logs sheltering the *Monitor*'s conning tower, carrying away the steering-gear and signal apparatus. . . ."

Worden's eyes and face were filled with powder, "utterly blinding and in a degree stunning me. The top of the pilot house, too, was partially lifted off by the force of the concussion, which let in a flood of light, so strong as to be apparent to me blind as I was and caused me to believe that the pilot house was seriously disabled."

Pete Williams, the quartermaster, by Worden's side at the helm and who had seen "right into the bore" of the enemy guns, was miraculously unhurt.

Keeler, not far away, was himself somewhat stunned by "a flash of light and a cloud of smoke." When it cleared, he saw Worden "stagger and put his hands to his eyes." As Keeler reached his side, the commanding officer cried:

"My eyes, I am blind!"

The paymaster called for Assistant Surgeon Daniel C. Logue and also Greene, the latter at Worden's request. The "exec." left the turret in command of Stimers and hurried to Worden to find him:

". . . a ghastly sight, with his eyes closed and the blood apparently rushing from every pore in the upper part of his face. He told me that he was seriously wounded and directed me to take command . . . and use my own discretion."

Worden was assisted to a sofa in his cabin.

Thus, both combatants, the *Monitor* and the *Merrimack,* were pursuing the battle with acting captains. There were other shared conditions: depletion of ammunition, of coal, and the near-exhaustion of both crews. One had fought the previous day. The other had fought, for a far longer time, a yet more implacable enemy: the sea.

As Greene would write: "My men and myself were perfectly black with smoke and powder. All my underclothes were perfectly black and my person was in the same condition . . . I had been up so long and been under such a state of excitement that my nervous system was completely run down . . . my nerves and muscles twitched as though electric shocks were continually passing through them, and my head ached as if it would burst . . . I thought my brain would come right out over my eyebrows."

Stimers estimated that a number of the crew were still "senseless" from having been in contact with the turret during hits.

Van Brunt, on the *Minnesota,* after two days of pounding, was feeling "to the fullest extent my condition." He added:

> I was hard and immovably aground, and they could take position under my stern and rake me. I had expended most of my solid shot and my ship was badly crippled and my officers and men were worn out with fatigue, but even then, in this extreme dilemma, I determined never to give up the ship to the rebels, and, after consulting my officers, I ordered every preparation to be made to destroy the ship after all hope was gone to save her.

Some guns were actually heaved over the side.

Aboard the *Merrimack,* Jones, although known in his younger Federal Navy days as quite a scrapper, had had enough of this confrontation. Like Phillips, he shifted the blame onto others as he advised Ramsay:

"The pilots will not place us nearer to the *Minnesota* and we cannot afford to run the risk of getting aground again. I'm going to haul off under the guns of Sewell's Point and renew the attack on the rise of the tide. Bank your fires. . . ."

To Ramsay the news was a sudden "wet blanket," Jones having "ignored the moral effect of leaving the Roads without forcing the

Minnesota to surrender." And, as anyone could see, the *Monitor* was buoyantly undefeated.

Lieutenant Hunter Davidson would recall bluntly, "Our men were completely broken down by two days' and a night's continuous work with the heaviest rifled ordnance in the world. . . . the ship was believed to be seriously injured by ramming and sinking the *Cumberland*. . . . if she should run aground and remain so in attempting to reach the *Minnesota* she would probably open forward where her horn had split the stem and become an easy prey to the enemy."

Colonel Cannon, still watching from the ramparts of Fort Monroe, heard someone exclaim of the *Merrimack*, "She is sinking!" Then, another's comment on the *Monitor*, "She sticks to her like a king-bird to a hawk!"

The analogy was no longer applicable. After trading final shots, the *Merrimack* set course for Sewell's, where the Confederate soldiers were already cheering; the *Monitor*, back to the side of the *Minnesota*. The latter was quickly surrounded by all manner of steamers and sailing craft from Newport News and the protected anchorage off Fort Monroe. Stephens wrote:

"Now from the decks and rigging of the vessels, from casemate and parapet of the fort, from the adjacent camp, from the beleaguered post at Newport News and the poor remnants of the crews of the *Congress* and *Cumberland* let one, loud, prolonged triumphant cry of victory and joy ring out . . . it is the Lord's Day!"

After some four hours, the battle was over. The *Monitor* had been hit at least twenty-one times and fired off about forty-three rounds. The indomitable *Minnesota* had expended, in the two days, 529 rounds of various caliber shot and shells up to ten-inch. The *Merrimack*, which had been hit certainly hundreds of times since Saturday, left no ordnance account of her twenty-four hours' action.

In Fort Monroe, Fox, an understandably emotional and now wearied spectator of the epochal engagement, prepared his telegram for Gideon Welles:

> The *Monitor* arrived at 10 p.m. last night and went immediately to the protection of the *Minnesota*, lying aground just below Newport News.
> At 7 a.m. to-day the *Merrimack*, accompanied by two wooden

steamers and several tugs, stood out toward the *Minnesota* and opened fire.

The *Monitor* met them at once and opened her fire, when all the enemy's vessels retired, excepting the *Merrimack*. These two ironclad vessels fought part of the time touching each other, from 8 a.m. to noon, when the *Merrimack* retired. Whether she is injured or not it is impossible to say. Lieutenant J. L. Worden, who commanded the *Monitor*, handled her with great skill, assisted by Chief Engineer Stimers. Lieutenant Worden was injured by the cement from the pilot house being driven into his eyes, but I trust not seriously. The *Minnesota* kept up a continuous fire and is herself somewhat injured.

She was moved considerably to-day, and will probably be off to-night. The *Monitor* is uninjured and ready at any moment to repel another attack.

The Lost Lamb

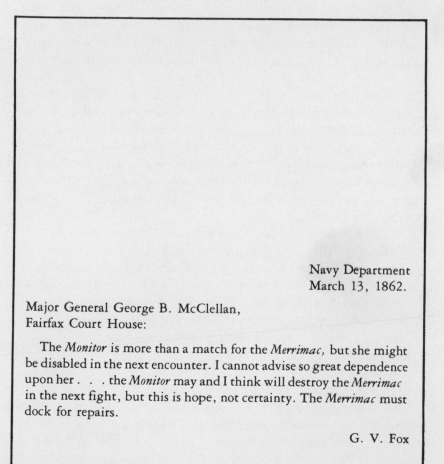

Navy Department
March 13, 1862.

Major General George B. McClellan,
Fairfax Court House:

The *Monitor* is more than a match for the *Merrimac,* but she might be disabled in the next encounter. I cannot advise so great dependence upon her . . . the *Monitor* may and I think will destroy the *Merrimac* in the next fight, but this is hope, not certainty. The *Merrimac* must dock for repairs.

G. V. Fox

Richmond's atmosphere that early March, as the Confederacy entered its second year of secession, was one of mingled apprehension and anticipation—not wholly dissimilar to the mood in Washington.

Martial law had been proclaimed in Petersburg and surrounding territory on March 1. Jefferson Davis had announced the suspension of habeas corpus in cities, towns, or areas threatened by the Federal forces. A troublesome stream of refugees was increasing daily from Norfolk. All of these transpirings were inherently foreboding.

At the same time, nature's blandishments were hinting at a crescendo. As a young resident, Constance Cary, whose family had refugeed from the estate Vaucluse near Alexandria, wrote, "When the spring opened, as the spring does in Richmond, with a sudden glory of green leaves, magnolia blooms and flowers among the grass, our spirits rose after the depression of the latter months. If only to shake off the atmosphere of doubts and fears engendered by the long winter of disaster and uncertainty, the coming activity of arms was welcome!"

A neighbor, Mary Boykin Chesnut, wife of James Chesnut, recently United States Senator from South Carolina and now an aide to Jefferson Davis, railed at "millionaires," war profiteers, "bloodsuckers . . . rolling by in their coaches" while "our children" allegedly had to content themselves with playing "in the gutter." Mrs. Chesnut couldn't help entertaining doubts even while others in the Capital of the Confederacy applauded the news from Hampton Roads. She soberly wondered:

"The worst of it is that all this will arouse them to more furious exertions to destroy us. They hated us so before, but how now?"

Taylor Wood had been delegated by Buchanan, wounded and "suffering greatly," to carry word of the naval engagement, as well as the tightly rolled flag of the *Congress,* to Richmond. There, together with Secretary Mallory and other dignitaries of the Confederacy, he provided a Sunday midnight briefing to President Davis, who "made many inquiries."

Realist Lieutenant Wood informed Davis, at his residence on Capitol Hill, that "in the *Monitor* we had met our equal, and the result of another engagement would be very doubtful." Finally, the South's President asked to see the trophy flag, which was "a very large one."

As it was unrolled by executive aides, it was discovered "in some places saturated with blood." Although Wood had done nothing to gloss over the slaughterhouse aspects of Saturday's battles, the sight and smell of such fresh blood was too much for the queasy Davis. He quickly ordered it rerolled and taken to the Navy Department—never to be seen again.

Another Richmonder, Commander Matthew Fontaine Maury, the hydrographer who had resigned his U.S. Navy commission, expressed joy at the loss of the ships and deaths of his erstwhile shipmates. He wrote, on the fifteenth, to a friend in the French naval service, a Captain de la Marche:

"Our *'Virginia'* by her performances in Hampton Roads, has, at a single dash, overturned the 'wooden walls' of Old England and rendered effete the navies of the world."

He then alluded to the lone *Merrimack* as one "little ewe lamb" which had "startled" Congress "from its dreams."

As an aside in the very long letter addressed to Paris, Maury, who, unlike his fellow officer Stephen Lee, seemed to have found the word "Virginia" in his original commission, denounced the "savage . . . Yankees" for blockading Charleston Harbor and obstructing its channels.

The "little ewe lamb," or "iron diadem of the South," as yet others knew her, meanwhile found herself in less than presentable shape. According to Jim Byers, of the tug *J. B. White*, still awaiting his chance to escape to Fort Monroe without being blown out of the water by the guns of Sewell's Point:

"The *Merrimac* came back into the river badly disabled, and almost in a sinking condition. Tugs had to be used to get her into the drydock . . . the crew pumping and bailing water with all their might to keep her afloat. I saw her in the dock at Norfolk the next day, was on board of her and made a personal examination of the ship.

"The effect of the *Monitor*'s guns upon the *Merrimac* was terrible. Her plated sides were broken in, the iron plating rent and broken, the massive timbers of her sides crushed; and the officers themselves stated that she could not have withstood the effect of the *Monitor*'s guns any longer, and that they barely escaped in time from her."

The beached monster became the object of earnest ministrations by platoons of workers. She needed many tons of new iron plate, especially under the waterline, one hundred additional tons of ballast, extensive repairs to her reinforcing oak beams, to her upperworks, including a new funnel, and an endless amount of tinkering with her engines. The latter remained the despair of Ramsay, who had learned that they could "not be relied upon" when he had served on her while she flew the United States flag. A familiar visitor bore witness.

Captain Gautier, of the *Gassendi,* calling at the Gosport yard, was taken aboard the *Merrimack.* When shown the engine compartment, he clapped his hands together and exclaimed, *"C'est un inferno!"*

His guide, Captain Benjamin Sloan, of Huger's staff, agreed, comparing the scene to "the darkness of Erebus, save for the flickering lights of a few dimly burning, smoking whale oil lamps."

From the start, the work proceeded at such a snail's pace that General "Prince John" Magruder raged at the "criminal tardiness," while Mallory informed the new captain of the Navy Yard, Captain Sidney Smith Lee:

"The crisis demands the extraordinary exertions of all loyal men, and if your subordinates fail from lack of zeal or ability we must supply their places at once."

The *Monitor* had fared much better, with only the damage to her pilot house and the dents in her turret, the deepest of which was four inches. In the past days, she had answered to two captains, first Tom Selfridge, then Lieutenant William N. Jeffers, a short, rotund ordnance specialist who had graduated fourth in the first class of Annapolis, 1846. Haunted by the question, Should he have carried the attack to the withdrawing *Merrimack?*, Dana Greene was deeply hurt that he had not succeeded to command.

Fox glossed over the passing up of the executive officer with a reference to his "extreme youth."

Worden, blind in one eye, had been taken by night boat to Washington Sunday, almost while the guns of his suddenly famous ironclad were still hot. Lincoln left a Cabinet meeting Monday morning to meet the slender, modest lieutenant whose head was bandaged. The latter opened the conversation:

"Mr. President, you do me great honor by this visit."

The Commander in Chief replied, "Sir, I am the one who is honored in this interview."

He thereupon hastened a message to Gideon Welles:

Hon. Sec. of Navy   Executive Mansion
My dear sir   March 10, 1862

I have just seen Lieut. Worden, who says the *"Monitor"* could be boarded and captured very easily—first, after boarding, by wedging the turret, so that it would not turn, and then by pouring water in her & drowning her machinery. He is decidedly of the opinion she should not go sky-larking up to Norfolk. Yours truly

A. Lincoln

The ink was scarcely dry when Lincoln dictated a telegram to Captain Fox, still at Hampton Roads:

"It is directed by the President that the *Monitor* be not too much exposed, and that in no event shall any attempt be made to proceed with her unattended to Norfolk. If vessels can be procured and loaded with stone and sunk in the channel it is important that it should be done. The *San Jacinto* and *Dacotah* have sailed from Boston for Hampton Roads and the *Sabine* in tow of *Baltic* and a tug from New York. Gun Boats will be ordered forthwith. Should it not be well to detain the *Minnesota* until other vessels arrive?"

Welles emphasized the proposal to block the Elizabeth River in a letter to Goldsborough, hastily brought back from the Burnside Expedition in the Albemarle Sound area.

Worden quickly received the adulation of a grateful North, convinced that the *Monitor* had come between the *Merrimack* and the wastage of port cities. "A new era was opened in the history of maritime warfare," it seemed to Secretary Welles, who formally conveyed the thanks of President Lincoln, and prepared papers promoting the lieutenant of many years to full commander. The U.S. Congress, state legislatures, city governments, chambers of commerce, all added their amens to the rising chorus of praise and gratitude. The only voice in discord, as might have been expected, was that of John Ericsson, who couldn't see why the *Merrimack* hadn't been sunk then and there. As reported by Charles W. MacCord, Ericsson's chief draftsman:

> The captain [Ericsson] was disappointed that the *Monitor* had not done her utmost during the engagement; by her subsequent inactivity he was simply enraged. He was, himself, the active voice incarnate, and the passive voice was to him absolutely incomprehensible; like the hot and angry bee, who never rests, and wonders how others can, he saw in the end of one task only the beginning of another. He had built his ship to *fight*; and I never heard him allude to the "excessive caution" which kept her idle after her one battle, without scathing denunciations

couched in language as fluent as it was vigorous, and more uncomplimentary than either.

At best, the testy Swede, who had never much favored Worden, felt that any success at Hampton Roads was directly attributable to Stimers being at the captain's "side."

Ericsson, however, should have been pleased. Not only had the *Merrimack* been stopped in the Confederate Navy's intent to break the blockade, but the monitor as a new class of warship had achieved, overnight, international fame. Secretary Welles's office was flooded with inquiries from sea powers around the world. Russia, Austria, and Italy, for example, wanted at least drawings.

Stimers, as an obvious engineering authority on the *Monitor,* when consulted, advised Fox that he did not "feel disposed to assist in swelling the naval powers of European countries."

Neither he, Ericsson, nor, certainly, Gideon Welles had to worry about overtures from the British Admiralty. In Parliament, the Duke of Somerset, as First Lord of the Admiralty, had gratuitously tagged the Hampton Roads confrontation as "anything but conclusive." The *Monitor* he described as "a vessel of very curious form . . . something between a raft and a diving bell." As for the life of her crewmen: "a sort of Calcutta Blackhole existence!"

With an eye to the future, the London *Times* was much more impressed. Its military editor wrote:

"Whereas we had available for immediate purposes 149 first class warships, we have now two, these two being the *Warrior* and her sister *Ironside* [also known as *Black Prince*]. There is not now a ship in the English Navy, apart from these two, that it would not be madness to trust to an engagement with that little *Monitor.*"

Despite unresolved problems of speed versus invulnerability and lack of seaworthiness, the navy let contracts for ten *Passaic*-class monitors, all somewhat larger than the original ironclad and mounting one 15-inch gun (firing a 450-pound ball) in addition to one 11-inch, as used in the *Monitor.* Some wanted monster 20-inch guns. Because of the extreme structural weakness of the first pilot house and its vulnerability, this control "brain" was located on top of the more heavily armored turret.

By the end of March, six were building, including two in Boston.

Meanwhile, Fort Monroe echoed to the whistling-scraping sounds of docking transports and marching feet as the Army of the Potomac at long last began arriving. The vanguard had embarked at Alexandria on March 17. Tented encampments stretched out from the Hampton–Newport News area like giant, blossoming cotton fields, filling all available ground that could be considered in firm Federal control. But McClellan continued to complain bitterly about what he believed to be numerical inadequacies of his troops—by early April, only "53,000 men in hand," with perhaps an equal number relegated to the rear as clerks, cooks, "horse valets," etc. Particularly irksome to the young commanding general was the fact that Lincoln had peremptorily relieved him of all commands except that of the Department of the Potomac. Disturbing as well was the acknowledged fact that the navy, at the moment, was far more interested in keeping the *Merrimack* holed up in Norfolk than planning coordinated compaigns with the army up the James and York rivers.

Perhaps none, on either side of Hampton Roads, was fully satisfied with the war's course this spring. In Norfolk they waited impatiently for the *Merrimack* to reappear. Every day that she did not strengthened the fear that the big ironclad had been more gravely wounded than generally supposed, or revealed. J. H. Dawson, secretary of the Norfolk Gas Company, while wondering how he was going to run coal through the blockade, wrote a friend:

"The *Virginia* is still in the dock, I believe, though she could go out any hour if necessary. They are keeping her there to finish putting on a coat of iron below the waterline, which will make her much safer against attack. I think she will be finished in two or three days and will probably go out and try her hand next week. I hope she will have a good time and get back safe."

Out of dry dock by early April, the *Merrimack* afforded her crew anything but a "good time." As Ramsay wrote:

> Steam was kept up continually. Our cabins were without air ports and no ray of light even penetrated the ward-rooms. There was nowhere to walk but on the upper grating—a modern prison is far more comfortable. Sometimes the sailors waded on the submerged deck, giving rise to the superstition among the darkies that they were the crew of the 'debble ship' with power to walk on the water.

C.S. *Merrimack*—the "Big Thing," as nicknamed by her opponents—had a new commander, old Josiah Tattnall, veteran of the War of 1812, over six feet tall, austerely striking in appearance, and, according to his chief engineer, "with florid complexion, deep-sunken blue eyes, and a protruding under lip." Jones, like Greene, had to face the fact that he was evidently not thought to be the best man to command the ship for which he was "exec." And, also like Greene, he had to live with his lack of victory over the enemy.

Commodore Tattnall, as all of his officers appreciated, was "burning to distinguish himself," but as with Jeffers on the *Monitor,* he was under orders not to risk destruction of the *Merrimack* or—worse yet—its capture. This would leave General Huger's division and Norfolk itself at the mercy of the Northern Blockading Squadron. Huger, for that matter, had already expressed grave concern over how long "the advantage" would remain with the Confederate Navy.

Nonetheless, he pleaded with Mallory "to pass the forts and strike elsewhere"—although not specifying exactly where.

On April 8 he issued a general order, aimed at the destruction of the *Monitor,* the "black Yankee cheese box on a raft," according to the Norfolk *Day Book:*

> It is supposed that in my conference with the commanders of vessels on the 6th instant the plan of boarding the *Monitor* with the four smaller steamers was well understood; but, to prevent the possibility of mistake, this general order on the subject is issued. The *Monitor*'s weak points are the smokestack, the ventilators, the pilot house, and the joint or opening between the revolving tower and the deck. She is also exposed through her openings to the action of inflammable materials.
>
> By stopping the smokestack with wet blankets or sail cloths or other suitable material, it is probable that the smoke and gas will drive the crew from below and out of the tower.
>
> A sail, or cloth of any kind, thrown over the pilot house will blind the pilot and render the helm useless.
>
> Wedges driven between the tower and deck will stop its revolving.
>
> To effect these ends, the captains of the vessels will supply themselves with the necessary material and will have officers and men selected for the performance of each particular duty. That is, a gang to cover smokestack, one to stop ventilators, one to cover tower, one to cover pilot house, a small one with bottles of turpentine and matches, and one with hammers and wedges.

The steamers *Patrick Henry*, *Jamestown*, *Beaufort*, and *Raleigh*, in the immediate command of Captain Tucker, will take a position as Captain Tucker may deem proper, considering the character of these vessels, while the *Virginia* engages the *Monitor*, and Captain Tucker with said steamers will hold himself in readiness to close and board the *Monitor* on signal for "close action" from the flagship. Until such signal is made Captain Tucker is to exercise his own judgment in regard to the four steamers, and he may, if he sees fit, board before the signal.

The mode of securing the vessels alongside the *Monitor* and the general details are left to the commanders of vessels.

Such an attempt, according to Jim Byers, was made on April 11. His tug was one of two (he himself had refused to go along) accompanying the *Merrimack*, manned by thirty "commando" type volunteers on each, "provided with iron wedges and top mauls" (heavy hammers, often with wooden heads). Byers added:

"The plan was to board her, a tug on each side landing the men, and throwing lighted tar balls down through the ventilators and wedge up the turret so it would not revolve."

As it turned out the *Monitor* was an elusive prize. Tattnall had to be content with prey of far lesser caliber than the Ericsson battery.

Two brigs and a schooner, only one with cargo (hay), were captured by the *Jamestown* without interference by the *Monitor*. While it made the blood of Keeler and others on board "boil," Jeffers was merely carrying out orders.

Some would report that the *Merrimack* fired one taunting shot before retiring.

However, the *Monitor* was now supported by a small (192-ton) one-gun ironclad, *Naugatuck*, and the liner *Vanderbilt*, donated by her namesake owner. The latter, with her bow shored up, was in the Roads for only one purpose—to cut the *Merrimack* in two. Considering her great size and speed of almost fifteen knots, she probably possessed the ability to do just that. But she needed a propitious moment and depth of water, and more aggressive spirit on the part of her merchant crew.

The day ended in complete frustration for those on both sides who had been spoiling for a return match.

According to Stimers, nonetheless, in a letter to Fox, the top command of the *Merrimack* was not nearly so anxious for an engagement with the *Monitor* as her other officers indicated:

". . . we had every reason to suppose nearly all day of the 11th that this whole question of the *Monitor* would be settled but a boat's crew from the Frenchman [probably still the *Gassendi*] in talking with our people on the wharf yesterday say that the commander of the *Merrimack* said that we had four vessels below here fitted as rams and that he was not coming down here to get punched—the battle must be fought up there."

A few nights later the *Merrimack* was on her way to Chesapeake Bay possibly to follow up a suggestion of General Lee to attack Federal transports in the York River. Then signal lanterns at Sewell's Point ordered her to return. According to Ramsay:

"Tattnall hesitated. He was of half a mind to disobey. 'Old Huger has outwitted me,' he muttered. 'Do what you [Lieutenant Jones] please. I'm going to bed.' And he went below in high dudgeon."

It was just as well for Tattnall, since the engines were behaving erratically.

On the twenty-seventh a Lieutenant O. C. Badger, aboard the U.S.S. *Anacostia,* on the Rappahonnock, wrote Lieutenant H. A. Wise, of the navy's Ordnance Bureau, with proposals similar to Tattnall's:

> It has occurred to me, from the movements of the *Merrimack* on her last visit to Hampton Roads, and from other reasons, that the enemy has some plan to draw the *Monitor* out from under the guns of the fortress, in order to capture her by boarding and towing her up Elizabeth River by her [the *Merrimack*'s] superior power or momentum.
>
> Suppose half a dozen men were to spring on the *Monitor*'s decks provided with grapnels and chains, and make them fast, just after her two guns had been fired; undoubtedly she could be towed off and they could not help themselves.
>
> It seems to me that it would not be difficult for them to provide a few men with armor to perform this duty, and with comparative safety, since only musketry could be used against them.
>
> In such an event it strikes me that the "liquid fire" with which you witnessed an experiment four or five months ago at the navy yard, Washington, would be a good thing to drive them off with. The pipe or a hose thrown out of the small holes in the "dome," or out of the pilot house, would, I think clear the decks sooner than the heaviest discharge of musketry that could possibly be brought to bear.

The "liquid fire" was probably the age-old "Greek fire" or phosphorus. The *Monitor,* in fact, had already received fifty "incendiary" shells, with the stated capacity of being able to burn for thirty minutes without being extinguished. Captain Jeffers, according to Keeler, was quite indignant at the whole proposition; as the paymaster reported, "He didn't object to killing all he could in the old fashioned way but this stewing, frying and burning human beings seemed to him rather barbarous. . . ."

On Sunday, May 4, Yorktown was evacuated. On the same day, Greene wrote a chatty letter to his father, George S. Greene, recently appointed a brigadier general of volunteers. His older brother George, Jr., and his wife, Susie, had been recent visitors to Fort Monroe and the *Monitor,* which had understandably become a "tourist" attraction of consuming interest. McClellan, he had heard, was pursuing the Confederates in "hot haste," though he admitted he possessed no information which was wholly "reliable." Dana continued:

"The *Merrimac* made her appearance this afternoon, but did not venture below Crany [*sic*] island. She was apparently on a pleasure trip, as we thought we could discover several ladies on board with our glasses. We expect her down every pleasant day, but she appears to have a wholsome [*sic*] fear of us.

"We remain just the same as when you were here; our pilot house has been completed and now we think our craft invulnerable at every point. . . . Capt. Worden is able to see from both of his eyes, and will probably be able to leave for New York in a week . . . Capt. Fox, Asst. Sect. of the Navy, visited us today with several people from Washington."

Events were accelerating faster than Dana Greene had any reason to appreciate. Goldsborough, for example, was writing Fox, back in the Navy Department, that deserters had informed him of "a regular stampede on board the *Merrimac*—every officer having left her. This however, after all, may be a ruse. She has been lying for the last three days at the buoy off the Naval Hospital, with her steam up and at every high tide, night and day, I have been expecting a visit from her."

Washington became convinced that Norfolk was going to be evacuated. On the fifth, Monday, Lincoln, Secretary of War Stanton, and Secretary of the Treasury Chase embarked aboard the revenue cutter *Miami* for Fort Monroe on a unique expedition, concocted by the President and his war secretary. Welles, surprisingly, had not been invited. So confident was the group of success that Brigadier General Egbert L. Viele, a fiercely moustached New Yorker recently engaged in operations at Port Royal, was brought along to become Norfolk's military governor.

The President proved a poor sailor. In rainy weather and a smooth Potomac River and then bay chop, the comfortable vessel steamed south. While most of the party partook ravenously of an excellent shore dinner, Lincoln, as Chase would write to his daughter, Janet, "gave it up almost as soon as he began and, declaring himself too uncomfortable to eat, stretched himself at length upon the locker."

On the sixth, Tuesday, the presidential party landed at Fort Monroe. The same day Williamsburg was occupied after two days of fighting. The total casualties were approximately four thousand. It seemed that the Peninsular campaign was swinging into high gear, with McClellan well started on the road to Richmond. The Confederacy, of the same mind, commenced preparations to evacuate Norfolk.

Wednesday, the seventh, the *Monitor* was visited by the Commander in Chief. Keeler found him "sad, worn and anxious." However, stooping as he moved around the narrow, low confines of the unusual warship, Lincoln gave the paymaster the impression he was "well acquainted with all the mechanical details of our construction."

On Thursday, the eighth, Jim Byers successfully ran the batteries in his tug and docked at Fort Monroe with the intelligence that Norfolk was being evacuated. This was all Lincoln, his secretaries of war and treasury, and his military staff needed to know. They could catch the enemy off balance.

The newly arrived ironclad *Galena,* with escorts, was hastily ordered to shell batteries just above the mouth of the James while the *Monitor* and others were sent across the roads to bombard Sewell's Point. The *Galena* silenced two of the batteries in short order while the *Monitor,* by Goldsborough's report, shot away Sewell's flagstaff "twice" and fired some of the buildings. The Rip Raps' big guns joined in. It became a standoff when the "great rebel terror," as Chase called the *Merrimack,* appeared.

Goldsborough wrote to Fox (who himself thought of the enemy vessel as an "ugly customer"): "The *Merrimac* came out and had a fair chance to engage the *Monitor,* but she was extremely cautious, and took good care not to expose herself to even half a chance in the way of a dash by this ship and the merchant rams to run her down. After remaining outside of the point for comparatively a little while, she returned and anchored under Sewell's Point, and there she now lies."

On Friday morning, the ninth, a singular and historic reconnaissance expedition led by the secretary of the treasury, including General Wool and General Viele, crossed the mile or two from the Rip Raps to Willoughby's Point or the Ocean View area, west of Lynn Haven Roads and some seven miles north of Norfolk. Too close to both the Rip Raps and Fort Monroe, this ground had remained undefended.

As had been known for the past year, this was, Secretary Chase discovered, "a good and convenient landing place" to assault Norfolk overland. He returned to Monroe to talk up the plan to Lincoln and Stanton, who then steamed over on a tug to see for themselves.

They at once were infected by Chase's enthusiasm.

A sort of musical comedy invasion, with no further preparation, was agreed upon. The Baltimore steamer *Adelaide,* which had carried the news of the *Merrimack*'s March 8 rampage, was halted an hour before sailing, her passengers, baggage, and freight unceremoniously hustled off and troops marched double-time aboard.

By midnight, the *Adelaide* and other transports were side-wheeling heavily to Willoughby's Point carrying, by Wool's estimate, "less than 6,000 men." A bombardment from the deep, throaty guns on the Rip Raps commenced, aimed at Sewell's Point with the intent of leading the enemy to believe the landing would be *there.*

Federal ammunition could have been saved. Huger's troops were gone, largely by railroad, moving ultimately to the defense of Richmond which now seemed dangerously threatened. Debarking troops on Saturday, May 10, marched past abandoned defenses to accept the surrender of Norfolk. General Viele had a new job—the military governorship of the Norfolk area, just as planned.

On the *Merrimack,* panic prevailed. Huger had abruptly left Norfolk without passing the prearranged signal to the ironclad. In fact, the only hint that the troops were gone was the absence of the flag flying from the Gosport staff and of smoke curling from fires in most of the yard buildings. Steam was raised, coal and ballast heaved overboard to lighten the heavy ship in order to enable her to pass Harrison's Bar in the James as she steamed to the defense of Richmond.

By late evening, the word from the pilots—she wasn't light enough. An unfavorable wind which had been blowing "down stream" all day had undoubtedly kept water shallow over the bar.

Tattnall, "unwell," had lost heart. He would neither have a try at the bar nor sink with guns blazing in the midst of the now powerful Federal fleet. Suddenly, the flag officer was faced with a lonely quandary similar to that of old Commodore McCauley the previous spring.

The decision: the same. Scuttle.

Even as Gosport, now partly aflame, swarmed with Union soldiers and, across Hampton Roads, the *Monitor* prepared to lead an exultant squadron toward the Elizabeth River, in fact aiming for the *Merrimack*'s very anchorage buoy, Mallory's "experiment" moved through the night for Craney Island. Her ever-imperfect engines throbbed a discordant requiem.

Cotton waste and trains of powder were strewn about the deck. A "slow train" led to the magazine containing nearly eighteen tons of powder.

At anchor, off the little island, the ironclad was abandoned in slow ferry trips to the Portsmouth shore. There were only two boats available for the process, after which the men started afoot for Suffolk, some fifteen miles distant.

Jones, the "exec.," the last to leave, applied the match. Ramsay wrote:

"Still unconquered, we hauled down our drooping colors, their laurels all fresh and green, with mingled pride and grief, gave her to the flames and set the lambient fires roaring about the shotted guns."

Lieutenant Samuel Franklin, now aboard the *Dacotah,* whose arrival he had awaited in early March, was but one of many who watched this Confederate version of the *Congress* going to her spectacular doom. He would write:

> I was called at midnight, and it was reported to me that the *Merrimac* was on fire. I went immediately on deck, and there she was, all in flames. The Confederates had decided to abandon her, and, to prevent our getting possession, they wisely set her

on fire. It was a beautiful sight to us in more senses than one. She had been a thorn in our side for a long time, and we were glad to have her well out of the way. I remained on deck for the rest of the night watching her burning. Gradually the casemate grew hotter and hotter, until finally it became red-hot, so that we could distinctly mark its outlines, and remained in this condition for fully half an hour, when, with a tremendous explosion, the *Merrimack* went into the air and was seen no more.

In the dark fields and marshes, alive with frogs, along the way to Suffolk, Ramsay heard "that last and low sullen, mournful boom [that] told our people . . . their gallant ship was no more."

On the opposite shore, Josh Lewis pronounced his own sparse amen, "thus ended the *Merrimack*."

It was truly the end of the *Merrimack/Virginia*, after eight short weeks of operational life. But the implications went beyond the mere loss of one warship.

Not only was Commodore Maury's "little ewe lamb" strayed —forever—but as Secretary Mallory knew, the war, for the Confederate Navy, was already lost.

" . . . hope and hang on . . . !"

MOST IMPORTANT FROM THE COAST
OUR IRON-CLAD *MONITOR* FOUNDERED AT SEA

We stopped the press to announce that a dispatch has just been received here stating that the *Monitor* on her way South foundered at sea and went down in the vicinity of Hatteras! No particulars have yet been received. The natural supposition is that all on board perished.

—The *Evening Star*
Washington, January 3, 1863

Badly in need of overhaul after seven months of almost continuous operation, her bottom barnacled and fouled, the *Monitor* in tow of the tug *Rescue*, equally war-weary, hauled into the Washington Navy Yard on October 1. A warm autumn drizzle was falling onto the tar and cinders of the bustling naval station.

". . . everything is confusion and excitement," Keeler wrote. "The hill tops in all directions are crowded with fortifications and their sloping sides covered with the canvass [*sic*] cities of our soldiers."

To a great extent, however, these were hospital "cities"—cities of pain and misery. There was ample reason.

Since the commencement of the Peninsular campaign in early May, North and South had suffered a combined total of not less than 120,000 casualties in killed, wounded, and missing, divided almost equally between the combatants. Neither side, as 1862 commenced, had envisioned the acceleration of the fighting and its staggering potential for slaughter and maiming.

The "Seven Days," ending on July 1, which also marked the close of McClellan's ill-starred campaign for Richmond, had accounted for 16,000 Union and 20,000 Confederate casualties. From the *Monitor*, helping to cover McClellan's withdrawal, Keeler wrote his testament to the human backwash:

"A tall stalwart fellow stands exposed to the rain on the end of the dock moodily leaning on his musket as though he were bidding defiance to both the elements and enemies. Here a sick one lies stretched out on a cast away plank, not even a blanket to shelter him from the rain. Here one limps painfully along through the mud and water by the aid of an old branch, with a wounded foot from which he has discarded the shoe, the suffering member tied up in a bloody dirty rag, sinks deep in the mud at every step."

There was also the heat. Of their duty at Harrison's Landing, Acting Master Stodder would write, "It was hell, being 170° in the fireroom, and on the berth deck it was 95°."

While never questioning McClellan's bravery or loyalty, Lincoln nonetheless complained that Little Mac was afflicted with "the slows." But it was more than that. The youthful major general could not exploit his victories, such as that at Malvern Hill when he needlessly withdrew to Harrison's Landing, inspiring General Phil

Kearny to speculate on his "cowardice or treachery." Historians would quip that the Federal commander had snatched his army out of the jaws of victory.

Lee outthought McClellan and instilled in him an "out-numbered syndrome." While the Confederate leader never counted more than 80,000 troops, the Army of the Potomac's commander led as many as 150,000, "McClellan's bodyguard," as Lincoln would wryly observe. Little more than one half of that assemblage, however, was ever in the field or frontline at one time. Instead of boldly committing the forces at his disposal, he sent pleas to Stanton for more men, while inching cautiously forward or not advancing at all.

Despite the narrowness and shallowness of the James, Goldsborough's squadron had pushed to within ten miles of Richmond, almost in sight of its spires, a few days after the loss of the *Merrimack*—as if to show cautious Mac the way. But the vessels would go no farther, stopped by the batteries of Drewry's Bluff. The *Monitor* could not elevate her guns to reach the fortifications. The *Galena*'s armor proved worse than ineffective. She lost thirteen killed and eleven seriously wounded.

Well-known leaders were sacrificed that summer. General Mansfield fell at Antietam, the dashing goateed Phil Kearny on September 1 at Chantilly, Virginia. Colonel Ellet, the Federal engineer who had warned of the destructive potential of the *Merrimack,* lived only long enough to see his wonderful rams prove themselves upon the Mississippi. He died from wounds received during the successful bombardment of Memphis on June 6, resulting in the capture of the city.

The battle had been widespread. Neither adversary could take heart that the scales had been tipped in either's favor by the year's fighting. If McClellan had been forced to abandon his campaign and General John Pope overwhelmed by Lee and Jackson at Second Manassas, so too Lee's own attempt to invade Maryland was disastrously thrown back at Antietam, September 17, by McClellan. The 12,000 Federal and 14,000 Confederate casualties there had added up to the bloodiest day of the war. Although McClellan had failed to follow up the retreating Lee, the North's morale was given a boost and Lincoln had been emboldened to issue his Emancipation Proclamation freeing the slaves in the seceded states.

What was not generally apparent then, however, was a fact of

187

simple arithmetic. The North could swallow its losses and fight on. The South's lifeblood was in far shorter supply. Grant, however, understood this.

Against this background, as the combatants paused to regroup and nurse their wounded, the *Monitor* was thoroughly cleaned and repaired: engines, blowers, shaft, guns—everything. She was inevitably an object of great curiosity.

"They went through the ship," wrote Acting Master Stodder, "like a flock of magpies, prying loose as souvenirs anything removeable. When we came to clean up at night there was not a key, doorknob, escutcheon—there wasn't a thing that hadn't been carried away."

By early November, the *Monitor* was on her way again. She hove to in Hampton Roads on the tenth "amidst a salute," according to Frank Butts, who had joined the crew at the Navy Yard. Already regretting his voluntary choice of the *Monitor,* Butts, from Rhode Island, would "venture to say that my feet were not dry once in the whole time I was on board the *Monitor.* . . . I remembered what I had been taught in the service, that a man always got into a mess if he volunteered."

Yet, for the remainder of November and all of December life was uneventful on the ironclad and, in the estimation of some, even enjoyable. On Thanksgiving, for example, Keeler would write, "We have had a most delightful day."

In mid-December, word of a crushing Union defeat: Fredericksburg, on the thirteenth, more than 12,000 casualties, a blow which the new commander of the Army of the Potomac, Ambrose Burnside, could not long surmount. The cost to the Confederates led by the formidable team of Lee, Stonewall Jackson, James Longstreet, and Jeb Stuart was about half of their opponents' loss.

Such a setback in part inspired Washington to push its plans for the capture of Wilmington, North Carolina. A defeat, according to military truism, should be balanced by victory, even a minor one, at the earliest opportunity. And so, in furtherance of the Wilmington operation, the *Monitor,* in tow of the *Rhode Island,* sailed from Hampton Roads on December 29.

Even though the weather had continued to worsen and the *Monitor* was wallowing helplessly in the angry seas, it was still difficult to comprehend Bankhead's shout: "The *Monitor* is sinking!"

Yet, somewhere off Hatteras, this was happening.

Captain Bankhead next ordered the towline cut since the cable was making the *Monitor* even more unmanageable. In a great display of bravery, Louis Stodder crawled to the bow of the thrashing ship, drenched with waves, and "by repeated blows from the hatchet which I carried in my hand, cut the rope uniting the two vessels."

Bankhead would report that the *Monitor* "ran down close under the lee of the *Rhode Island* at times almost touching her. Water continued to gain upon the pumps and was now above the ash pits."

"Two boats reached us from the *Rhode Island,* when I ordered Lieutenant Greene to put as many men into them as they would safely carry. . . ."

Butts was "disgusted" at what he made out to be a "scramble" to go aboard the rescue craft.

At this point, the *Rhode Island,* struck by a broadside of wind, drifted down, stern first, on the *Monitor*'s starboard quarter. To Stodder, "it seemed certain that our iron edge would go through the big steamer's side and thus send us all to the bottom, but in the end the *Rhode Island* cleared our side in a hand's breadth . . . [and] was soon a safe distance to leeward."

All in all, according to Keeler, "it was a scene well calculated to appal the boldest heart. Mountains of water were rushing across our decks and foaming along our sides; the small boats were pitching and tossing about on them or crashing against our sides, mere playthings on the billows; the howling of the tempest, the roar and dash of waters, the hoarse orders through the speaking trumpets . . . and the whole scene lit up by the ghastly glare of the blue lights burning on our consort . . . a panorama of horror which time can never efface from my memory."

Keeler, nonetheless, was impelled by duty to go below once more to collect his various books and accounts. In water "nearly to my waist and swashing from side to side with the roll of the ship," he groped through "darkness that could be felt" into his room.

The conscientious paymaster had succeeded in making a bundle of his records when it belatedly occurred to him that it was so "large and utterly unmanageable a mass" that he couldn't possibly take it with him into a boat. Then he removed his watch, hanging on a nail in the bulkhead, placed it in his pocket, and, next, procured his safe keys with the intention of salvaging the government "greenbacks."

He located the safe, but it was wholly under water. Giving up his attempts, he returned topsides and onto the turret, the highest refuge above the seas.

About 11:30, Bankhead found the engines still working slowly, the pumps "in full play," but water gaining rapidly. "Sea very heavy and breaking entirely over the vessel, rendering it extremely hazardous to leave the turret . . . a bailing party had been previously organized not so much with any hope of diminishing the water but more as an occupation for the men.

"The engine being stopped, and no longer able to keep the vessel head to sea, she having fallen off into the trough and rolling so heavily as to render it impossible for boats to approach us, I ordered the anchor to be let go and all the chain given her, in hopes that it might bring her up."

There were members of the *Monitor*'s complement still too sick to move from their berths. Butts, sloshing through "water just above the soles of my shoes" in the wardroom, came upon the young third assistant engineer, Samuel Lewis, still in his bunk.

"Is there any hope?" he asked.

Butts, without much conviction, replied the obvious, "As long as there is life there is hope." At the same time, he recalled "an old saying among sailors . . . 'hope and hang on when you are wrecked.' "

Moving nervously about the ship, he next started up the turret ladder only to be knocked off his feet, "and at the same time the steam broke from the boiler room, as the water had reached the fires, and for an instant I seemed to realize that we had gone down. Our fires were out and I heard them blowing the water out of the boilers."

The *Monitor* was now fully "dead" in the stormy seas, off Hatteras.

Butts decided that inside the stygian turret was better than outside. He assumed position there, "all alone" besides the two big eerie cannon, passing buckets to the men on top.

> . . . I took off my coat—one that I had received from home only a few days before—and rolling it up with my boots, drew the tompion from one of the guns, placed them inside, and replaced the tompion. A black cat was sitting on the breech of one of the guns, howling one of those hoarse and solemn tunes which no one can appreciate who is not filled with the supersti-

tions which I had been taught by the sailors who are always afraid to kill a cat.

He decided the safest place for the cat was inside the other gun —and he tucked and sealed her away as he had his coat. When he hoisted his next bucket up, there was none to grasp it. . . .

> By this time [Bankhead continued] finding the vessel filling rapidly and the deck on a level with the water, I ordered all the men left on board to leave the turret and endeavor to get into the two boats which were then approaching us. I think, at that time, there were about twenty-five or thirty men on board. The boats approached very cautiously, as the sea was breaking upon our now submerged deck with great violence, washing several men overboard, one of whom was afterwards picked up by the boats. I secured the painter of one of the boats (which by the use of its oars was prevented from striking the side) and made as many get into her as she would safely hold in the heavy sea that was running.

Stodder braved the blackness belowdecks to make one more search for crewmen. He found Engineer Lewis still bedded—"I told him the ship was sinking, and that he had better take his chances in the open. He refused, however, to do so and, not being strong enough to carry him, I had to leave him to his fate."

Keeler, hearing an order from Bankhead, "led the men to the boats," stripped down, and started from the turret to the deck. He found the ladder "full of men hesitating but desiring to make the perilous passage of the deck."

The paymaster, grasping a rope, started to slide down, only to be picked up by a wave and carried "ten or twelve yards from the vessel." Then another fortuitously hurled him back against the ship. He grabbed a stanchion "with all the energy of desperation. . . ."

Butts, leaving the turret, realized he was not really the last crewman aboard. He saw a boat "made fast on the weather quarter filled with men. Three others were standing on deck trying to get on board. One man was floating leeward, shouting in vain for help; another, who hurriedly passed me and jumped down from the turret, was swept off by a breaking wave and never rose."

Butts had an experience similar to Keeler's except that he managed to cling to a succession of lines, including at one time a funnel brace. Through the force of a wave he found himself "dangling in the air nearly at the top of the smoke stack." (It was a new, taller one, provided at the recent overhaul.) Tough, he still hung onto a rope as yet another wave hurled him from the ship:

"I thought I had nearly measured the depth of the ocean, when I felt the turn, and as my head rose above the water I was somewhat dazed from being so nearly drowned and spouted up, it seemed, more than a gallon of water. . . ."

Surgeon Grenville M. Weeks quoted Bankhead as exclaiming, "It is madness to remain here longer; let each man save himself!"

The captain believed that several of the crew, even in this extremis, might be aboard, including a few "still left upon and in the turret who either stupefied by fear or fearful of being washed overboard in the attempt to reach the boats would not come down." Nonetheless, he rationalized he had "done everything in my power to save the vessel and crew," and "jumped into" a "deeply laden boat."

He was certain the "heavy, sluggish motion" of the *Monitor* testified that "she could float but a short time longer."

Keeler, already in the boat, noted that its sides were crushed and thought that water was "rushing in streams" through the cracks. With the craft filled with so many persons and projected through the heavy seas, he wondered if they would ever reach the *Rhode Island.*

Butts, helped by a boathook, had struggled into this same last skiff to push away from the thrashing *Monitor.* In the confusion, Greene was shouting, "Is the captain on board?"

Soon, it was apparent that he was.

After what Butts described as "a fearful and dangerous passage over the frantic seas," the lifeboat reached the *Rhode Island.* A number of the exhausted survivors, including Keeler, had to be hoisted on deck by means of looped lines.

As rain and spindrift beat into their faces, the little group huddled on deck watching, as Stodder wrote, "the red and white lights that hung from the pennant staff above the turret of the *Monitor.*

"About one o'clock on the morning of Wednesday, December 31st, she sank and we saw her no more."

III
A SEA CHANGE

The Quick and the Dead

. . . by the slow thunder of the drums, the flare of dying cities, I have come to this dark place. And this is the true voyage, the good one, the best. I will now prepare my soul for the beginning hunt. I will plumb seas stranger than those haunted by the Albatross.

Thomas Wolfe
Look Homeward Angel

America in 1897 bore scant resemblance to the America of January 1, 1863. The forty-seven survivors of the *Monitor*, very few of whom still lived, would not have felt at home on any of its main streets with their electric trolleys, electric lights, pavements, and even an occasional gasoline-powered vehicle.

Open most any door on Main Street, and walk into a new world of electricity, telephones (half a million already), indoor plumbing, and perhaps central heating. To hurry up and simplify correspondence, typewriters were plentiful and relatively cheap.

To help daughter or junior learn the waltz, there was the Edison phonograph. For nostalgia in depth and, hopefully, in focus—several brands of cameras.

That year, on a mild October day, the eighteenth, the obituary of a distinguished naval officer shared page one prominence in the *Evening Star* of Washington with an article speculating on the possible annexation of Cuba. Rear Admiral John Lorimer Worden had died at the age of eighty of pneumonia at his residence, 1428 P Street, in the northwest section of the city.

The sea warrior had just begun to fight when he was hurt in his battle with the *Merrimack*. Two months after the sinking of the *Monitor*, he commanded her sister *Montauk* in an attack upon Fort McAllister, on the Ogeechee River, guarding Savannah. His ironclad, struck forty-six times, kept up the bombardment, which failed, however, to reduce the formidable defenses. Nonetheless, on February 28, Worden destroyed the privateer *Nashville* under the guns of the same fort.

From April 1863 until 1866, the then Captain Worden assisted in superintending the construction of *Monitor*-class ironclads, of which seventy-one would be ordered during the remainder of the century and fifty actually commissioned. They evolved into ocean-crossing double-turreted warships of six thousand tons, one hundred feet longer than the first *Monitor*, topped with a bridge, mast, and superstructure that easily heralded the battleship of the twentieth century.

In fact, "modern" battleships, or "armored cruisers," such as the *Oregon, Maine,* and *Olympia* of the Spanish-American War, were already knifing across the Atlantic and Pacific by Worden's last years.

The aging naval officer was superintendent of the Naval Academy and commander of the European Squadron before his retirement in

1886. His neighbors knew Admiral Worden as a kindly gentleman of exceptional modesty. Indeed, none would have been more surprised than he to know that President McKinley and most of his Cabinet attended his funeral at St. John's Episcopal Church across Lafayette Square from the White House. He was buried in the family plot in Pawling, New York.

There was no leader of the Lincoln Administration left to pay final respects to Admiral Worden. They were all gone—Secretary Stanton died in 1869, shortly after President Grant had appointed him to the U.S. Supreme Court; Seward, three years later; Secretary Chase in 1873; and Gideon Welles in 1878. General Grant passed on to his reward in 1885, McClellan the same year, and General Sherman in 1891.

John Ericsson survived until his eighty-sixth year, on March 8, 1889. "Give me rest," were quoted as the last words to his doctor, who had been treating him for a kidney ailment. But the imaginative Swede did not know the meaning of "rest," having almost to the end been working on torpedo designs, on solar energy and solar motors, formulas aimed at perpetual motion—indeed, to his very few intimates, his own body had proven the closest approximation to perpetual motion. He had confided in them:

"I propose to continue my work so long I can stand at a drawing board." And that he did—at 36 Beach Street.

Somewhat over a year later, his remains were moved for return, aboard the "armored cruiser" *Baltimore,* to Sweden, even though no immediate next of kin survived. A reporter wrote:

> The day selected for the departure was fair; the First and Second avenues were bathed in a flood of summer sunlight as the casket of the great inventor was brought from the vault of the little Marble cemetery and placed upon draped pedestals near the main gate. Across it lay the old banner of the *Monitor,* which together with the Swedish flag was encircled by a laurel wreath. The Swedish singing societies, two hundred strong, gathered about the bier and sang the sweet, sonorous battle prayer of Sweden, which constituted the only service. At its close the casket was placed in the hearse drawn by four splendid black horses, and the solemn procession moved through Second avenue to St. Mark's place, through Astor place to Broadway, thence to the Battery.
> An immense multitude of people were massed along the line

> of march, thronging the windows and roofs of the buildings, as
> well as the sidewalks, the colors of Sweden and our own red,
> white, and blue everywhere displayed at half-mast and a rever-
> ent silence one of the striking features of the imposing scene.
> The procession was an hour and a half in passing any given point
> . . . one carriage which preceded the platoon of police bore a
> model of the old *Monitor*. The strains of the Swedish national
> hymn, heard in the distance, announced to the waiting crowds
> at the Battery the approach of the funeral cortege. . . .

Admiral Worden himself had been among the mourners.

History had been kind to Worden and Ericsson. This was less so for
others. Commodore William N. Jeffers died in Washington in 1883.
While the short obituary recalled he had served as chief of the Bureau
of Ordnance, it was wholly overlooked that he had been commander
of the *Monitor* for several eventful months in the James River.

Three of the old *Monitor* crew stuck together for their next assignment: Greene, Keeler, and Bankhead, serving, respectively, as they
had on the lost ironclad, as executive officer, paymaster, and captain
of the blockader *Florida*. She was a comfortable, converted side-
wheeler that saw a modicum of action. Keeler was slightly wounded
twice. He became the recipient thereby of a pension of ten dollars a
month.

After the war, Keeler moved to Mayport, Florida, where he variously tended his orange grove, worked in a factory manufacturing
furniture and ironware, and wrote a chatty weekly column for the
Florida *Times Union* of Jacksonville. Not wanting to flaunt his war
background in the home ground of the Confederacy, Keeler signed his
column simply "Major" or "Silex."

An accident in the factory robbed him of his right eye, but did not
curtail his chronicles. Since "Dear Anna" was now with him, there
was no point in maintaining his erstwhile voluminous correspondence. So he kept a journal of his own life's anticlimax, replete with
terse comments and clippings about his old friends, and this and that.

The day after Thanksgiving, November 1885, Keeler entered,
"Sick—but little done." Anna and a daughter, Lizzie, took over his
journal for him. On February 27, 1886, Keeler died.

Then and only then did Anna and Lizzie release to the newspapers
the true identity of "Major Keeler."

One clipping in his journals, under a December date, 1884, was particularly sad. It recounted how Commander Samuel Dana Greene, then equipment officer of the Portsmouth (New Hampshire) Naval Base, had "in a state of high nervous excitement" entered a "ship house" there and blown out his brains.

To those who knew Dana, the surprise was leavened by their long-standing apprehensions. He had become something of a paranoid, feeling that his services on the *Monitor* had never been properly recognized and that, somehow, within the labyrinth of his mind and memory he could justify his not following up the battle as Worden *perhaps* would have, had he not been injured. Greene brooded so constantly that three years after the war, in 1868, the sympathetic Worden sat down to write a long letter to Gideon Welles, hoping, in some manner, to assuage Greene's hurt. It read in part:

> Recently learning that Lieut. Comdr. S. D. Greene, the executive officer of the *Monitor* in her conflict with the *Merrimack* in Hampton Roads on the 9th of March, 1862, has been annoyed by ungenerous allusions to the fact that no official record existed, at the Department, in relation to my opinion of his conduct on that occasion, I desire now to remedy a wrong, which I regret should so long have existed, and to do justice to that gallant and excellent officer, as well as to all the officers and crew of the *Monitor* who, without exception, did their duty so nobly in the remarkable encounter—by placing in the files of the Department the following report. . . .

Worden then penned the only account he ever wrote of the voyage from New York and of the engagement, finally explaining, "the fact that the battle with the *Merrimack* was not more decided and prompt was due to the want of knowledge of the endurance of the XI-inch Dahlgren guns with which the *Monitor* was armed and which had not been fully tested . . . had I been able to have used the 30 lb. charges which experience has since shown the guns capable of enduring, there is little doubt in my mind that the contest would have been shortened, the result more decided."

Greene, he summed up, ". . . handled the guns with great courage, coolness and skill and throughout the engagement . . . exhibited an earnest devotion to duty, unsurpassed in my experience, and for which I had the honor, in person, to recommend him to the Department and to the Board of Admirals. . . ."

But apparently it wasn't enough, not then or afterward.

Through importunings of Greene, and others of the *Monitor,* Worden, in 1874, petitioned Congress to appropriate $200,000 "prize money" for the crew, a reward for presumably saving the Federal fleet and eastern ports. Opposition arose from North and South. Survivors of the *Cumberland,* for example, asserted unequivocally that the damage that sloop wrought on the *Merrimack* caused the latter to be relatively ineffective the next day. And old *Merrimack* hands growled that not the *Monitor* but the Confederate ironclad's own many limitations kept her from "running amuck" in Hampton Roads and elsewhere. The matter went unresolved, though debated for a decade.

After 1885, no more was heard of *Monitor* prize money claims.

In 1864 Bankhead was sunk again—this time by a Confederate torpedo while commanding the gunboat *Otsego* in the Roanoke River. At war's end, in 1865, Commander Bankhead, as captain of the screw sloop *Wyoming,* was hunting, without success, for the raider *Shenandoah.* Since word of the surrender at Appomattox, on April 9, had not reached her Confederate captain, James Waddell, the big vessel continued throughout that spring to capture and burn New Bedford whalers in the remote and frosty Bering Straits.

Two years later, Bankhead fell ill in Aden, Arabia. He died—on April 27, 1867—en route home. At the age of forty-six, he had joined his sixteen shipmates he had abruptly left behind somewhere off Hatteras.

Others, too, did not long survive the war. Dahlgren, after various commands, including that of the Pacific Squadron, dropped dead of a heart attack in 1870 while back at his old post, commandant of the Washington Navy Yard. He had never ceased to mourn his twenty-one-year-old son, Ulric, cavalry colonel killed in Brigadier General Judson "Little Kil" Kilpatrick's daring cavalry attempt, in March 1864, to reach Libby and Belle Isle prisons in Richmond and thus rescue Union officer prisoners. Ulric had lost a leg at Gettysburg.

Since the eminent gun designer died during a blistering July heat spell, undertakers resorted to the unusual if macabre expedient of completely encasing his body in ice so that his many friends could view him one last time.

Dahlgren's associate, Gustavus Vasa Fox, left the navy to superin-

tend woolen mills in Lowell, Massachusetts, an earlier occupation.
He died on October 29, 1883—just two weeks prior to the then Rear
Admiral Trenchard's demise.

The corpulent Goldsborough, as if to demonstrate that excessive
avoirdupois did not necessarily add up to a shortened life-span,
slipped his anchor in 1877, at seventy-two years of age. He had
previously been commander of the European Squadron.

Paulding, staunch supporter of the *Monitor* and of Worden, made
yet another contribution to the war effort in July 1863. During the
draft riots in New York City, which claimed upwards of a thousand
lives, he ordered ships to stand by in the East and Hudson rivers, and
sent sailors ashore to reinforce hard-pressed police and militia. When,
at the age of eighty-two, he passed away at his home in Huntington,
Long Island (on October 20, 1878), his obituaries recalled that he was
the last survivor of MacDonough's long-ago victory in Lake Champlain in 1814.

Their specific adversaries in the Rebellion did not prevail past the
1870s.

Josiah Tattnall was court-martialed and exonerated for scuttling
the *Merrimack*. He could not understand why General Huger himself
wasn't on trial for evacuating Norfolk with little or no forewarning.
Now, unsure of his popularity in either the North or the South, the
aging commodore fled to Nova Scotia. In 1869 Tattnall, in failing
health, was pleasantly surprised when his native Savannah invited
him home to become the city's harbor inspector.

He lived only two more years, succumbing at seventy-six, on June
14, 1871. Following a city-wide funeral, dustily resplendent with the
old gray, already shrinking uniforms, the old sea fighter's remains
were interred among the moss-covered cyprus trees of the family
plantation, Bonaventure.

Catesby ap Jones did not sail away so peacefully. After the
Merrimack, he returned to Selma to supervise the ironworks that he, at
least partially, owned. There, among other things, were cast cannon
for the great ram *Tennessee*. Afterward, until 1869, this sometime
soldier of fortune hired out to Chile in her flash-in-the-pan war with
Spain.

But then the pages of the family Bible for this Virginia-born
(Clarke County) Alabaman became stuck, and to this day his descen-

dants don't particularly care to unglue them. He died on June 17, 1877, in Selma in what is obliquely described as "something like a duel."

Stephen Mallory, Gideon Welles's counterpart, was imprisoned for nearly a year after the war. Paroled, he returned to Florida in a frustrating quest to pick up the pieces of a life shattered by wrong decisions. He died in Pensacola on November 12, 1873.

Buchanan, too, was interned following Farragut's furious fight for Mobile Bay in August 1864. His formidable ironclad ram *Tennessee* fought off most of the Federal fleet and struck her colors only after she was rendered virtually as helpless as the *Congress* had been two years previously. The scrappy Buchanan was again wounded.

Exchanged for a Federal officer of similar rank, Buchanan returned to Maryland, becoming the president of Maryland Agricultural College, an antecedent of the University of Maryland. He soon, however, retired to his estate, "The Rest," where at long last he found his own rest, May 11, 1874.

In October of that same year, the Norfolk newspaper *Virginian* announced that salvage operations of the *Merrimack/Virginia,* which had been attempted sporadically since the end of the war, were being resumed. Baker and Company, which had raised her the first time, again held the contract. Timbers, iron plates, other bits and pieces of the old hull had already been fished up: In fact, a gold-handled cane was fashioned from the ironclad's oak and presented to Jefferson Davis even while he was languishing in his small cell at Fort Monroe.

Two years later, in late May 1876, the entire hull, blackened and shattered, was actually raised, with the aid of pontoons, and towed back to the old stone dry dock. The *Virginian* carried a long story, reporting in part:

"All day yesterday [May 30, 1876] the navy yard was crowded with parties curious to look at the remains of the once famous old vessel, and a good opportunity will now be offered for doing so while the hulk is in the dry dock."

Souvenirs, again many taking the form of canes, for which there was great demand especially throughout the East, were wrenched from her remaining metal and wood. Her bell presumably went to St. Paul's Catholic Church in Portsmouth, where it hung until the edifice was destroyed by fire in 1897.

Then commenced a mystery not fully resolved to this day. The

"*Merrimack* bell" subsequently was presented to the Norfolk Museum of Arts and Sciences after being snatched from a Baltimore foundry's melting crucible. (Recently the museum was renamed the Chrysler Museum.) However, on display at the Museum of the Confederacy in Richmond (once known as the White House of the Confederacy) is another bell claiming a *Merrimack* pedigree. Thus the question— which is authentic?

Perhaps both are, since a second C.S.S. *Virginia* was launched in 1863, then scuttled two years later in the James before the fall of Richmond. Local historians feel the bell at Norfolk is the authentic toller of changing watches from the original *Merrimack/Virginia.*

Her shaft and anchor also went to the Museum of the Confederacy on Capitol Hill. Her cranky engines, which had proven so loyal to the Union during her short career as the *Virginia,* vanished onto some foundry's scrap heap.

And so, the actors, their strident lines, and their "props" all were fading. Even in 1876 the face and preoccupations of America had changed so markedly that the entire War of the Rebellion became imbued with improbable overtones.

Some spanned generations. William Conant Church, the biographer of Ericsson, lived until a month following America's entry into World War I, in 1917. He fought with the Army of the Potomac in the abortive campaign for Richmond in 1862, advancing to lieutenant colonel in the Volunteer Army. Continuing his career as a writer and editor, he founded the *Army and Navy Journal* among other publications, and also established the National Rifle Association.

New names had appeared and as soon faded in the nation's newspaper columns during Tom Selfridge's long life, which was eventful as well. He was sunk on the gunboat *Cairo* the same year he lost the *Cumberland.* At the turn of the century he witnessed the coronation of Czar Nicholas II. Selfridge had lived through the advent of the dreadnought, the battle cruiser, the fast light cruiser and destroyer, submarine, even the aircraft carrier. He could read how they all clashed at Jutland in the world's mightiest naval engagement.

Farragut and Porter were long forgotten, and even George Dewey at Manila Bay, Robert Peary at the North Pole, or William Sims who took the doughboys "over there" were now the substance of young people's history books.

Tom Selfridge survived into an era of automobiles, high-speed trains, airplanes, dirigibles, radios, the corner drugstore—the jazz and flapper age and its many delineators, from F. Scott Fitzgerald to Gertrude Stein.

On February 4, 1924, the day after Woodrow Wilson died, Rear Admiral Thomas O. Selfridge, eighty-eight, in a house in Washington but a few blocks distant from that of the War President, took his own leave of a world that had become at once unfamiliar and, certainly, too fast for the courtly old man. Curiously, he had just penned the last pages of his memoirs.

But he wasn't the last surviving witness to the *Monitor-Merrimack* contest. Four years later, in May 1928, Bill Drake, the latter's crew member, passed on in the North Carolina Confederate Soldiers Home, Raleigh. The Raleigh *News and Observer* expressed the opinion that the old warrior was the "last survivor" of the famous battle at Hampton Roads.

Perhaps so. There is no record of the statement being challenged.

The two very elderly gentlemen, briefly pitted one against the other by the whimsy, or perversity, of fate, had survived into the electronic age. Its technology would one day make it possible to find the lost *Monitor*, whose particular course, or courses, had paralleled both of their lives.

Somewhere off Hatteras

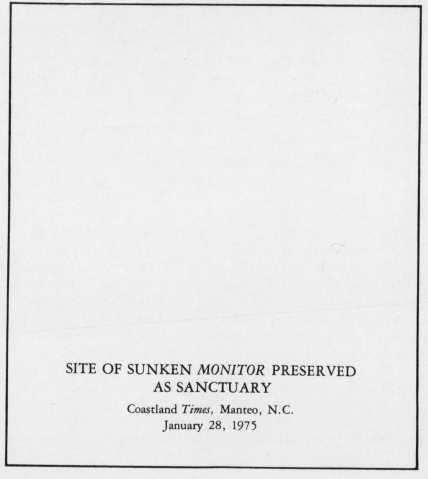

**SITE OF SUNKEN *MONITOR* PRESERVED
AS SANCTUARY**

Coastland *Times*, Manteo, N.C.
January 28, 1975

The *Monitor* was long at rest, as were the bones of those who perished with her that storm-tossed night. Yet the sailors had left clues behind them as to the whereabouts of their famous vessel, like artifacts from a lost civilization.

Captain Trenchard's quartermaster on the *Rhode Island* had logged at 1 P.M. that long-ago December 30:

"Cape Hatteras lighthouse bearing W.S.W. 14 miles distant."

Then, "at sunset . . . 17 miles S.E. of Cape Hatteras."

Again, "at 8:45 P.M. Cape Hatteras light bore N. ½ W. distant 20 miles"; and at 11 P.M., "when about 30 miles S.S.W. of Cape Hatteras."

Bankhead would later surmise for Navy Department questioners that the *Monitor* sank "about 25 miles south of Cape Hatteras." But considering the confusion of the night, Bankhead could scarcely have known where he was.

If the crew of the ironclad had found peace, this was in no way true of the inhospitable waters that had claimed U.S.S. *Monitor*. The bleak, gray-green reach of ocean shares doubtful honors with Sable Island, south of Nova Scotia, as a prime "graveyard" of the Atlantic. Off Hatteras, cold northerly currents collide with the warm Gulf Stream to produce a witch's brew of turbulent, often confused seas and weather.

Hydrographic charts admonish in laconic understatement, "Navigation in the area is extremely hazardous to all types of craft."

Diamond Shoals, a few miles east of Cape Hatteras, remains a mariner's nightmare, shifting so often and so markedly that the same maps warn, "Hydrography is not charted on Diamond Shoals due to the changeable nature of the area."

The backwash of two world wars added to the havoc of storms, shoals, and unlucky or inept navigation to leave a legacy of anywhere from two hundred to seven hundred wrecks which can be plotted "somewhere off Hatteras." This marine boneyard is littered with everything from trawlers and "pleasure" craft late of the Sunday fleet to torpedoed tankers and oceangoing vessels of similar size.

The variable in totaling these squadrons of the lost: Just *what* are the boundaries "off Hatteras"? A few, or hundreds, of square miles? Responsible navigators think of "Hatteras" as extending many miles north and south of the cape itself.

Only the boldest or most reckless sailor will tarry in these waters if he has no special purpose for doing so. Thus, it was not mere whim or happenstance that Hatteras Lighthouse, when built in 1798, of brick and stone, raised its warning beacon 191 feet above the surface to become among the tallest in the world.

That still did not seem sufficiently lofty, so the government built another one on the site in 1870 which was 208 feet high, but with a "focal height" only two feet above that of its predecessor. Captain Trenchard obviously saw the friendly yellow wink "distant 20 miles." The new structure throws a beam but four miles farther to sea, depending on visibility. Radar, loran, various electronic fixes have now become more important aids than lights.

However, in addition to being famous in its own right, Hatteras light, in the minds of a few, would become closely identified with the foundered *Monitor*. Navigators even in the last century could take Trenchard's final sightings, allow for drift, wind, and weather conditions, magnetic discrepancies, erroneous speed logging, and errors in sighting and come up with at least a five-by-fourteen-mile rectangle southeast of Cape Hatteras—that is, seventy square miles of ocean, or probably more, in which to find one small ship.

World War I witnessed dramatic advancements in deep-sea diving. Sturdy divers in their immense suits, lead-weighted boots, and breathing line "umbilicals" made headlines in the 1920s and 1930s by submarine rescue or salvage operations, most noteworthy that of the *Squalus* off Portsmouth, New Hampshire, in 1937.

Yet it took another world war for the blossoming of additional sciences essential to the location of underwater "mysteries." These principally were "MAD" (magnetic anomaly detection), improved sonar or marine sounding devices, and advanced underwater cameras and lighting equipment.

While skin divers would become almost as numerous as strong swimmers, the fearsome currents off Hatteras discouraged even the most daring. When a few skin divers did seek the *Monitor* in the 1950s, they did not venture into deep enough waters to find the old ironclad's resting place. Instead they found other wrecks, several times reporting objects awash at low tide resembling the distinctive turret.

An army corporal in 1955 swore that he spotted the wreck from a small airplane. Such reports served at least to keep interest warm. In the same year, for example, an entity in Dundee, Michigan, labeling itself the Monitor Historical Society, offered a reward of one thousand dollars for finding the ironclad.

But irrespective of individual courage or tenacity, none at that time seemed to appreciate the magnitude of the quest. No "loner," not even an adventurous team of skin divers, would ever locate the *Monitor*. Her quest was expedition-size, demanding a range of expertise, utilizing several sciences, and—as it would turn out—supported by the United States Government itself.

While there would ultimately be a marriage of such diverse elements, disagreement persists as to the genesis of the plan. It can, however, be stated that the National Science Foundation provided the technological muscle for making such a search possible, in that it funded the construction of the 117-foot research ship, *Eastward*, belonging to Duke University, Durham, North Carolina. This would be operated out of Beaufort, North Carolina, on Bogue Sound and the Intracoastal Waterway, by the university's Marine Laboratory.

While an abiding interest in the *Monitor* was shared by many, two gentlemen in particular became unusually involved: John Newton, marine superintendent of the oceanographic program at Duke's ocean laboratory; and Dr. Harold Edgerton, MIT Institute Professor Emeritus, long active in photography and related fields, having pioneered in intense, high-speed strobe/flash lighting. His efforts have contributed to making indoor snapshots simpler for the general public and aerial navigation safer, with the use of strobe approach lights for airports. He has made many developments in underwater photography.

Dr. Edgerton's previous underwater archaeological expeditions off Greece made use of his cameras and "side-scan" sonar to provide silhouette tracings of underwater objects. He had concluded that modern expertise and equipment "should give us the means to find the *Monitor*," even though he had no proof that it was not buried in the sand or broken up and scattered.

He thought of John Newton, Civil War buff as well as oceanographer-cartographer-geologist. During his ten-year tenure at Duke, Newton had located many wrecks off the North Carolina coast. Specifically he had worked with Dorothy Nicholson, of the *National Geographic* research staff, on that magazine's map of known wrecks off Hatteras. Newton had also contributed to *An Oceanographic Atlas of the*

Carolina Continental Margin, published by the North Carolina Board of Science and Technology. It contains maps of wreck locations.

Thus, Newton had already established himself as a knowledgeable "wreck man." And it came as scant surprise to the senior MIT professor when Newton confessed to being long infected with *"Monitor* fever," regarding perhaps the greatest wreck of them all.

"We met," Edgerton recalled, "for the first time in January 1973, when I was on a side-scan sonar expedition out of San Juan, Puerto Rico. We struck it off immediately and began to plan for a serious search. He would organize a ship and crew. My job would be to bring a side-scan sonar and support equipment."

August of the same year was targeted as optimum with respect to sea and general weather conditions. The composition of the party took shape:

Gordon Watts, young underwater archaeologist with the Department of Cultural Resources, state of North Carolina.

Dr. Richard Sheridan, geologist at the University of Delaware.

Ed Jaeckel, of *Industrial Research* magazine, who lives in Ridgefield, Connecticut, friend of Edgerton's and deepsea diver who has explored many wrecks worldwide.

Fred Feyling, of Cambridge, another associate of Dr. Edgerton's and also adept at navigation and map reading. He owns a shipyard in St. Thomas, the Virgin Islands.

Fred Kelly, of Duke, chief of the oceanographic party.

Funds, if less than munificent, were forthcoming, including $27,160 from the National Science Foundation to support the *Eastward* operating costs, $10,750 from the *National Geographic* to John Newton and another grant to Edgerton.

While the *Monitor* hunt was indisputably foremost in the scientists' minds, the NSF specified that, tantalizing and glamorous as it might well be, it must constitute only a segment of the two valuable weeks allotted for underwater investigations. The other and scientifically more important portion would be devoted to examination of a "geologically interesting" ridge-and-swale (depression) feature twelve miles off Ocracoke Island. The latter is the site of an early settlement and lair of Blackbeard the pirate in the eighteenth century, some twelve miles south of Cape Hatteras and the windswept Outer Banks.

The modest expedition, supported by two small U.S. Army Reserve coastal craft, got under way in late August 1973, in calm seas and under clear, hot skies. These were conditions Captain Bankhead might have prayed for but never enjoyed. According to Sheridan, the operation appeared to go off "like clockwork."

Not all of the *Eastward*'s company, however, completely agreed with Sheridan's approving assessment. Dorothy Nicholson, one of two women aboard (the other being Cathie Newton, senior at Duke and daughter of John Newton) would wryly observe that "Murphy's Law" was proving its reliability—anything that could possibly go wrong did so. Newton himself would amplify:

> The search for wreck of U.S.S. *Monitor* commenced with great enthusiasm immediately following completion of the geological work, but it very rapidly became mired in technical problems. Buoys floated grandly for a period of minutes, then vanished beneath the sea, reception of the signals from the transponders of the precision navigation system was inexplicably nil and the identification of sonar and magnetometer targets was more difficult than had been anticipated. One by one, the problems were resolved, or bypassed to provide a smoothly functioning search system.

From the outset numerous sonar contacts disclosed an underwater potpourri from outcroppings of rocks to sunken ships. Sheridan would label only two of the contacts as "crisp," or significant with respect to the skeleton of the lost warship for which the scientists were on the prowl.

The sonar was backed up by something much more intricate and exact: transponders or electronic position "senders" of the Del Norte Navigation System—Trisponder/202A—which Dr. Edgerton attached to the top of Hatteras Lighthouse and also Diamond Shoals light tower.

"Without it," Jaeckel has said, "the project might have failed." The four-year-old Del Norte Technology, Inc., of Euless, Texas, had loaned the equipment.

According to Bob Wilson, associate director of the Duke University News Service, Newton, Watts, and Dorothy Nicholson "plotted the fixes on an 1857 Coast and Geodetic Survey chart of Cape Hatteras, then transferred the data to a current chart—No. 1109—by taking into account set and drift, plus time elements from historical records."

"It was Fred Feyling," recalls Edgerton, "who located our first target with the side-scan sonar during a midnight watch on August 23 . . . excitement was high.

"Unfortunately, several days of photography and television 'looking' convinced us that the round pilot house of the sunken fishing ship was not the *Monitor*'s turret."

This was the first of the two "crisp" contacts. It only substantiated what Sheridan also referred to, the sophisticated electronic aids notwithstanding, as the "incredible odds" against finding a 172-foot disintegrating wreck in an expanse of ocean.

The morale, Dorothy Nicholson recalls, was "pretty low." According to Ed Jaeckel, "Everyone was tired and very disappointed." Hopes had been raised unwarrantedly. The failure, by the estimate of those aboard the *Eastward,* was of scarcely less effect than that attending McClellan's Peninsular campaign. It assumed the aspects of a retreat.

However, with time and money running out, the research vessel continued to poke around the relatively shallow waters "somewhere off Hatteras." Four days later, the twenty-seventh, the *Eastward* was moving northward, at 3 A.M., across a glassy surface, slowly, following a depth contour of about two hundred feet.

Nicholson and Watts were on deck trying to "rethink," like detectives, the tangle of frustrating clues. Fred Kelly, whom Jaeckel described as "a super guy," was lolling against the railing, fishing for sea bass or anything else he could catch.

Inside a small cabin known as the electronics center or "wet lab," the sonar was tracing its peaks and valleys on the instrument's paper roll—much like an electrocardiagram. However, "Doc" Edgerton's wonderful, precision side-scan sonar was at the moment not fully functioning. This left the conventional "fish-finder"—a Raytheon depth finder—to continue the search for the foundered Civil War gunboat.

Fred Kelly decided it was time to eat or at least have some coffee. He went below to stow his gear, glancing at the depth finder as he did so. The operator had "apparently" fallen asleep, something not surprising considering the tedium of the duty, and the hour.

Kelly paused, looked again at an "enormous spike," or peak, on the finder's tracings. The characteristic wavy line indicated some fifteen feet above the sea floor and "about the right length."

He called the bridge and ordered the vessel put about—which was like a general quarters in its effect of awakening all who were asleep and sending most everyone on board, not excluding the cooks, jamming into the little room or the adjoining passageway.

Somehow, in spite of the profound disappointment of four days before, there seemed to be an exhilaration and a sudden realization, without a shred of confirmation beyond the "enormous spike," that a great historic and emotional moment was at hand.

None would be positive as to the first remarks, although Jaeckel remembers "a lot of shouting." Most, however, recalled Kelly saying something, after notifying the bridge.

It was the word "Target!" according to Edgerton, while Newton quoted him as saying, "Hey, that looks like something!"

Dorothy Nicholson recalls the "intense excitement" as the ship swung completely around, 180°.

The depth, 220 feet, and the distance—about fifteen miles from Diamond Shoals Light—were about correct if indeed the *Eastward* was actually above the *Monitor*. Edgerton, with only a few hours' sleep, would write:

"Next came the camera. The pictures on the first roll [at once developed in the 'wet lab'] showed promise. So we sent the camera down again. But on the last exposure the camera became entwined in the wreck. It would not come up. A surge of the ship caused the steel cable to break; the camera, strobe and a pinger were left in the wreck."

Again, Murphy's law seemed to be working.

A buoy was dropped at what was now tagged "Wreck Site No. 2." Next, a television camera was lowered. Newton would write:

"There on the black sand seafloor at a depth of 220 feet the camera's light illuminated a flattened hulk that in numerous features fit *Monitor*'s description. . . ."

Dorothy Nicholson observed, "Look at that flat surface—iron plates with rivet holes!"

"Speculation continued," according to Ed Jaeckel, "about what portions of the *Monitor* we were seeing." He theorized that the *Eastward* must have "literally run right over the wreck."

Bob Wilson reported, "Anticipation aboard the *Eastward* rose to a palpable level" as the narrow armor belt and large circular structure came across the screen.

". . . shouts of excitement—There it is! There it is! That's it! —suddenly broke the tension."

Edgerton observed, "It's obviously not the paddle wheel of a steamer, and clearly not the gun tub of a modern warship. It has to be the turret of the *Monitor* . . . but it is underneath the ship, half covered. . . ."

Geologist Sheridan, perhaps the calmest person on board, appreciated the relative clarity of the image, since he knew the upside-down wreck had to be obscured and encrusted with calcium carbonate and even coral growth. Even so, like Newton, he was "convinced" that the "elusive" *Monitor*—more than 110 years after her final plunge—had been found.

"We were all fascinated," Jaeckel added, "by what we were seeing and I think we were struck by the historical significance of the moment. Many of us had spent years working toward it."

The Duke research ship kept being pulled away from the wreck by what Jaeckel described as "the vicious currents over it. One moment we would be looking at the *Monitor* on the video screen and the next moment the camera would be looking at the sea floor.

"We would try and try to maneuver the *Eastward* back over the wreck only to catch a glimpse of it and drift out of view. Sometimes two and three hours were lost in these efforts. It was maddening. But with the Del Norte we always knew we were close."

The wreck continued to be studied by television and the partially repaired side-scan sonar. The television sweeps tended to show the stern and midships section rather than the bow because of the particular mooring of the research vessel.

Yet, when the *Eastward* poked her nose back into Beaufort, the work had just begun. Had crew and passengers *really* seen the *Monitor?* As Gordon Watts would write:

Identification of the *Monitor* was a cumulative process. It required five months of comparing measurements of the wreck we found with descriptions of the ironclad . . . the configuration of the lower hull was unique even among the other classes of Civil War monitors. It was made with a flat bottom and sides that rose sharply up the underside of the armor belt at an angle of 36 degrees. Later monitors had a more conventional lower hull configuration.

The coal chutes of the *Monitor* were located slightly inboard of the armor belt . . . where our television pictures show them. The most famous feature . . . was its revolving turret. It is upside down on the ocean floor, and the hull of the ship is resting on it at an angle. The brass ring at the base of the turret coincides exactly with the specifications . . . the turret was 20 feet in diameter, with 8-inch thick armor. Our measurements match those of the original descriptions.

The location of the *Monitor* generally corresponds with the locations given by the ironclad's commander and that of the tow ship *Rhode Island* shortly after the sinking. Sonar records show the long axis of the hull is aligned southwest to northeast, with the bow to the southwest. Since the crew had released the anchor before the *Monitor* sank, this orientation is most logical considering the prevailing winds and surface currents at the time of the sinking.

The wreck is very fragile . . . rivets holding the iron plates together have deteriorated.

The winter passed. Not until March 7, 1974, did Duke University host a well-attended press conference to announce its discovery. At this time Newton proudly declared:

We are now prepared to say that we have found the *Monitor*. She lies under 220 feet of water, about 15 miles south of Cape Hatteras [at the head of what is known as Hatteras Submarine Canyon] . . . the shell-strewn sandy floor where the *Monitor* lies is beyond what we consider safe scuba-diving range, and the area is scoured by strong and treacherous currents. . . .

Even so, all concerned still wished to be more positive. The navy—quite a Johnny-come-lately considering its prize had been sunk since 1862—now was interested, enough so to locate eleven wrecks in the area through airborne magnetic detection equipment. Directly concerned were the Naval Research and Development Center, Annapolis; the Naval Research Laboratory, Washington; and the Naval Academy's "Project Cheesebox." Midshipmen under the enthusiastic leadership of Ensign E. M. "Ed" Miller had not only studied the history of the *Monitor* but painstakingly fashioned a scale model.

Yes, historically minded naval officers agreed, it was time to positively identify the good old *Monitor*. The department dug down and came up with a modest $50,000 to lease a unique aluminum-hulled exploration ship, the 1,700-ton *Alcoa Seaprobe,* operated by a subsidiary of the Aluminum Company of America. Featuring an oil-rig type derrick (in much the design of her far bigger sister, the CIA's *Glomar Explorer*), the *Seaprobe* is 243 feet long with cycloidal propellers fore and aft allowing her to hover in position over a "target."

She is a floating electronic-photographic laboratory with the most sophisticated sounding and viewing equipment known (the fittings of the *Glomar Explorer* not being a matter of record). The most remarkable feature is a rectangular "well" amidships through the hull from which grapples can recover 200-ton payloads from 6,000-foot depths, or bottom samples four miles deep. The object this time, however, was not to raise the *Monitor.*

Alcoa had made the *Seaprobe* "available," noting that the navy's check covered only operating expenses. Duke added another $20,000, the *National Geographic* (which, officially, does not publish its financial favors) further funds, with additional "backup support," in the words of Edgerton, from MIT and the Army Reserve. Ed Jaeckel believed the *Geographic* to be "the prime source of financial assistance."

The *Seaprobe* put out from Morehead City, North Carolina, on March 31, 1974. The very next day, April 1, and on the first pass, she "homed," according to Newton, "on the wreck with wondrous precision . . . the bones of the *Monitor* stood out in bold relief on the sonar."

Television and other cameras were lowered on the end of drill pipes above the old ironclad as pictures and videotapes were made from stem to stern. A sonar device, known as a "pinger," was placed in position thirty feet north of the wreck's center. The scientists didn't want to lose their precious find.

For nearly a week, in rough seas, the *Seaprobe* hovered obediently while thousands of single photographs were obtained—the tiny "crystals" that the Naval Photographic Laboratory would ultimately fashion into a photo-mosaic.

The next month the *Eastward* went to sea again to dredge up several dozen relatively small artifacts from the *Monitor:* iron plates, one with a bolt hole, a nut, and an encrusted "deck light" cover, much like a street's manhole cover. All are in a southern preservation laboratory, where the delicate operation is under way of restoring them as close to their original state as possible without their crumbling into metallic dust and splinters.

However, this continual teasing away at the wreck worried North Carolina's Governor James E. Holshouser, Jr., who nominated the *Monitor* tomb to be a ward of the U.S. Department of Commerce by terms of the Marine Protection Research and Sanctuaries Act of 1972. In turn, Commerce's NOAA (the National Oceanic and Atmospheric Administration) would assume jurisdiction.

On January 30, 1975, in Washington, Secretary of Commerce Frederick B. Dent formally took jurisdiction of the *Monitor,* saying "she was . . . bold, innovative and unique in her time. . . . to this day . . . has a mystique which is extremely real to millions of Americans."

ACKNOWLEDGMENTS

> . . . from the decks and rigging of the vessels, from case-
> mate and parapet of the fort, from the adjacent camp, from the
> beleaguered post at Newport News and the poor remnants of the
> crews of the *Congress* and *Cumberland* let one loud, prolonged
> triumphant cry of victory and joy ring out . . . !

So wrote James Stephens, of the 20th Indiana; at the conclusion of
the great battle at Hampton Roads. Though living memory is mute,
eyewitness testimony in all its dimension, immediacy, and inherent
excitement has been preserved through the written or printed word.
For this treasure the author is indebted to many sources—and in the
particular instance of James Stephens, to Tom Rumer, of the Indiana
Historical Society Library, Indianapolis, Indiana.

From the same source came the correspondence or recollections of
Amos Ireland, J. M. Doubleday, and Francis A. Osbourn, all
Hoosiers stationed on the shores of Hampton Roads.

The Erasmus Gilbreath and Joshua Lewis manuscripts belong to
the companion Indiana Division of the Indiana State Library.

As always, risking the grave offense of inadvertently omitting a
helpful source, the author wishes as well to say "thank you" to these
other libraries, societies, universities, associations, etc.:

To Mattie Russell and David W. Brown, of the William R.
Perkins Library, Duke University, Durham, North Carolina, an
exceptionally fine library which has measurably assisted the author to
re-create segments of the past for previous books. This time they
kindly made available the papers of Alexander M. McPheeters (including the Henry Ghiselin correspondence), of Jackson Ward, and of
Thomas Baxter (including J. H. Dawson).

Among newspaper clippings on file in this library was that, princi-

215

pally of the William F. Drake obituary, in the Raleigh *News and Observer* of May 1928, describing in some detail his brief career on the *Merrimack.*

To Kathryn E. Kresge, of the Casemate Museum, Fort Monroe, for much general information and photographs, in particular the "John" letter, believed to be that of Acting Master John J. N. Webber, of the *Monitor.* There are maps, photographs, and models faithfully re-creating the Civil War days at this famous fort, together with a cell furnished as it was when Jefferson Davis was prisoner.

To John Lochhead, Librarian of the Mariners Museum, Newport News, who, once again, unlocked his treasure house of maritime history to offer gracious and unstinting aid. In this he was aided by his "colleague without portfolio," as it were, Alexander Crosby Brown, former book/literary editor of the Newport News *Press Herald,* and well-known author on naval and marine affairs and authority on Tidewater Virginia.

The files of letters, manuscripts, diaries, and clippings plus books and periodicals made available at the library of this splendid museum are almost too vast to list. Many are reflected elsewhere in the acknowledgments. However, specifically cited should be: Franklin Buchanan letter, dated March 27, 1862; Louis Goldsborough letters, dated April 12, May 5, and May 12, 1862; Dana Greene letter to his father, May 4, 1862; John Worden letter to Welles concerning Greene and the battle, January 5, 1868.

Among the newspaper articles made available by Lochhead: November 11, 1959, Newport News *Times-Herald,* by-line James S. Avery, telling of the recovery of the *Cumberland*'s anchors and chain in November 1909; Norfolk *Virginian-Pilot,* March 6, 1966, by-line George H. Tucker, recounting in detail the raising of the *Merrimack;* Newport News *Daily Press,* March 7, 1965, by-line Alexander C. Brown, report on the Hampton Roads battle.

To Ellen Neal, Southern Historical Collection, University of North Carolina Library, Chapel Hill, Buchanan papers, James B. Jones letter, et al., part of the John B. Massenberg collection.

To Elizabeth C. Fake, Alderman Library, University of Virginia, custodian in particular of the correspondence of the diehard Confederate officer Charles Phelps.

To T. J. Dunnings, Jr., New York Historical Society, Alban Stimers and John Ericsson letters, diaries, sketches, etc.

To Anthony M. Cucchiara, Long Island Historical Society, for background information on Greenpoint, Brooklyn, in the last century, and the Rowland shipyard.

To William M. E. Rachal, Virginia Historical Society, for general information on the *Merrimack* and Norfolk and on Buchanan and Tattnall, in particular.

To Alice Hanes, Portsmouth Naval Shipyard Museum, photos and general "leads."

To Margaret Cook, Curator of Manuscripts, College of William and Mary, Williamsburg, Virginia, the Colonel and Mrs. William Lamb Diaries, and other information on old Norfolk.

To Marcia Le Franc, of the Rhode Island Historical Society, Providence, Rhode Island, for the Francis B. Butts reminiscences of the *Monitor*. They are to be found in various forms in several publications, primarily that read before the Rhode Island Soldiers and Sailors Historical Society, in 1890. His account is also to be found at the Mariners Museum and the Library of Congress.

To Robert Krauskopf, Director, Navy and Old Army Department of the National Archives, for logs of the *Monitor, Minnesota, Roanoke,* and *Rhode Island.*

To the Manuscript Division of the Library of Congress for the papers of Louis Goldsborough, John Ericsson, and Matthew Fontaine Maury.

To Mrs. Charles A. Potter, Librarian, Essex Institute, Salem, Massachusetts.

To William R. Emerson, of the Franklin D. Roosevelt Library, Hyde Park, for information on *Monitor* paintings.

To these libraries, especially for their old-date books and magazines: District of Columbia Public Library, the Library of Congress, Army Library (Department of Defense), Montgomery County (Maryland) Public Libraries, and New York Public Library.

To Janet Susa, Charles Scribner's Sons, for permission to quote from Thomas Wolfe, from *Look Homeward Angel* (New York: Scribner's, 1929).

> U.S.S.*Monitor* was truly the forerunner of a new era in naval warfare . . . rarely if ever has a single ship so captured the imagination of the people. . . .

Speaking was Vice-Admiral Edwin B. Hooper, Director of Naval History. He is among the very many persons, not already acknowledged, who aided the author in this book preparation. Since generally the author finds it impossible to group these generous individuals in the order and degree of their helpfulness, he is compelled to rely on that familiar "alphabetical order."

Yet, since every rule or otherwise robust intention is invariably accompanied by an exception, the author, first, wishes to pay respects to the "founding father" of this study, Dennis Fawcett, Senior Editor, Trade Books, Prentice-Hall, whose idea it was in the first place.

Too, the author desires again to acknowledge the tireless efforts of Alec Brown, of Newport News. In the already sweltering heat of early summer, Alec made every effort to show the author not only the theater of naval operations in the Newport News–Norfolk area, but the yet broader staging for the old armies. As well, he has continued to answer, via the Postal Service or vis-à-vis, the author's many questions, the majority of which might well have seemed quite elementary to an expert.

For yet another exception the author says thanks to his wife, Mary, who, in spite of no special devotion to things martial, patiently proofread, edited, counseled, and sometimes typed—to say nothing of listening to a typewriter during what sane people label as outrageous hours.

To continue, he expresses appreciation to Mrs. Whitney (Gurney) Ashbridge, of Chevy Chase, Maryland, descendant of Hiram Paulding; to Clay Blair, Jr., of Miami, Florida, author, presently challenger of the JFK naval "mystique" in World War II, and who tried vigorously to locate the *Monitor* in the 1950s; Windsor Booth, Chief, News Service for the *National Geographic;* William J. Brennan, with NOAA, U.S. Department of Commerce; Dr. Ford Keeler Brown, of Annapolis, a descendant of Paymaster Keeler; Robert A. Carlisle, head of the Still Photos Branch, Office of Information, Department of the Navy; Edward L. Dischner, ALCOA Marine Corporation, in Washington, and John E. Wright, Supervisor, Marketing Communication, in Pittsburgh (Ed Dischner gave much of his time in presenting slides and motion pictures resulting from the *Seaprobe*'s quest and generally discussing the technical aspects of this second expedition); Dr. Harold E. Edgerton, Department of Electrical Engineering, MIT, whose assistance included permission to quote from his article in *Technology Review* (of MIT) of February 1975; Commander James Finkelstein, of the Office of Information, Department of the Navy, and his colleague, Anna C. Urband, who has proven a crutch to the author in researching other books involving the sea and ships; Booton Herndon, of Charlottesville, Virginia, author of many books and invariably a clearinghouse of leads for his colleagues baying on fresh scents; Mary Huie, of Augusta, Georgia, who did most of the "clean" typing; Tim "Tiny" Hutton, history-minded staffer with Congressman Thomas N. Downing, of Virginia; Ed Jaeckel, of Ridgefield, Connecticut, on the staff of the magazine *Industrial Research* and a member of the *Monitor* locating expedition; Mary Johrde, head of the Office for Oceanographic Facilities and Support, National Science Foundation; Catesby P. Jones, Alexandria, Virginia; Virgil Carrington "Pat" Jones, of Manassas, Virginia, whose *Civil War at Sea* is a Bible for those thrashing about in imperfectly charted rebellious seas.

Lieutenant Commander Thomas W. Kuhn, CHC (USN) Chaplains Division, Bureau of Naval Personnel, Department of the Navy, who confirmed that Chaplain Lenhart, aboard the *Cumberland*, won the dubious distinction of being "the first naval chaplain to lose his life in the service of his country";

Alexandra Lee Levin, of Baltimore, author of *The Szolds of Lombard Street* and chronicler of the Lee family. She supplied information on Admiral Sam Lee, who remained faithful to the Union; Diane S. Liebman, Information Office, Association of American Railroads, Washington; Lieutenant Commander Arnold S. Lott, USN (ret.) Editor, Books, Naval Institute Press, who kindly granted permission to quote from the Keeler letters as edited by the late Professor Robert W. Daly, of the U.S. Naval Academy;

Robert F. Marx, of Satellite Beach, Florida, diver, who sought the *Monitor;* Ensign Ed Miller, who, along with John Newton, Robert Sheridan, and Gordon Watts has already been introduced; Dorothy Nicholson, of the *National Geographic,* who, too, has spoken from these pages, but nonetheless must be thanked again for her special help, friendliness, and encouragement in aiding the author;

Lieutenant Thomas J. Nixon, III, of Elizabeth City, North Carolina, a survivor of the U.S.S. *Lexington* in World War II, who ably assisted the author in an earlier work, *The Lexington Goes Down,* and again reached for his literary cap, magnifying glass, and pipe to Sherlock another quest;

M. J. O'Leary, Manager, Public Relations, Western Electric

Acknowledgments

Company, New York, longtime friend of the author, who, like Nixon, did his own gumshoeing, on his part, to open doors to the Greenpoint of more than one hundred years back; Rear Admiral Schuyler N. Pyne, USN (ret.), of Annapolis, a descendant of John Pyne Bankhead, forced, by circumstance, to leave the *Monitor* abruptly, and who noted in passing that not all of his ancestors lived by the sword or cannon ("Many members of my family on the Pyne side were clergymen of the Anglican Church in England and the Episcopal Church here");

Joseph E. Suppiger, Curator, Lincoln-Civil War Collection, Lincoln Memorial University, Harrogate, Tennessee; Frank Uhlig, U.S. Naval Institute, Annapolis; Henry Vadney, Assistant Head, Curator Branch, Office of Naval History and, as well, from the same office of the Department of the Navy: Dean Allard, Head, Operational Archives Branch, William "Bert" Greenwood, Librarian, Frederick Meigs, Assistant Librarian, and Charles "Chuck" Haberlein, photo section;

Ed Weems, historian, of Waco, Texas; Bob Wilson, of the Duke University News Service who, while quoted earlier, still deserves continuing thanks from the author for his patience and his readiness to field questions and, in general, for being a morale booster during moments of confused seas; and last, but certainly not least "Mrs. Greenleaf," from Kent City, Michigan, who tore out "a few pages . . . from my old high school history book" to further the author's travails on the *Monitor*.

There are certainly others, whose names unhappily are misplaced.

BIBLIOGRAPHY

> Taken as a whole, the winter was not very unpleasant. It was
> very cold sometimes, and we had no fires, as we were liable to go
> to quarters and open the magazine at any moment . . . we
> drilled and kept watch and ate our meals with great
> regularity. . . .

Dr. Edward S. Shippen's memories of life on the *Congress* were
published in *Lippincotts Magazine,* February 1878, in the *Century,*
August 1885, and in book form in 1879 (*Thirty Years at Sea*
[Philadelphia: Lippincott Co.]). Certainly, shipboard duty was far
preferable to that ashore, where Corporal Ranson wrote that "water in
the Horse Stable is up to their knees." Ranson's bleak testimony
appeared in *Hobbies—The Magazine for Collectors* in September 1959.

It is not, however, within the intent or even the capability of the
author to list every reference source—magazine, book, newspaper,
etc. Such a labor of love has been prepared by David R. Smith, "The
Monitor and the *Merrimac,* a Bibliography," published by the
UCLA Library Occasional Papers, # 15, Los Angeles, 1968, which
contains, as well, citations of government documents and unpub-
lished articles and manuscripts.

These are selected source periodicals:

Bulletin of the University of North Carolina, 1926, "The
 Merrimack and the *Monitor,*" by Benjamin Sloan.
Century, March 1890, an article concerning the turret of the
 Monitor.
Confederate Military History, Vol. 12 (Atlanta: Confederate Pub-
 lishing Co., 1899), William H. Parker and other accounts.
Everybody's, December 1900, article by Louis N. Stodder.

Harper's Weekly, many articles, especially in the 1861–63 period. In the April 20, 1912, issue, the writer speculated in "The Grave of the *Monitor*" that the ironclad was lying "some 50 miles southeast of Cape Hatteras Light." While more or less on course, the guess put the wreck more than three times too distant.

Magazine of American History, January 1881, "John Ericsson, the Builder of the *Monitor,*" and, same magazine, January 1885, another article on the ironclad by Francis Wheeler.

Marine Technology Society Journal, December 1974, "Finding the Ironclad *Monitor,*" by Bob Wilson.

Mount Pleasant Citizens Association, Washington, D.C., "The First Battle of the Iron Clads," a paper read before it, October 1923, by William E. Rogers, printed the same year by the Hayworth Printing Co., of the same city.

National Geographic, January 1975, "How We Found the *Monitor,*" by John G. Newton.

New England Magazine, February 1899, article concerning Seaman Curtis, of *Congress.*

Newport News Historical Committee, 1969, "Endless Harbor, the Story of Newport News," by Parke Rouse, Jr., published by the City of Newport News, Virginia.

North American Review, October 1889, Charles W. MacCord's recollections of building the *Monitor.*

Outing, August 1889, recollections of R. F. Coffin, of tug *Mystic.*

The Quaker, April 1889, recollections of an unidentified crewman aboard the *Congress.*

Revue Maritime et Coloniale, Paris, April 1862, account of Ange Simon Gautier, aboard the *Gassendi.*

Shipmate, January-February 1975, article on Rear Admiral John A. Dahlgren.

Southern Bivouac, March 1887, article by Surgeon Dinwiddie Phillips, of the *Merrimack.*

Southern Historical Society Papers, Vol. 16, 1888, quoting the Duke of Somerset, First Lord of the Admiralty on *Monitor,* "a sort of Calcutta Blackhole existence"; Vol. 20, 1892, recollections of Virginius Newton; Vol. 32, 1904, William R. Cline's report on the *Merrimack.*

U.S. Naval Institute *Proceedings,* many articles on the subject of the *Monitor,* which can easily be retrieved through the publication's own cumulative indexes. Dana Greene's account is published in 1923, Vol. 49.

Virginia Magazine of History and Biography, Vol. 73, 1965, "Notes on Life in Occupied Norfolk, 1862–63," by Lenoir Chambers.

While many newspapers were researched, the principal ones are mentioned in the text.

*Additional report of Chief Engineer Ramsay, C. S. Navy,
regarding the engines of the C. S. S. Virginia.*

Lieutenant JONES,
Executive Officer.
C. S. S. VIRGINIA,
[*April–, 1862.*]

SIR: The engines of this ship are not disconnected, and one can not be worked alone. As long as the vacuum of the forward engine holds good, the engines might be run by working the after engine high pressure, but as the vacuum of either engine is at all times precarious, and if the vacuum of the forward engine should fail, the engines would stop. Using one engine high pressure would also require a great deal of steam, which the boilers can not generate for any length of time.

The air-pump valves are now being overhauled, and unless there is something more serious than I now anticipate I hope to be ready by night.

Respectfully,
H. ASHTON RAMSAY.

This is but one of the literally hundreds of messages, dispatches, or reports pertaining to the *Monitor* and *Merrimack* to be found in the Official Records of the Confederate and Union Navies—principally in Series I, Vols. 6, 7, and 8, (Washington: U.S. Government Printing Office, 1897, 1898, 1899).

In these volumes are contained dispatches from all of the principals mentioned in this book, and a number of the secondaries, referenced for the most part in the text.

Other books:

Armbruster, Eugene L. *The Eastern District of Brooklyn.* Brooklyn: G. Quattlander, 1912.
Battles and Leaders of the Civil War. Edited by Robert Underwood and Clarence Clough Buel. New York: Century Co., 1887–88. (This basic reference source for the Civil War contains articles originally published in the *Century* magazine. Vol. 1 was principally used for this book, including accounts by Taylor Wood, R. E. Colston, Henry Reaney, John M. Brooke, Dana Greene, John Ericsson, Frank Butts, and others.

Bennett, Frank M. *The Monitor and the Navy Under Steam.* Boston: Houghton Mifflin, 1900.

Blair, Clay, Jr. *Diving for Pleasure and Treasure.* New York: World Publishing Co., 1960.

Browning, Orville Hickman, *Diary.* Edited by Theodore Calvin Pease and James G. Randall. Springfield, Ill.: Historical Society, 1925.

Cannon, Le Grand Bouton, *Personal Reminiscences of the War of the Rebellion.* New York: Burr Printing House, 1895.

Chesnut, Mary Boykin. *A Diary from Dixie.* New York: D. Appleton and Co., 1905.

Chittenden, Lucius. *Recollections of President Lincoln and His Administration.* New York: Harper & Brothers, 1901.

Church, William Conant. *The Life of John Ericcson.* New York: Charles Scribner's Sons, 1890.

Dahlgren, Madeleine Vinton. *Memoirs of John A. Dahlgren.* Boston: James R. Osgood Co., 1882.

Daly, Robert W. *How the* Merrimac *Won.* New York: Thomas Y. Crowell, 1957.

————, ed., *Aboard the USS* Florida, *1863-65.* Annapolis, Md.: U.S. Naval Institute, 1968. (The letters of Paymaster Keeler)

————, *Aboard the USS* Monitor, *1862; The Letters of Acting Paymaster William Frederick Keeler, U.S. Navy, to His Wife Anna.* Annapolis, Md.: U.S. Naval Institute, 1964.

Dew, C. B. *Ironmaker to the Confederacy.* New Haven: Yale University Press, 1966.

Dorr, Eben P. *A Brief Sketch of the First Monitor and Its Inventor.* Buffalo: Printing House of Matthews & Warren, 1874.

Drury, Clifford M. *The History of the Chaplain Corps, United States Navy Bureau of Naval Personnel.* Washington, D.C.: U.S. Government Printing Office, 1948.

Durkin, Joseph T. *Confederate Navy Chief.* Chapel Hill: University of North Carolina Press, 1954.

Ellet, Charles, Jr. *Military Incapacity and What It Costs the Country.* New York and Philadelphia: privately printed, 1862.

Fox, Gustavus V. *Confidential Correspondence of . . .* Published for the Naval Historical Society by the Vinne Press, New York, 1920.

Franklin, S. R. *Memories of a Rear Admiral.* New York: Harper & Brothers, 1898.

Iles, George. *Leading American Inventors.* New York: Holt, 1912.

Jones, Charles C. *The Life and Services of Commodore Josiah Tattnall.* Savannah, Ga.: Morning News Steam Printing House, 1878.

Jones, Virgil Carrington. *The Civil War at Sea,* Vols. 1 and 2. New York: Holt, Rinehart and Winston, 1960.

Lamb, Robert W., ed. *Our Twin Cities of the Nineteenth Century.* Norfolk: Barcroft, 1887.

Lammers, H. J. *The Untold Story of Hampton Roads.* Norfolk: privately printed, 1893.

Leech, Margaret. *Reveille in Washington, 1861–65.* New York: Harper & Brothers, 1941.

Lewis, Charles Lee. *Admiral Franklin Buchanan.* Baltimore: Norman Remington, 1929.

Lull, Edward P. *History of the United States Navy Yard at Gosport.* Washington, D.C.: U.S. Government Printing Office, 1874.

McCordock, Robert Stanley. *The Yankee Cheese Box.* Philadelphia: Dorrance and Co., 1938.

Maclay, Edgar Stanton. *Reminiscences of the Old Navy.* New York: G. P. Putnam's, 1898.

Monitors of U.S. Navy. Washington, D.C.: Naval History Division, U.S. Navy Department, U.S. Government Printing Office, 1969.

Nicolay, John G. and John Hay. *Abraham Lincoln: A History.* New York: Century Co., 1890.

Parker, William H. *Recollections of a Naval Officer.* New York: Scribners, 1887.

Porter, David Dixon. *Incidents and Anecdotes of the Civil War.* New York: D. Appleton & Co., 1885.

Pratt, Fletcher. *The Monitor and the Merrimac.* New York: Random House, 1951.

Rebellion Record, a Diary of American Events. Edited by Frank Moore. New York: G. P. Putnam's, 1863–65.

Schuckers, J. W. *Life and Public Services of Salmon Portland Chase.* New York: D. Appleton & Co., 1874.

Selfridge, Thomas O., Jr. *Memoirs.* New York: G. P. Putnam's, 1924.

Still, William N., Jr. *Iron Afloat.* Nashville: Vanderbilt University Press, 1971.

Wallace, Elizabeth Curtis. *Glencoe Diary, the War-Time Journal of Elizabeth Curtis Wallace.* Edited by Eleanor P. Cross and Charles B. Cross, Jr., Norfolk County Historical Society of Chesapeake, Va.: privately printed, 1968.

Welles, Gideon. *Diary of Gideon Welles.* Cambridge, Mass.: Houghton Mifflin, 1911.

Wertenbaker, Thomas J. *Norfolk, Historic Southern Port.* Durham, N.C.: Duke University Press, 1962.

White, Ruth. *Yankee from Sweden.* New York: Henry Holt, 1960.

White, William Chapman and Ruth. *Tin Can on a Shingle.* New York: E. P. Dutton & Co., 1957.

Worden, John Lorimer. *The Monitor and the Merrimac; Both Sides of the Story.* Told by Lieut. J. L. Worden, USN, Lieut. Greene, USN, of the *Monitor,* and H. Ashton Ramsay, CSN, chief engineer of the *Merrimac.* New York and London: Harper & Brothers, 1912.

INDEX